22 Days in May

22 Days in May

The Birth of the
Lib Dem–Conservative Coalition

David Laws

First published in Great Britain in 2010 by

Biteback Publishing Ltd
Westminster Tower
3 Albert Embankment
London
SE1 7SP

ISBN 978-1-84954-080-3

10 9 8 7 6 5 4 3 2

A CIP catalogue record for this book is available from the British Library.

Set in Adobe Garamond by Soapbox

Printed and bound in Great Britain by
CPI Cox & Wyman, Reading, RG1 8EX

Contents

Introduction

The twenty-two days from 6 to 27 May 2010 changed British politics, and changed my life.

In just five days, a coalition government was formed for the first time since the Second World War. After years of expectation of a great alliance of the 'Liberal–Labour centre-left' and in defiance of the general assumptions of most politicians and political commentators, the coalition that emerged was actually between the Liberal Democrats and the Conservatives.

I was fortunate enough to have a vantage point as these remarkable events unfolded. Indeed, I was one of those at the centre of the discussions and negotiations which led to the formation of this historic coalition. Just over two weeks later, however, my own political career moved rapidly from triumph to disaster, and I will not claim that it has been easy to 'treat those two impostors just the same'.

In the twenty-two days covered in this book, I went from being a Liberal Democrat parliamentary candidate to being re-elected as the Member of Parliament for Yeovil, with a record majority for that constituency. I then helped to negotiate the coalition agreement, before joining the Cabinet as Chief Secretary to the Treasury – the first Liberal/Liberal Democrat to hold that post and the first Liberal Treasury minister since 1931.

Alongside the Chancellor, I implemented within ten days the

government's commitment to slice £6bn off public spending, and embarked upon some of the early work necessary to deliver an emergency budget statement. Then, after twenty-four turbulent hours, I resigned from the Cabinet and entered the record books once again, but less gloriously, as the shortest-lived holder of a Cabinet Office for 200 years.

A cartoon published in *The Times* just after my resignation has me reaching the peak of Everest, with my front foot about to rest on its snow-capped peak, on which sits a giant banana skin.

This was a turbulent and traumatic period for me, and those close to me. I regret, of course, the personal hurt experienced, as well as the fact that I am no longer able to contribute to the coalition government I helped bring into being. Waiting eighty years for a Liberal government to come along, and then not being part of it is a pretty frustrating experience.

I offer this memoir as a contribution to the historic record of British politics, rather than as a personal indulgence. I remain a very private person, even after the events and revelations of late May, and in spite of the demands which fall on all those whose life is spent in public office.

My intention in writing this book is not to describe an all too brief Cabinet career.

It is, instead, to inform those who are interested in this important period of British politics, and to make sure that an accurate account is left of what really happened in May 2010, before memories fade, myths grow and evidence is lost.

I also wish to ensure that an accurate and honest account is left of how the Liberal Democrats made difficult decisions after 6 May, before others seek to put their own spin on our motives and judgements. I am pleased to say that the other members of our negotiating team are too busy delivering in government to have time themselves for this task.

I have contributed in the Appendices a detailed written record of the key documentation involved in the coalition negotiations. I have considered carefully whether this breaks any implicit understanding of confidentiality, since some of these documents are being published for the first time. However, their contents have already been openly discussed by key participants in the talks. I do not, therefore, think that the arguments for secrecy are particularly strong. In any case, I hope that students of British politics will find these papers to be of interest.

In this book, I do not pretend to be providing a 'rounded' account of the coalition talks, seen from all sides. That work is for others to complete. My account is very much my own, and is written from my perspective and that of my party.

Doubtless this will mean that I have missed some other important aspects of the negotiations, including the significance of direct talks between the party leaders. I have seen transcripts of some of these discussions, but not all were formally recorded in this way. No doubt the weight which I attribute to certain events will also be open to dispute. But that is a hazard common to all historical records.

I have put into quotation marks some of the words used by the key players in this political drama, but only where I have been able to rely on the written transcripts of some of the meetings, or my own notes made at the time, or indeed my clear memory of some parts of our discussions. Where these sources are not available, I have sought to summarise the conversations that took place, rather than seek to artificially reconstruct them.

I have also included an account of my all too brief period in government, in order to give a flavour of how the coalition established itself and began meeting the challenges facing it. Many of the most important early challenges relate closely to the responsibilities of the Treasury, where I was a minister.

I finish with a brief assessment of the coalition to date – why it came about, its strengths and its weaknesses, and the challenges that lie ahead.

I would like to thank all those who helped me to cope with the events surrounding my resignation, including those many thousands of people who are not known personally to me, but who wrote, e-mailed or telephoned their support and encouragement.

I would particularly like to thank my family and friends, my constituency party in Yeovil, including Chairman Cathy Bakewell MBE, my agent Sam Crabb, Jill and Garry Shortland, and Tim Carroll, as well as my brilliant office staff of Sue Weeks, Sarah Frapple, Claire Margetts, Sadye McLean, Tom Powsey and Jeremy Gale. On the 28th and 29th of May I also particularly benefited from the loyal support of Paddy and Jane Ashdown, Jeremy Browne MP, Jonny Oates, Olly Grender, Julian Astle, Sean Kemp and Nick Clegg MP.

Finally, thanks to those who have read all or parts of this book, to check on my recollections and to suggest improvements: Olly Grender, Julian Astle, Paddy Ashdown, Jonny Oates, Tom Powsey, Danny Alexander MP, Andrew Stunell MP and Chris Huhne MP. I am particularly grateful to Alison Suttie, who supported the Lib Dem negotiating team and sat in on almost all of our meetings. Alison lent me copies of her detailed, contemporaneous, notes of these meetings and of some of the discussions between the party leaders. These notes saved me from many an error, and they have added enormously to the detail and reliability of this account.

Above all, I thank James for his patience, love and support.

David Laws MP, October 2010

Thursday 6 May 2010

General election day

My alarm clock went off at 5am. My second alarm went off at 5.05am. Logic would suggest that after a long general election campaign, and with many an hour without rest ahead, I should be sleeping soundly until at least 7am or 8am. But it is the curse of Liberal Democrat MPs that we are not expected to leave the hard work on election day, or any other day, to our activists and supporters.

In my Yeovil constituency, this Lib Dem tradition of 'leading by example' had, over time, been bolstered even further by my predecessor as MP, Paddy Ashdown. Paddy used to be the last to leave constituency fund-raising events after personally sweeping the floor of the relevant village hall – a precedent with obvious, undesirable, implications for his successor.

So, after weeks of pavement pounding and media performances, after eight hours a day of knocking on doors for almost two months, I dragged myself out of bed to join our local volunteers for a 6am leaflet drop in the centre of the town of Yeovil.

All political candidates hope that their election day will be sunny or at least that it won't rain. We dread the thought of trying to drag unwilling voters out to the polling station on a wet evening and always assume that our own party voters will be peculiarly susceptible to the rain, wind or the cold, while the supporters of other parties trudge bravely out to cast their votes.

I had, therefore, prayed for sun, but a glance outside my bedroom window confirmed the worst: a cloudy day with rain threatening. The gloom outside offset my pleasure that, at last, the 2010 general election campaign was almost over.

I sighed, showered, started my car and headed off to Yeovil, dressed in my 'delivery' clothes and not my usual suit.

I had first been elected as MP for Yeovil in 2001, but this was my fourth time as a parliamentary candidate, having first lost to Michael Howard in Folkestone and Hythe in 1997.

My majority in the Yeovil constituency had climbed from 3,928 in 2001 to 8,562 in 2005. In early 2010 I had feared that the result in Yeovil might be closer this time. However, Nick Clegg's strong performance during the election campaign, and the positive reception we were getting on the doorstep, made me dare to hope that my majority might rise into five figures or even exceed the total of over 11,000 achieved by Paddy Ashdown in 1997.

I met up with three members of our hard-working campaign team at the bottom of Westfield Road in Yeovil at 6.10am. Our task was to deliver 'Good Morning' leaflets to the residents of Yeovil West, just in case they had somehow managed to miss the fact that this was the day of the general election.

After leaving the others to cover the huge Westfield estate, I drove off to Freedom Avenue and Springfield Road to deliver my 300 leaflets.

I passed the occasional early riser, including those who were amazed, baffled or impressed to see their MP out delivering leaflets at 6.15am.

After I had completed Freedom Avenue, I switched on my mobile phone for the first time since the previous evening.

On my phone was a text message, asking me to call Nick Clegg's chief of staff, Danny Alexander, who was up in his constituency in Scotland. I noted that the message was timed as having been left sometime on the previous evening, but I was confident that Danny would be up and about, and so phoned him, at around 6.45am.

Danny answered straight away. He wanted to know when I was expecting to be back in London after the election count in Yeovil. The polls were still pointing to a high possibility of a hung parliament and I was one of four MPs who had been asked by Nick Clegg to be part of a negotiating team to deal with such an outcome. We were due to meet early on Friday morning to assess the election results and be ready to advise Nick on his return to Westminster.

The team had been secretly established at the end of 2009. It was done without great fanfare or consultation to avoid the party becoming distracted by post-election game playing, when people needed to focus on getting our policy messages across, and winning as many seats as possible.

Sensibly, Nick did not chair this team himself – he selected the members, told us what he wanted and left us to get on with the work. Nick knew that the party needed to be ready for a hung parliament outcome, but – refreshingly for a Lib Dem leader – he did not spend all his time obsessing about this.

Nick's focus was always on building the long-term future for our party. It was not obvious, even privately, which of the two other parties he would prefer to do business with. In private, as in public, he was instinctively equidistant between Labour and the Conservatives and he was acutely aware that in most hung parliament scenarios the choice of viable partner would be made by the voters and not by us.

The team which Nick selected to advise him on strategy in a hung parliament, and to do the negotiating itself, consisted of four MPs –

Danny Alexander (MP for Inverness, Nairn, Badenoch & Strathspey), Chris Huhne (MP for Eastleigh), Andrew Stunell (MP for Hazel Grove) and me.

Danny Alexander was to chair our team. Danny was only elected in 2005 and he was the youngest of the four of us. He had quickly shown himself to be hard-working, pragmatic, ambitious and effective. He had helped run Nick's leadership campaign in 2007 and had then become Nick's trusted chief of staff. Danny's great skill was to be able to get on with people of very different political views, without losing a hard edge on policy and strategy.

Chris Huhne was our Home Affairs spokesman and the runner-up to Nick in the 2007 Lib Dem leadership election. After he lost to Nick in 2007, and following a fairly rough leadership contest, Chris had won respect for his loyalty and hard work. He had lost, and lost narrowly, but he accepted it. He was still clearly ambitious for himself and for the party. But he knew that this ambition could only now be realised through Nick as leader and so had become part of Nick's trusted inner team. Chris played 'Gordon Brown' to my 'David Cameron' in the mock leaders' debates with Nick Clegg before the general election.

Chris had been a respected economics journalist and had gone on to help run a credit ratings agency in the City. He was elected to the European Parliament but had switched to Westminster in 2005. Chris is strongly pro-European, dry on economic matters and formidably intelligent. And although Chris would more easily relate to centre-left politics than to the Conservative Party, he is an ambitious realist – admirable characteristics in a party where both these qualities are too often in short supply.

Andrew Stunell, the third member of our team, was a former Chief Whip with lots of local government experience. He is an expert on green issues, political reform and campaigning. Andrew was trusted not only by the party in Parliament, but by our councillor and campaigning base beyond Westminster. Andrew was on the team in part to ensure that the wider party's perspective would be properly represented. I am not sure if Andrew is actually a sandal-wearing Liberal Democrat in his spare time, but he looks as if he could be.

Andrew also brought to the table the pragmatism of someone who is used to Liberal Democrats sharing power with both other parties in local government. No one would ever class Andrew as a 'right-winger' politically, but his local government background meant that he was used to fighting both other parties and that he understood the need to strike the best deal when no party had a majority.

Nick also attached to our group his trusted aide and deputy chief of staff, Alison Suttie, who has years of experience of Lib Dem politics and personalities. Alison had worked with both Nick Clegg and Chris Huhne in Brussels, and therefore had a good understanding of the process of negotiation between political parties.

This was our planning team for a hung parliament eventuality and it was also to be our team of negotiators after the general election, in the event a hung parliament materialised. It was a team capable of dealing with either Labour or the Conservatives.

Our team had met on four or five occasions in early 2010, largely in February and March, and had talked through in detail all of the different post-election scenarios.

Our common view was that if any party had an outright majority it was highly unlikely that there would be any 'deals' or coalitions, and in such a scenario we firmly expected to be sitting on the opposition benches.

But the polls continued to suggest that the election outcome might be close, with a hung parliament a distinct possibility. Our planning assumption, in line with almost all of the opinion polls, was that the Conservatives were likely to be the largest party, and that a Lib Dem–Conservative arrangement of some sort was the more likely outcome. But given the workings of the British electoral system, we could not rule out the possibility of a Lib Dem–Labour working majority. So we were determined to be prepared for every possible scenario.

Our team was united in the opinion that in any hung parliament the Lib Dems would need to play a constructive and positive role in forming a government. To do otherwise would not only confirm the widespread prejudice that hung parliaments lead to weak governments – a particular risky and unpopular result given the difficult economic decisions that were likely to be necessary – but could also rapidly lead to a second general election.

We all considered that a second general election would be damaging to our vote if we could be blamed for failing to play a constructive role in forming a stable government. We were absolutely determined not to let that happen. 'Doing nothing' in a hung parliament would be the worst possible outcome, and one that we would do everything to avoid.

If the Conservatives emerged as the largest party, we fully expected David Cameron to make a bold offer to bring the Lib Dems into a coalition government. The Conservatives seemed to have all to gain, and little to lose, from making such an offer – whether we responded positively or not.

We were conscious that to walk away from such an offer, to be seen to be afraid to take responsibility, could be very dangerous for us and bad for the country – not least given the state of the economy and the financial markets. Britain's deficit was one of the largest in the developed world, and if the markets concluded that Britain's government was too weak to tackle this deficit there would be a high price to pay in falling bond prices and rocketing interest rates.

But most of us doubted that the Conservatives would be willing to offer what had long been a key Lib Dem condition for any coalition – a referendum on voting reform.

A few years before, I had spoken privately to George Osborne in his Westminster office and had told him bluntly that the Lib Dems would never go into coalition without the prospect of electoral reform, but neither he nor any senior Conservative had ever seemed keen to pursue this possibility. In fact, there didn't seem to be any real support within the Conservative Party for voting reform or any movement in this direction.

So despite increased media speculation about the scope for Lib Dem–Conservative co-operation, it was difficult to see how it could work in practice.

As a result of this, Danny, Andrew and I all believed that in a Conservative-dominated hung parliament the most likely outcome was a 'confidence and supply agreement' in which, in exchange for a commitment on some of our key policies, the Lib Dems would promise to support the government on economic issues and on confidence votes, while remaining on the opposition benches.

We were not, however, confident that such an arrangement would last long. Taking the tough decisions on the deficit would be unpopular and the risk was that both parties would look to end the agreement at a time of maximum political advantage to them – a dangerous game at a time of national economic emergency.

That was certainly the view of the fourth member of our team, Chris Huhne. Chris argued strongly that a confidence and supply arrangement would be the worst of all worlds, resulting in the Lib Dems taking no credit for the government's achievements, but all the pain for sustaining it in office.

Chris can be a tiger when he gets an idea into his head, and he continued to push the full coalition option hard, whether we secured voting reform or not.

After weeks of work and debate, the negotiating team was due to report its conclusions to Nick Clegg at a meeting on Wednesday 17 March. Danny Alexander, as chair of our team, had produced a fifteen-page summary of our conclusions.

Many of the conclusions were uncontroversial – including the identification of our four key policy objectives, which were simply those highlighted in our election manifesto and in our election campaign. We were clear that we would need progress on all four policy objectives in order to consider an arrangement with another party.

Danny also set out a strategy for consulting our party on the negotiations and recommended provision be made for a special conference, if needed, no later than nine days after polling day. This appeared to be the requirement of a 'triple lock' provision which had been passed by a party conference way back in 1998, when party members feared being bounced by Paddy Ashdown into a coalition with Tony Blair's Labour government.

So, on 17 March, we met to discuss these issues. As well as Nick Clegg, we were joined by Vince Cable, Chief Whip Paul Burstow and Party President, Ros Scott.

To my surprise, the night before our meeting, Chris Huhne had tabled a 'Minority Report' pushing the coalition option very hard indeed.

In his twenty-point, two-page note Chris argued forcefully that a full coalition for at least four years had to be our negotiating objective, whatever the balance of each party's MPs in a hung parliament.

Chris concluded that arms-length confidence and supply deals lead to a lack of willingness by parties to take tough decisions on the deficit and on public spending. He argued that without a strong coalition arrangement the result would be 'worse policy outcomes and a higher budget deficit'.

Research Chris had commissioned showed that minority governments rarely deliver big fiscal consolidations, while he claimed that seven of the ten biggest fiscal consolidations in the OECD area since 1970 were carried out in hung parliaments with coalition governments.

Chris went on to claim that 'half pregnant' deals 'are weak and look weak. . . they are more likely to lead to a loss of market confidence . . . and a full-blown economic and political crisis.'

If we were blamed as a party for such a crisis, Chris noted, the political costs would be huge. So good economics would also be good politics, and both in his view pointed to coalition.

I did not disagree with this economic analysis, and nor I think did Nick Clegg, Danny Alexander or Vince Cable. Indeed, Danny had highlighted the risks of economic instability very clearly in his summary of the group's conclusions. We even proposed to publish an 'Economic Stability Plan for Britain' on the day after polling day so that we should be seen to be acting early and responsibly to reassure the markets and tackle the budget deficit.

But the issue for us was what our bottom-line negotiating position should be. And the majority of us believed that voting reform had to be key to any coalition agreement.

Without some credible mechanism to progress voting reform, we thought it would prove difficult to argue for a coalition.

This was, of course, much more likely to be an issue if the Conservatives were the only coalition partner – which always looked the more likely scenario, given the state of the polls.

As well as the possible impasse on voting reform, the majority of the negotiating team thought that it might prove difficult to resolve our other policy differences with the Conservatives in a credible way. And although we expected 'an immediate, very warm, and very public approach from David Cameron' (Alexander, 'Post Election Strategy Recommendations', 17 March 2010), we were of the view that the private preference of the Conservative leadership might still be to govern as a minority, rather than seeking a full coalition deal.

Our conclusion was that while we would draft both a Lib Dem–Conservative coalition document and a Lib Dem–Conservative confidence and supply document, we felt that the former was much less likely to ever see the light of day.

Nevertheless, I produced a first, full draft of a coalition 'partnership agreement' on 21 March, which was based on a similar approach to that used in Scotland in the first Scottish Parliament coalition in 1999. It was entitled: 'A Partnership for Renewal', and ran to a length of about sixteen pages. I also produced a much shorter 'confidence and supply agreement' (see Appendix 6).

Paul Burstow, our Chief Whip, drafted two 'operational annexes' for the 'coalition' and 'confidence and supply' agreements, setting out in detail how the two parties concerned would co-operate, and dealing with detailed issues such as allocation of ministerial posts, arrangements for Cabinet committees, details of collective responsibility and whipping arrangements, public appointments and so forth.

In the less likely circumstance of a hung parliament in which Labour and the Liberal Democrats had a majority, our team felt that the likely outcome was clearer – a full coalition. This was because Labour had already committed to a referendum on the Alternative Vote. Our challenge would then be to open the door to more fundamental voting reform, going beyond the AV system.

Little would be gained by propping up a Labour minority government with a 'confidence and supply agreement', and we never gave this possibility any serious consideration.

We therefore drafted a Lib Dem–Labour coalition document, with a similar set of key policy pledges to that in the Lib Dem–Conservative scenario.

So the conclusions of our 17 March meeting were: firstly, that outright coalition was our favoured endgame; secondly, that this was much more likely if a Lib Dem–Labour arrangement was electorally possible; thirdly, that a confidence and supply agreement was the most likely scenario if we found ourselves dealing with the Conservatives, unless they conceded both on our key pledges and on progress on electoral reform.

We also discussed the major complication that would arise if Labour and the Liberal Democrats were to form a coalition – the future of Gordon Brown. This was not just a 'post-election' issue. At the time, it seemed highly likely to be an issue in the election campaign itself.

In the Conservative–Lib Dem battlegrounds a 'Vote Clegg, get Brown' message could hardly be more damaging, given the desire for change and the deep-seated hostility to the Prime Minister amongst many voters.

My view was that the Conservatives would repeat this message endlessly during the campaign, and that it could cost us hundreds of thousands of votes and potentially many seats.

So in late 2009, I went to see Nick Clegg and suggested that we might need to rule out supporting a Brown-led government after the election, given how toxic this issue could become.

I even suggested that Nick might make the announcement in one of the three scheduled election-time 'leader debates'. It would certainly have sent a dramatic signal and, I argued, it would be important in Lib Dem–Conservative marginal seats.

My view was that even if the public accepted a Gordon Brown-led coalition, and I did not believe that they would, he would turn out to be an impossible person to work with in a coalition government. As I argued to Nick: 'If his own Cabinet cannot work with him, what chance do four or five Lib Dem ministers have?'

I expected Nick to be sympathetic, knowing that he had never found Gordon Brown to be an easy person to work with.

But Nick was strongly against any announcement, delayed or otherwise, that ruled out working with Gordon Brown after the election. He argued that this would simply raise other questions about who else we would work with and what their mandate would be.

I understood these concerns. But in our six or seven practice sessions for the TV leader debates, when I played David Cameron, I endlessly challenged Nick on whether he would prop up a Brown-led government. 'I agree with Nick on many issues,' was my line, 'but he cannot rule out putting Gordon Brown back into Downing Street – vote Clegg on Thursday, and you could wake up on Friday with Gordon Brown.' Nick developed some good counter-attacks, but I admit to continuing to feel nervous about how effective this line of attack on us could be. To my surprise, it was not a line which the Conservatives exploited as effectively as I feared during the election campaign.

All of this background work – potential scenarios debated and discussed, the documents prepared, and the challenges which we could soon face – were in my mind as I stood in a chilly Freedom Avenue, on the phone to Danny, grasping a pile of leaflets and hoping that it wasn't about to rain.

'It seems to be going OK here in Yeovil,' I reported.

'My election count should be at around 2.30am and I hope to be away by 3am. I will drive back to London, and expect to be back in Westminster at around 6am. So I can meet anytime after that.'

I had pressed hard for all of us on the negotiating team to meet as early as possible on the Friday morning, riling those who thought that a few hours sleep would help to get a sense of perspective.

What I felt we would need was not a sense of perspective, but a sense of urgency and professionalism. The media demands would be huge and any notion that we were 'taking our time' would merely reinforce the journalists' natural instinct to think that Liberal Democrats aren't quite serious enough about life.

I imagined what the 24-hour media would make of: 'The Lib Dem team has gone home to get some sleep.' It was not a headline I wanted to see.

Before getting back to my leaflet delivery, I took the opportunity to check on the party's latest prediction of the number of Lib Dem seats.

'Eighty-five plus' was Danny's cheerful forecast, which seemed in line with general expectations following the Lib Dem poll bounce after Nick Clegg's strong performances in the three televised leader debates.

'Great,' I replied to Danny. 'That would be fantastic. Well, the election could hardly have gone better. Nick must be feeling very satisfied. Well done. I will see you in a few hours time. Good luck in your own election.'

So I signed off feeling confident about our national prospects, and convinced that there was a real possibility of our negotiating team having serious work to do.

The rest of the day went quickly: back home; a call in to Winsham

Primary School, near Chard, to observe their own election day event; and then off to the towns of Ilminster, Crewkerne and finally Yeovil to 'rally the troops' and get our vote out. To my relief, the rain held off and the voters seemed to be turning out.

I spent the end of the day in the Liberal Democrat heartlands of Yeovil East, as is my tradition, and by around 8.30pm I pulled stumps and drove back to my house near Chard.

There I had a shower, changed clothes and scribbled down a few notes for what I hoped would be an acceptance speech as Yeovil's MP in just a few hours' time.

I then set off for the village of South Petherton to have dinner with local party activist and stalwart, Joan Raikes. Joan and her husband Myles, now sadly deceased, had a tradition of laying on dinner for our parliamentary candidates on general election night. We would receive a hearty and healthy meal while watching the early results come in, and listening out for the phone call from our election agent, which would be the first news of how my own count was going.

The news from across Somerset seemed to be good. Everyone was very positive and optimistic. It looked as if we were going to hold our three seats and possibly win a further seat – Wells. This would leave only one Conservative seat in Somerset – hardly the sweep of the West Country which the Conservatives had promised.

I arrived at Joan's house just in time for the close of poll and for the first exit poll from the BBC. We settled down for a pre-dinner beer, expecting to hear that we were on track for 26% or 27% and for a big increase in our total of seats.

For weeks, the whole Lib Dem election campaign seemed to have been going so well. But the first, unexpected, dark cloud arrived just after 10.00pm when the results of the exit poll were revealed.

The shock was that the BBC was projecting Lib Dem seats of under sixty – net losses of seats against our expectations of big gains.

'What rubbish,' I scoffed. 'All that work,and they have got a totally duff result. How can we possibly end up with fewer seats?'

The results were so at variance with the other polls and expectations that even the BBC seemed dubious of their own figures. Determined to remain upbeat, we tucked in to a large dinner of three courses.

At about 11.30am the telephone rang. I knew it must be Sam Crabb, my election agent, from the count. I looked as disinterested as I could while Joan went out to take the call. This is a nervous moment for all election candidates. No matter how confident you are, or what your own canvas figures show, you are never quite certain until the real votes are counted out.

But Joan reported that the news was good – Sam had told her that his early sampling of the vote count indicated that we were heading for victory in Yeovil – with a majority of over 11,000. I dared to hope once again that we might even exceed the 11,400 majority that Paddy Ashdown had amassed in 1997.

Friday 7 May 2010

First moves in a hung parliament

At around 1.00am, my election agent, Sam Crabb, rang again, and instructed me to come to the count, which he assured me was proceeding faster than expected.

I made the fifteen-minute drive into Yeovil to the Westland Centre. I parked in the packed car park, rang my mother and then James Lundie, to tell them what result I was expecting and to put them out of their misery.

The Westland Centre was packed, as the Yeovil vote count was taking place alongside that of the next-door Somerton and Frome constituency. For months I had dreaded the prospect of this ultra-marginal seat falling to the Conservatives and losing my friend and colleague, the Lib Dem MP for Somerton and Frome, David Heath.

David is a fantastic local MP and one of the most dedicated and professional of parliamentarians. He was first elected in 1997 and only held what on paper looked like a natural Tory seat by virtue of his ability to attract votes from across the political spectrum. In 1997, 2001 and in 2005, David's majority had never risen to the four-figure level, and in each election the Tories poured in cash and made little secret of their expectation that the seat would 'go blue'. Each time David had defied these expectations, but the national swing to the Conservatives in 2010 made this seat look a particularly tough one to hold.

But both our counts seemed to be going well, and my result finally came in at around 2.30am – a majority of 13,036, the largest in the one-hundred-year history of the Yeovil constituency.

I was absolutely delighted and made my acceptance speech from the stage of the Westland Centre, thanking our hard-working team that had run one of the best Lib Dem local campaigns in Britain, with more canvassing than in any other constituency in the UK.

About forty-five minutes later, the Somerton and Frome count was completed, and it was clear that – in spite of most expectations to the contrary – David Heath had pulled off his fourth election win since 1997. Indeed, David had increased his majority for the first time to four figures – 1,817.

I stayed to listen to David's acceptance speech, standing behind his tearful wife and elated party workers. The defeated Conservative candidate, Annuziata Rees-Mogg, then made a gracious acceptance speech, followed by the other candidates, and then the whole thing was over.

We also heard news from the counts in both Taunton Deane and Wells predicting that we would win these two seats. It was a good night for the Lib Dems of Somerset.

I thanked our own Yeovil constituency workers, who were celebrating in the bar, and then announced that it was time for me to get back to London to be ready for the possibility of a hung parliament and the negotiations which would surely follow.

I had promised to give a lift back to London to one of our hard-working constituency interns – Oliver Carter – and we set off at around 3am, while listening to the election results programme on BBC Radio 4.

I left the Westland Centre in Yeovil with the news that in Somerset we were doing much better than could have been expected – taking four of the five seats and increasing our majorities in all our existing seats.

This all seemed consistent with a nationwide 'Clegg bounce' from the general election leader debates and I expected to hear reports of similarly good results from across the country.

But the results that I was hearing on the radio seemed anything but good.

Barely were we out of Yeovil, when we heard of the defeat of Lembit Öpik in Montgomeryshire, and this was followed shortly after by losses in other unexpected places – to the Conservatives in Harrogate and in Oxford West & Abingdon, and to Labour in Chesterfield and Rochdale.

I had hoped that these disappointments were just aberrations, but it was soon clear that the gains we were expecting in large numbers against Labour were simply not materialising, even in places such as Liverpool Wavertree and Hampstead & Kilburn, where hopes had been running high.

It was these Labour seats that we needed to gain if we were to increase our overall seats total and it was clear that something had gone badly wrong.

The longer we listened to the radio reports, and the closer we got to London, the clearer it was that we were going to be nowhere near the figures of seventy-five to ninety seats which had been implied by the most recent polls. The BBC's 'rogue poll' was turning out to be remarkably accurate.

There was a silver lining, however: no party appeared to be achieving its objectives. Labour had clearly lost power, but the Conservatives looked like finishing well short of an overall majority.

Increasingly it looked as if what we lacked in seats we would make up for in influence.

It was around 6am when I arrived back in Westminster. I drove to the Palace of Westminster and in through the large gates on Parliament Square.

The policeman on the gate was very friendly and reported that I was the first Member of Parliament back since the election. He congratulated me, but reported that since my parliamentary pass had now expired, I could not gain access to the parliamentary estate.

After a number of phone calls and presentation of the paperwork which I had received from the returning officer in my constituency, it was decided that my pass should be reapproved. I drove around New Palace Yard, through the security check and down into the underground car park, which descends five levels below the ground outside the historic Westminster Hall.

I then made the short, five-minute journey on foot to the Liberal Democrat party headquarters at 4 Cowley Street.

I knew exactly what to expect over the next forty-eight hours, because we had planned all of this in detail just days before.

As well as our weeks of deliberating on strategy before the general election, our negotiating team and other key party officials had all met up on Sunday 2 May in central London, to review the polls and to make preparations for a hung parliament.

The meeting was chaired by Danny Alexander and included Chris Huhne, Andrew Stunell, Chris Fox (chief executive), Jonny Oates (director of communications), Chris Saunders (economics adviser), Alison Suttie (deputy chief of staff to Nick Clegg), Ben Williams (secretary to the Parliamentary Party), and me.

We had discussed the likely election result and how to react, how to handle the other parties, when to start negotiations, how to consult with the party and communications with the media.

We wanted to ensure in particular that our party communications were rather more effective than they were in the hung parliament of 1974, when Edward Heath's office tried to contact party leader Jeremy Thorpe on election night, only to be told: 'He's not available right now. He is leading a candle-light procession through the streets of Barnstaple.' I could not see Nick Clegg leading any candlelit processions through the streets of Sheffield, but we wanted to leave nothing to chance.

At our meeting on 2 May, we had agreed that Nick Clegg would make a short speech about the election result at his own count in Sheffield, and then return to Cowley Street to make a more general statement at around 7.00am. This was based on a 3am result in Sheffield, which turned out to be wildly optimistic.

We also agreed to concentrate our internal party consultations on the Saturday – the first viable day on which we would be able to bring together the whole shadow Cabinet, Parliamentary Party and Federal Executive. If there was a hung parliament, we would need to share our negotiating strategy with party colleagues to ensure unity and have a clear mandate with which to open talks.

We had to think not only about how to cope with our own party members and MPs, but also with the British media. They were not used to coalition-forming and their reporting would frame the public's view of what was taking place.

Chris Huhne felt it would be important to brief the media on how long coalitions take to put in place in continental Europe (apparently many weeks). Any lowering of expectations might help but I pointed out that neither the British media nor the financial markets nor the public would tolerate a prolonged period of uncertainty.

We also had a discussion about the possible need for a special party conference to ratify any coalition deal, and Chris Fox – the chief executive – set out the arrangements that he was already making to hold such a conference on the Sunday, a week after the election (16 May).

On the substance of the decisions we might face, it was generally agreed that allowing Gordon Brown to stay in power after his and Labour's poor election performance would be very toxic.

Our views on this issue had hardened over the course of the election, not least because Gordon Brown was regarded as having had a pretty poor election campaign and it was now fairly certain that Labour would suffer big losses on election night.

So in any arrangement with Labour we decided that we would need to press for Brown's departure. This decision would only be altered by a huge and unlikely surge in Labour's performance before polling day.

We debated again the likelihood of delivering a full coalition agreement with the Conservatives. Danny, Andrew Stunell and I continued to doubt that we could secure the policy agreement that would make this possible. Most of us still felt that a confidence and supply agreement with the Conservatives was the most likely outcome from a situation where the Conservatives were just short of a majority.

However, Chris Huhne again warned that in his opinion a 'soft' arrangement with the Conservatives would be very bad for UK financial markets, as hard economic choices on the deficit were more likely to be ducked.

He remained of his view that we had to aim for a full coalition. Anything else, he felt, would be bad for the economy and could lead to an early second general election, fought before the benefits of taking tough decisions had materialised.

Chris argued that the crisis in Greece, which was in danger of spreading to other European markets, meant that the context had changed materially since our discussions in February and March.

'The urgency of securing a stable government is much greater,' he said, 'as is the need for tough action on the deficit.'

He argued that a minimum agreement with the Tories would need to be for four years, as it would take this long to sort the economy and the deficit out.

Chris also suggested that David Cameron would be more pragmatic over issues such as electoral reform than we imagined.

Danny insisted that we were not going to reopen the detailed discussions which we had had before the election. So while we had clear plans for process, party management and the media, there was still an uncertainty over what the most likely and preferred outcome was should there be a hung parliament where a majority government could only be formed through a Lib Dem–Conservative coalition.

These detailed preparations at least meant that when I arrived at party headquarters in Cowley Street in the early morning of 7 May, I had a very clear idea of what we had to do next.

What I had not anticipated was the sombre atmosphere of the press office on Cowley Street's ground floor, where staff and volunteers were watching the election results coming through.

Our press and campaigns team had worked incredibly hard for weeks on end and, after Nick's superb performance in the election debates and our surge in the polls, there were high hopes that we would make a major breakthrough in our number of MPs. Now we faced a huge gap between high expectations and the rather disappointing results.

There was also real sadness at some of the colleagues who had lost their seats – including Willie Rennie in Dunfermline & West Fife, Julia Goldsworthy in Camborne & Redruth, Susan Kramer in Richmond, and others. Increasingly, it looked as if we would struggle to even hold the sixty-three seats that we had entered the election with.

But if we had failed to emerge as the election 'winners', it was difficult to see who else had. Labour were still clearly heading for defeat with a massive loss of seats, but the projections still showed the Conservatives falling short of an overall majority. The final election projections had the Conservatives on around 306 seats, Labour on 258 seats, the Liberal Democrats on 57 seats and the smaller parties with around thirty seats combined.

It was therefore pretty clear that we were in hung parliament territory. It looked as if only a Liberal Democrat–Conservative deal could deliver a majority government, and that a Lib–Lab deal would fall short.

The press office kept me busy with a few media interviews on the green outside the Palace of Westminster and in the media centre at 4 Millbank. I stuck firmly to the line that none of the parties had secured an overall mandate and that we now needed to wait for the final results before determining how to act.

It was plain that as the Conservatives were emerging with the largest number of seats and votes, we would be obliged to enter talks with them first, based on the commitment that Nick Clegg had made during the general election campaign.

Nick had been expected to arrive at Cowley Street between seven and eight o' clock in the morning, but his own constituency count was running very late and his return could not be expected until late morning.

I therefore returned home, washed, shaved, put on a change of clothes and set off back to Cowley Street to be ready to do more media.

On the way down Black Prince Road, I called Lord (Andrew) Adonis, Labour's Secretary of State for Transport. Andrew and I were old friends, and we had met informally twice before the general election to ensure that lines of communication were open in case a Lib–Lab deal was possible after 6 May.

Andrew had been a Liberal Democrat but had left the party in 1994 to work for Tony Blair. He had been a powerful member of the Downing Street Policy Unit and was widely viewed as exercising more influence over education policy than most Secretaries of State.

Andrew had personally pushed through the Academies programme and was also a driving force behind the government's plans for higher and variable tuition fees.

All of this had made him rather unpopular both with some Liberal Democrats and on the left of the Labour Party. I do not think he expected to survive for long after Gordon Brown became Prime Minister. But Mr Brown had the good sense to realise that he could not afford to be seen to sack the most competent of Blairites, and later on he also seemed to discover Andrew's value as a most effective, respected and results-focused minister.

Andrew's position had now become particularly important for a number of reasons. Firstly, he was not only a former Liberal Democrat, but someone who was as liked and as trusted as people can be when they are in different parties.

Secondly, Andrew had long believed in centre-left realignment, with a partnership between the Liberal Democrats and Labour – as did his political hero, Roy Jenkins.

Finally, although there still remained a few links amongst the more senior members of the two parties, such as Paddy Ashdown and Peter Mandelson, or Menzies Campbell and Gordon Brown, the links with the new Lib Dem generation were not very strong. Andrew, however, was one such link. If anyone was going to deliver a Lib–Lab partnership, it was Andrew.

By contrast, few in Labour's younger generation seemed committed to links between the two parties. People like Ed Balls were deeply tribal, and made little effort to engage with the Liberal Democrats.

Even Ed Miliband, notionally far less tribal and aggressive than his namesake, notably failed to follow up on his occasional suggestions that we should meet to talk about our 'common interests'. Indeed, on the only occasion when I did chat with Ed in his ministerial office in the Commons, he merely emphasised to me how 'toxic' the Lib Dems presently were in the Labour Party, due to our success in taking council seats off them in their northern heartlands.

As a possible candidate for leadership, it seemed likely to me that Ed Miliband considered any proximity to the Lib Dems as damaging to him personally rather than it being of any value to his party to forge a relationship with us and help keep Labour in power.

Andrew Adonis's position was therefore important. He was liked by the Lib Dems. He knew people of both the older and younger generations in our party and was committed to better Lib–Lab relations and to voting reform.

Although in the past he would not have been the most obvious conduit to Gordon Brown, it was clear that his relations with Gordon Brown were now much closer, and that they were talking more regularly than might have been expected.

Clearly, Mr Brown must have already been thinking beyond the general election, and he must finally have realised that without a deal with the Lib Dems he had almost no chance at all of staying in power. It was, indeed, a deathbed conversion to the merits of co-operation with the Lib Dems.

Andrew had invited me to meet him in February 2010, for a glass of white wine in his large office in the Department of Transport in Marsham

Street. He had then told me that he was sure there would be almost no problem at all agreeing on policy with the Lib Dems in the event of a hung parliament. Our conversation turned instead to the more difficult issues such as voting reform and the Prime Minister's own political position.

I suggested to Andrew that Labour could include a commitment to AV in their own election manifesto, which might mean a referendum would not be necessary if both parties could secure explicit ratification through their manifestos. This was, of course, rather an outside shot – both with Labour and given our own commitment to the Single Transferable Vote method of proportional representation. It was also a piece of policy freelancing on my part.

But in any case Andrew was clear that Labour could go no further than the offer of a referendum on AV.

'I am afraid that there are probably around seventy Labour MPs who hate AV and who think it could cost them their seats. We have pushed these people as far as they are willing to go. If we went further, there would be resignations,' he said.

Andrew also referred directly to media speculation that we might insist on Gordon Brown's resignation as a price for any coalition. This speculation accurately reflected the debate going on with and around Nick Clegg at this time.

Andrew surprised me by saying: 'That just will not work. It will be a deal with Gordon, or no deal at all. In any situation where a Lib Dem–Labour coalition is possible, that will be regarded almost as a triumph for Gordon, given where we are in the polls.'

'And you just cannot come along and dictate to us who our party leader should be. It would not work. Just imagine what our MPs would think of that, or what you would think if we told you who your leader should be.'

'I can see the difficulty,' I said. 'But see things from our perspective – Gordon Brown is incredibly unpopular. And I personally believe that he would be impossible to work with in government. Look how he deals with his own colleagues. I can imagine how he would deal with us. I really don't think we could accept him as Prime Minister, because I do not think the British people would, and I think he would be an impossible coalition partner.'

But Andrew was insistent: 'This could be a huge, historic opportunity. Don't get hung up on this personality issue, or we will lose the opportunity. However, you might want to insist on Alistair Darling remaining as Chancellor,' he said. 'That could be rather better for you than the alternative!'

We agreed to meet once more before the election. This was on Thursday 18 March at a restaurant called Loose Box, in Horseferry Road, just down from the Department of Transport.

Over breakfast we chatted about the same issues and agreed to stay in touch. Given the state of the polls neither of us felt that a Lib Dem–Labour coalition was the most likely outcome of the election, but it was not impossible either.

Andrew remained insistent that Gordon Brown would have to remain PM. I did not push the point, and I respected Andrew's loyalty, but in truth I could not imagine a scenario where we would put this man back in as Prime Minister.

Andrew suggested that we should talk during the election period, but I was insistent that we should wait until the general election was out of the way.

I did not relish our conversations being leaked by someone less decent than Andrew. And the headline 'Lib Dems in secret talks to prop up Brown' would be absolutely deadly to us.

Andrew clearly believed that there could and should be a Lib–Lab coalition if the numbers permitted this in a hung parliament. He regarded all of the policy issues as being resolvable and he clearly thought that a deal on AV could be struck.

Now that the election was over and the results were almost all in, I decided that the time was right to make contact with Andrew again. Andrew answered the call almost immediately and it was clear that he had already spent some time weighing up the emerging parliamentary arithmetic.

'What do you think?' I said to him.

'Well, it is clearly a hung parliament,' he said. 'We need to look carefully at the numbers.'

I volunteered the view that however close things seemed, the seats in Parliament just did not look as if they could deliver a stable Lib–Lab coalition of any kind.

I pointed out that the support of the minority parties would be necessary in order to secure a majority, and with difficult economic decisions to take this did not seem like a prospect to relish.

I expected Andrew to sell the possibilities of a Lib–Lab deal to me very hard. But Andrew is a realist and does not have the usual politician's ability to talk palpable nonsense.

'It won't be easy,' he acknowledged, '. . . but I don't think it's impossible. And Gordon is very much committed to trying to make it work. Let's stay in touch.'

It was a pretty awful telephone line and as I reached the Embankment the sound of traffic drowned out parts of the conversation. But we agreed to talk later, once the final results were in.

Back at our Cowley Street headquarters, there were more media bids to be fielded and some good news, that of Sarah Teather's victory, against tough odds, in Brent.

Sarah had faced some difficult boundary changes and had been engaged in a bitter battle with Labour MP Dawn Butler for the best part of two years. The arithmetic said that Sarah should lose, but – to borrow from Peter Mandelson – she is a 'fighter, not a quitter' and had been working flat out for months on end with no holidays at all. It was great news that she would be returning to Westminster.

Eventually the news came through that Nick Clegg had arrived back in London, by train, and was expected to reach Cowley Street at around 10.30am.

I bumped into an old friend and the party's former director of communications, Olly Grender, outside Cowley Street. She asked me whether I had heard that a decision had already been made to rule out talks with Labour and to go straight for a Conservative–Lib Dem agreement of some kind.

I was rather shocked by this, as I felt it was much too early to take any firm decisions other than that we should talk to the Conservatives first.

My predecessor as MP for Yeovil, Paddy Ashdown, was in Cowley Street and had been talking to Nick Clegg on the phone as he came down from Sheffield.

Paddy asked me to come out with him for a quiet word on the balcony at the back of the Cowley Street press office and, while he puffed on a cigarette, reported to me that he and Nick had decided any deal with Labour was very unlikely because of the parliamentary arithmetic. Paddy continued that when Nick returned to Cowley Street he would make a clear statement of his intent to give the Conservatives the first opportunity to form a government.

I was a little unclear whether this was merely the logical extension of the position we had taken during the election, or whether a more fundamental decision had been taken that the Labour option was undeliverable.

My own view was that it was clear we had to start our negotiations with the Conservatives first, as we had promised to do, but I saw no reason to rule out other options until we had at least had a chance to explore them. Nor did it make sense to weaken our bargaining position by indicating there was only one party that we could do business with.

Nick arrived outside Cowley Street at around 10.40am and made his announcement to the waiting press. Behind him were gathered a large number of party staff who were under strict instructions to look happy, upbeat and positive, and who at least managed to look pensive and awake.

Nick made clear that he would hold to the commitment he had made during the election campaign: to talk first to the party with the largest number of seats and votes,which was clearly the Conservative Party. I was surprised to discover later that a few Liberal Democrats had argued after the election that we should open talks with both the Conservatives and Labour simultaneously,but Nick made clear privately that he would stick to the promise that he had made.

Nick then came into Cowley Street, where he was applauded warmly. Staff gathered on the main staircase and Nick, speaking from the first floor outside the general election 'War Room', thanked all those who had worked so hard over the previous weeks and months.

Nothing could disguise the disappointment that Nick felt and nor did he try to pretend that the results were as we had been expecting. Had this outcome been predicted a few months before, nobody would have been surprised and some would have regarded this as a success. But expectations were raised hugely by the general election leader debates and by the party's poll surge, so the final result fell a long way below what we had all hoped for.

Nick had been absolutely brilliant throughout the general election, and his performance merited a much better result.

I had helped Nick prepare for the leader debates before the election and had been with him for the twenty-four hours before the final debate in Birmingham. We had arrived the evening before the debate in a hotel outside the city, and had spent that evening and the next day on preparations.

The pressure on Nick to perform was immense but he was a point of calm in the middle of the storm around him. I realised that in his election performances he had finally delivered everything that those of us who had supported him as leader from the beginning believed he could achieve. And, like us all, the better his performances were, the more his self-confidence blossomed.

As Nick finished his speech to party staff there was again warm applause and he turned left and into the small first-floor conference room, visibly chocking back the tears and emotion. 'That was the toughest speech of my life,' he said to me as he entered the room. The gap between yesterday's hopes and today's reality was a big one.

Some coffee and biscuits were soon pulled together. Waiting for Nick in the room was the negotiating team: Danny Alexander, Chris Huhne, Andrew Stunell and me, along with Party President Ros Scott, the chair of the general election campaign, John Sharkey, and other key party staff such as Jonny Oates, Chris Fox and Ben Williams.

We exchanged brief pleasantries about the election results in a subdued atmosphere. But although there was a deep sense of disappointment, we also realised that the overall election result had delivered just the outcome for which we had planned in such detail, and that this was such a huge opportunity and responsibility.

And although the moral strength of our bargaining position was weakened by the disappointing total of seats won, the brutal reality was that our support would be necessary for a stable government to be formed. We might not have the seats we wanted, but we had the leverage we needed.

After a couple of minutes of banter, we sat around the conference table and prepared to consider our options.

Danny Alexander started by confirming that he had spoken to David Cameron's chief of staff, Ed Llewellyn, at 5am, and made clear that we were ruling nothing in and nothing out.

Nick, looking tired, then said: 'Well, after my statement the ball is now firmly in David Cameron's court. As we agreed in our election planning, I expect David Cameron to appear painfully reasonable while preparing for a second general election.'

'By the way, Gordon Brown has already been in contact with Vince Cable, and he is talking about forming an anti-Tory "rainbow coalition"! I am not sure that the numbers really work for that – do they?'

The general view was that a rainbow coalition was unlikely, but not impossible.

I spoke next. I said that if the Conservative strategy was to reach out to us publicly but to hope privately that the talks did not succeed, we would have to be very careful not to be blamed for the failure to create a stable government.

I pointed out that all our pre-election preparations had led to the conclusion that in a hung parliament we had to be seen to be working for an outcome that was right for the country as a whole. If we were seen to be putting ourselves first we would be blamed for instability and we could then be the big losers in any second general election. This was even more the case given the difficult economic environment.

I also emphasised that if we went into any arrangement with the Conservatives, we needed to consider a fixed-term parliament, to build up trust and stability.

Chris Huhne said: 'Look, it is absolutely vital to strengthen our bargaining position, by making the rainbow coalition a real possibility. If we can do this, we might even persuade David Cameron to accept a referendum on voting reform.

'However, let's be realistic, the danger of a rainbow coalition is that it might fall to pieces. Plaid and the SNP, for example, would be a nightmare to deal with, and this would make deficit reduction very difficult indeed. However, we have to make the rainbow coalition a serious option if we are to strengthen our negotiating position.

'Of course, if we do end up in a rainbow coalition, David Cameron will simply wait for it all to unravel. This is a leader who has a "Napoleonic control" over his party, and who can afford to wait to fight another election,' finished Chris.

Nick intervened again. 'I have to say that based on the existing arithmetic in the Commons I am incredibly dubious that a rainbow coalition can deliver.

'I also think the markets would go nuts,' he said. 'It would be really difficult to take tough action to tackle the deficit, and that could mean higher interest rates and the UK being targeted by the markets in the same way as Greece, Portugal and the other high debt countries. I am seriously worried about that prospect. And as for Gordon Brown, I have to tell you that I believe that he would be incapable of leading a coalition government, and that he would be unacceptable to the country.

'But, let's be absolutely clear, a minority Conservative administration would lead quickly to a second general election. This would be bad for the economy, bad for the country and would be a big political risk for us.

'I think it will be tough to negotiate what we want from either the Conservatives or Labour. But failure would condemn us and the country to a second general election.'

Andrew Stunell felt that the election result made an autumn general election difficult to avoid. 'We just have to accept that this is where we are, and get on and plan for it,' he said. 'And let's be clear – the rainbow coalition option is just not deliverable. It would be impossible to tackle the deficit with all the horse-trading that a rainbow coalition would require.'

We had a brief discussion about the arithmetic of the new House of Commons. Someone attempted to write up on the office white-board the latest projection of the number of seats for each party. There was a rather frustrating few minutes while people debated whether the Speaker's seat was included in the Conservative total, how many seats the Irish had and so on. Nobody seemed to be clear about whether there was a genuine, credible, alternative to a Conservative administration of some kind. And this was a rather important decision to get right.

In front of us we had various policy briefing papers from our superb team of advisers, as well as the 'Coalition Agreement' and 'Confidence and Supply Agreement' which I had drafted before the general election was called.

We all agreed, in line with Nick's statement, that we should be ready to open negotiations with the Conservatives and that any communication with Labour should be on an informal basis.

Ed Llewellyn, Cameron's chief of staff, contacted us at around 12.30pm to acknowledge Nick's speech and to help arrange the first Lib Dem–Con talks. He also informed us that David Cameron would be making a statement later in the afternoon, and would want to talk privately to Nick.

During our meeting we were also interrupted by a call for Danny Alexander from Lord (Peter) Mandelson. We adjourned the meeting while Danny went next door to take the call.

Peter Mandelson told Danny that he wanted to commend Nick for his statement on the Cowley Street steps, but he urged that parallel discussions should be held with the Labour Party. Danny replied that he had made clear to Peter that we had to keep our promise to talk first with the Conservatives.

Nick agreed with this. 'Look,' he said, 'we must act here with honesty, openness and integrity. I have said that we will negotiate first with the Conservatives, and that is what we must do. That doesn't mean refusing to even listen to Labour, but we have to act privately in a way that is consistent with what we are saying publicly.

'Meanwhile, I want to make sure we are prepared for every eventuality. I want a contingency paper prepared immediately for another general election in the autumn – this year!'

The thought of a second general election filled us all with dread, not least on a personal level. That, of course, was not our official party position!

We finished the meeting with agreement that Nick would speak to David Cameron after a planned 2.30pm statement by the Conservative leader. We would then meet again in the evening in Cowley Street to review our strategy. Saturday would, as planned, start with meetings of the Lib Dem shadow Cabinet and the Parliamentary Party. The Federal Executive of the party would also meet in the afternoon. The plan was that this consultation with the party would take place before any serious talks.

My own view was that we needed to get on with negotiations as soon as possible, as the media and the public would expect some sense of urgency. The needs of the country should come before internal consultations.

We were all keenly aware that there would be a huge amount of speculation in the media and in the financial markets about whether or not a stable government could be formed, and about our intentions.

We also knew that there would be pressure for early progress and action, and that we couldn't afford to sit around talking. Any sense that hung parliaments automatically lead to dithering and indecision would be more damaging to us than to either of the other two parties – unless they and not we could be shown to be clearly to blame. This was unlikely to be the case, given our excessive requirements for party consultation, which at times seemed designed to bind party leaders in unbreakable chains.

We had discussed a timescale for action before the election and I had pressed consistently for us to move as swiftly as possible. While some wanted to consult, get some sleep and not start talking until Sunday or Monday at the earliest, I wanted swift action and early talks.

I had envisaged preliminary talks starting on Friday 7 May, with party consultation on Saturday 8 May (along with further talks), and I had wanted the whole negotiation completed by Tuesday 12 May.

This was, I felt, the very fastest possible timetable for completing the coalition talks, but I also felt that the media and markets were unlikely to tolerate much more delay than this. It was, in a sense, both the fastest and slowest timescale possible. And with the international markets already in a febrile state, a failure to form a stable government could have a real impact on the UK bond market and on UK interest rates, as well as on confidence in the pound.

Nevertheless, I did not relish the prospect of trying to get a decision out of the Liberal Democrat Party in this timescale or anything like it. Liberal Democrats love debate, discussion and consultation, and it was always clear that the whole Parliamentary Party would want to be involved in making a decision, and not merely the shadow Cabinet.

Having been involved in the negotiations to create the first coalition government in the new Scottish Parliament in 1999, as well as the negotiations over the Welsh Assembly government in 2000, I knew just how difficult the process of securing party agreement could be.

I also knew that other members of our negotiating team were definitely on the 'don't rush things' end of the spectrum.

The hugely experienced Andrew Stunell advised against decisions taken without enough sleep, and felt that the serious negotiations should really start after the weekend.

Even the normally businesslike Chris Huhne argued for stately progress and bubbled with international statistics about how long it took to form coalitions in other European countries. Chris is quite brilliant and normally very media conscious, but I could not support his suggested weekend media strategy of intensively briefing the British press on just how many weeks it took to form coalitions on the Continent and elsewhere.

My view was that the *Sun* or the *Daily Mail*, or even the BBC, were unlikely to change their views on the speed of coalition building as a consequence of a Lib Dem press officer suggesting they look up Italy or Malta in an international league table to find out how long it took their politicians to cobble together a deal.

The fact is that we are not Germany, Italy or Malta. We are Britain. And the British press and British people are used to seamless and swift transfers of power. I was sure that the speed and smoothness of the transfer would make a very big impact on people's initial views of the credibility and competence of any coalition or partnership. That was certainly the impression I had gained from our experiences in Scotland in 1999 and Wales in 2000.

I was also of the view that the amount of discussion and negotiation would swiftly expand to fill any amount of time allocated to it. And I felt that more time was no guarantee of a better agreement. It seemed to me that we just had to use the available time effectively.

Fortunately both Nick and Danny had agreed on the necessity for us to act quickly and so plans had been put in place for a swift start to the negotiations, as well as for early internal consultation to reduce the risk of 'noises off', by ensuring that everyone was kept informed and given a chance to express their views.

We confirmed our plans for the following day's meetings of the shadow Cabinet, Parliamentary Party and Federal Executive. MPs and others were now paged to let them know where and when they would be expected to meet. This was vital for securing party unity and a coherent media message.

Once all of these plans had been put in place, Nick set off back to his house in Putney to see his family and to snatch a few hours of much needed rest.

The ball was now in David Cameron's court and we waited to see how he would respond.

Before the election we had expected David Cameron to react boldly to a hung parliament, by offering us talks on a full coalition with important concessions on policy. And we needed to be able to respond in kind.

It seemed to us that an offer of this kind fitted the bold nature of Mr Cameron's political personality, his pledge to reach out to others in politics and the electoral interests of the Conservative Party.

From Mr Cameron's perspective, a Lib Dem–Conservative coalition could put him into No. 10 as Prime Minister and give him a large enough majority to deliver on the tough choices necessary to sort out the British economy and public finances.

There was clearly another reason for David Cameron to be bold. If, as seemed more likely, we had to turn down such a coalition because of the absence of agreement on key policies, including voting reform, or for reasons of political caution, then the absence of 'strong government' might be blamed on us. This would be damaging in the event of a second election and could help the Conservatives to secure an outright majority.

David Cameron's 'big, open and comprehensive' offer did not take long in coming. It was announced by the Conservative leader from St Stephen's Club, Queen Anne's Gate, at 2.30pm.

This was less than an hour after Gordon Brown had also publicly signalled his willingness to talk to us and had pledged to stay in Downing Street to see if an agreement between the Lib Dems and Labour could be reached.

We now had two coalition offers on the table.

This was exactly what we had expected under these circumstances, indeed we never seriously considered that full coalition would not be the 'opening pitch'" of both other parties. It is quite simply what the public would expect.

However, we strongly suspected that the Conservatives would be resistant to any form of voting reform for Westminster, and we thought it likely that a coalition agreement would founder on that rock, as well as on some of the key policy differences between us, for example on tax and Europe. We believed, at least before the general election, that this would be the Conservative expectation and strategy.

Nevertheless, there were some strong clues in David Cameron's statement that his offer of a full coalition was more than just a political manoeuvre.

The Conservative leader talked of Britain having 'voted for a new politics'. That sounded like an expectation of more than just a minority government, even with some sort of loose confidence and supply agreement.

And the wording on a confidence and supply arrangement in Mr Cameron's statement was lukewarm at best: 'It's been done before, and yes we can try to do it again.' That hardly sounded like a ringing endorsement.

On the other hand there was, according to the Conservative leader, 'a case for going further' into a full coalition. The case was based in part on the need to tackle 'the biggest threat' to our national interest – Britain's huge budget deficit.

That required, according to Mr Cameron, 'a strong, stable government that lasts [and] . . . which has the support of the public to take the difficult decisions that are needed. . .'

There was, of course, a passage setting out Conservative bottom lines – on the deficit, on defence, immigration and Europe.

But the statement also contained a detailed description of the scope for delivering key Liberal Democrat manifesto commitments – on schools funding, a low-carbon economy, taxation, civil liberties and political reform.

In Downing Street, Gordon Brown and his inner circle were apparently unimpressed by Mr Cameron's performance. They thought it was a mistake to be reaching out to such an extent to the Liberal Democrats, almost an admission of failure. Theirs was a typically tribal reaction and a serious misjudgement.

Also watching Mr Cameron's performance was a wiser and less partisan representative of the Labour cause: Lord Mandelson. This veteran political strategist wrote later that: 'I was almost alone in our ranks in being impressed. Gordon and his team told me they felt it was a mistaken show of weakness, given the fact that the Tories had won the largest number of seats. To me, it sounded like the new politics . . . In the past, I had felt that Cameron was not bold enough about changing his party . . . But now he was acting boldly.' (*The Third Man*, pp. 544–5)

Lord Mandelson was right. This was a bold, almost Blairite, attempt to seize the initiative and to capture the public mood.

The truth was that the Conservatives had failed to secure a majority, in spite of the recession, Gordon Brown's leadership and thirteen years in opposition. That had to be recognised.

The enthusiastic offer of a 'new politics' is undoubtedly what Tony Blair would have made in 1997. But the scale of his majority in 1997 and in 2001 made this unnecessary, and perhaps even impossible.

For David Cameron, the failure to secure a majority under the peculiarly favourable circumstances of 2010 now made such boldness both possible and, perhaps, necessary.

The prizes for Mr Cameron were obvious: government, not opposition; stability, not chaos; joint responsibility for tough decisions, not sole blame for the painful cuts to come; and an opportunity to change the entire perception of the Conservative Party and to reshape British politics.

In the incredibly busy and pressured atmosphere of that afternoon, I am not sure that the significance of these aspects of Mr Cameron's speech was immediately taken on board in our Cowley Street headquarters. We had expected a 'big, open and comprehensive offer', if there was a hung parliament, and that is what we had got.

But was it a bluff or was there serious intent? Was it the preferred Conservative position in private or just a public posture? And if it was the Conservatives' preferred outcome, what price would they be willing to pay for it?

We didn't know how serious the offer was or what concessions would be made to help deliver it. But we did not have to wait long to find out.

At around four o'clock in the afternoon, Nick Clegg and David Cameron spoke on the telephone for the first time since the election results were in. Nick was, by now, back in his house in Putney, trying to get a bit of rest.

David Cameron started the conversation: 'Look, Nick, I really appreciated your statement. You said during the election that you would allow the party with most seats and votes to have first go at forming a government, and you've been true to your word. Thank you. I just want to say that I believe that you and I can get on. I believe that this is doable, and for the good of the country we need a decent government that delivers stability and which works.'

Nick replied: 'Thanks for that. I made a promise and I am keeping it. Look, I saw your statement, and I listened carefully. I am very happy to explore the scope for agreement further, but I must be honest that there are some key issues which will be very difficult for both sides to agree on, and which are really important to both parties – for example, Europe. We have to see if we can handle these "red line" issues.'

'I understand,' said David Cameron. 'Let me make clear that I am open to any agreement from a full coalition to a confidence and supply arrangement. I am open to all thoughts – what we have to deliver is economic stability. Right now that is crucial for the country. I am not one of the "old guard" – I favour doing things differently. We are ready to start talking to you on a formal basis. I will throw in my top four people. My negotiating team will consist of William Hague,

George Osborne and Oliver Letwin, as well as my chief of staff, Ed Llewellyn. They know my views and they know my party well. And Oliver probably knows our respective policies better than we do! All of this team support me in thinking that a full coalition would be best for Britain. That includes William Hague, who is very much onside.'

'OK, that's helpful,' said Nick. 'My team will be led by Danny Alexander, and with him will be David Laws, Chris Huhne, and Andrew Stunell.'

Mr Cameron was keen to get the negotiations going as soon as possible: 'We really need to start the talks this evening and make good progress. Pretty soon people are going to say "who the hell is running this country?" Perhaps we can have a first meeting of the teams this evening at 7pm? It would send out a really good signal to the country and the markets. I really want to avoid this process stretching out for too long. We must try to conclude things by Monday morning, for when the markets open.'

'I would also like us to speak, face-to-face, pretty soon. If you want, I am ready for a really big agreement, with Cabinet posts. If not, and you want us to go ahead by ourselves, I would not be as happy, but I am genuinely open to exploring what works best. I would prefer a bit more of a binding deal, but I would settle for less. Our teams could meet at 7pm in 70 Whitehall, which as you know the Civil Service has prepared for our talks. I just think we need to get on and finish this as soon as possible – within one or two days, not into next week, if we can avoid this. I think Monday morning will be a key moment, with the markets opening. Can we aim for that? That would be pretty powerful.'

Nick replied: 'Look, look, I'm happy to start this evening. But I have a meeting of my Parliamentary Party tomorrow morning, and we cannot decide anything until I have consulted people. Also, we mustn't rush this. We have to get the details right. I don't want to sound terribly po-faced, but we have to sort out the substance of all this. That will drive everything as far as I am concerned – can we deliver on the substance?

'And I don't deny that I have concerns on some areas. You know where the problems will be. Europe may be a red line issue for your party, but it is for me too – it is something I feel very passionately about. But I am serious about these talks, and we will enter them in a spirit of compromise. By the way, you should also know that I have been contacted by the other side. But I am clear about the chronology of this – we are talking seriously with you lot first.'

Mr Cameron responded: 'Well I just wanted to reassure you that Gordon hasn't been in contact with us! I just think it would be ridiculous if Gordon Brown stayed in Downing Street, after losing one hundred seats. Yes, there are "red lines" for both parties. On Europe, our view is clearly that there should be no more passing of powers to the European Union in this parliament. But I understand what you are saying on delivery – you want to show that the Liberal Democrats are really delivering on the bread and butter domestic issues. Let's press ahead, and again I want to shoot higher than just a confidence and supply arrangement.'

Nick said: 'I enter this in a genuine spirit of compromise, to see what we can agree. Let's get our teams together.'

The conversation closed on a positive note, and with agreement for the two leaders to meet over the weekend, with the timing dependent on the momentum of the talks. In the meantime it was agreed that Danny Alexander and Ed Llewellyn would get in touch, and that a first meeting would be set up within a few hours. This was the first substantive post-election discussion between David Cameron and Nick Clegg. It set the right tone and had lasted just twelve minutes.

One or two of our negotiating team had gone off home to rest and recuperate, but they soon found themselves being phoned and woken up by Alison Suttie, Nick Clegg's deputy chief of staff, with instructions to meet at the National Liberal Club at 7pm.

This would allow for a pre-meeting of our team, before going over to the Cabinet Office for the first talks with the Conservatives. In the meantime, a second party leader was keen to talk to Nick Clegg: Gordon Brown.

The Prime Minister's call came through to Nick's home in Putney at around 5pm, just an hour after discussions with David Cameron. Peter Mandelson listened in on another phone, as did Alison Suttie.

The discussion started well enough, with the Prime Minister congratulating Nick on his performance during the election campaign: 'Hi, Nick. Well, history never quite repeats itself in quite the same way, does it?

'Nick, well done, this was a triumph for you. You got your message across. You presented yourself very well,' said Mr Brown, with one of his rather charmless and double-edged comments. Nick replied: 'That's nice of you to say so, but I don't seem to have delivered the seats we wanted!'

Gordon Brown continued, slowly and in measured tones: 'Look, you did well, Nick. Now, you know the Civil Service will be available to offer their support to us?'

Nick explained that the Conservative and Lib Dem negotiating teams would meet that evening for early talks, and these would focus on issues of substance and whether there was scope for agreement. 'I spoke to David Cameron about one hour ago. We've all seen what we've said to each other in public. I have made clear that what I do will be driven by the substance, including on political reform. I need to look first at whether there is common ground with the Conservatives.'

Mr Brown then launched into a great pitch for a Lib Dem–Labour coalition. It sounded almost as if he was reading from a prepared script.

'Look Nick, whatever the Conservatives are offering on policy, I am sure we could match them immediately. I have already prepared a note on our policies, another note on the policy differences between us and a third note on the constitutional process moving forward. We need our sides to meet as soon as possible.

'We have so much in common on the constitutional reform agenda, which I know is so important to you. I want you to understand my commitment to the political reform process. I just would not want you to undervalue my commitment on this, but I do think a referendum would be needed – though I am open about how we go about all this. Reform of the Commons and Lords is clearly vital. This is a once in a generation chance to clean up the political system. There is electoral reform, reform of the Lords, freedom of information.

'There is also Europe. I would emphasise that a major crisis in the Euro area now seems likely. Perhaps we should get Vince and Alistair Darling to talk? There will be a G7 discussion this evening on this. Europe really needs a strategy for growth. We must be part of this. I want you to know that I attach importance to Europe, where I think we can find common ground.'

By this stage there was no holding Mr Brown back.

'Look Nick,' he continued, 'On tax, spending and the economy, there are not big ideological differences between us – not big stumbling blocks. I have looked at all this. We both want to help the low paid on tax, the issue is how. We can look at property taxes, but that will take a bit of time on the revaluation. But there is common ground.

'Turning to civil liberties. ID cards and "28 days", I think we can thrash it out. I'm going through all the possible difficulties, but I have not found anything that cannot be resolved.

'Nick, the recent political scandals have really changed my view on political reform. We need to make progress on that. Now, perhaps I could also go through all the other issues that came up during the recent campaign as well if. . .'

A desperate-sounding Nick swiftly interrupted: 'No! No! Don't. Please don't! I think I know where you are heading. And, look, I am genuinely grateful that you've clearly given this amount of thought to it. I'd very much like to see the written description of all this that you referred to. I just need to say that there is a chronology to this. I have to start with the Conservatives, I gave that pledge. . .'

Mr Brown interrupted: 'But I am worried about the constitutional precedent here . . . anyway, I am not going to argue,' he said.

'Look, Gordon, how do you see the politics of all this?' said Nick. 'How could our parties overcome the accusations about two parties which came second and third forming a government, and could we actually form a stable government?'

Mr Brown plunged in: 'Yes, I have thought about all this. Nick, people want change, and two parties working together would mean change. Also, we have together over 50% of the vote. The Conservatives received about 36%. I would not pursue this if I didn't think it was possible. And, yes, we can command support in the Commons. We can form an understanding with all the Northern Ireland parties, based on the economic needs of Northern Ireland. I am thinking of the SDLP, the Alliance, the Unionists. You know, the DUP are not positive towards the Conservatives at all. I would see an economic understanding with all the Northern Ireland parties, with their backing on confidence issues and on major legislation. This would guarantee us a majority on those crucial issues.

'Nick, I could prove to you that this would work, but I think we both need to meet soon in private to discuss all this. So, yes, we can get a majority. Yes, it is change if two parties work together. Yes, we would have a changed agenda. Look, I have spoken to Vince already. I am happy to invite some of your people into the Cabinet, indeed I wanted to do this some time ago. We would need a fixed-term agreement, so we know when it is ending.'

'Fixed for two years or longer?' asked Nick.

'Curtailed or four years,' replied Mr Brown. 'But we would need some time if we are to get the constitutional changes through.'

'Look,' Nick interrupted. 'Thanks for getting in touch. Sorry you had difficulty reaching me. I. . .'"

Mr Brown broke in again: 'I understand you have said you will talk to David Cameron first, but can you also talk to us on policy today?'

Nick replied: 'I have said I will talk to the Tories first. Let's see tomorrow how those talks go, and then consider how we proceed.'

But Mr Brown was determined to force his way into the negotiations as soon as possible. He started to press harder and more insistently: 'It would surely be worthwhile to have parallel discussions?'

'Why not send me a paper I can look at?' replied Nick.

'Nick, can you put someone in charge with consulting with us? I want progress as soon as possible. This could be a problem. We must make progress before Monday morning, when the markets open. They will want to know whether there is stalemate or progress. I just want to confirm our good intentions.'

Nick began to get somewhat exasperated by Gordon Brown's obvious attempts to undermine his 'Conservatives first' commitment on talks: 'Gordon, I know how you feel, but I don't want to trip up over my own shoelaces on this. I have made this clear publicly. There is a process here, a chronology. Look, who are you thinking of on your team anyway?'

Mr Brown replied: 'Peter Mandelson. Andrew Adonis and Ed Miliband. With Alistair or Ed Balls, depending on the issues. Andrew Adonis would be the best person on policy. But Peter will lead on the process here. Look Nick, I really want to honour the constitutional process here. I want to know, to recommend to the Queen, to know if there is progress. I want to know first thing tomorrow and we need to meet in private – there are things I don't want to say to you over the phone.'

Nick replied that he understood Mr Brown's desire to talk, but he needed more time: 'My shadow Cabinet meets tomorrow morning. I understand that speed is of the essence, but you will just have to give me more time. . .'

'Putting it another way,' interrupted Mr Brown, 'If you decide to talk to the Conservatives, can you not talk to us too? Surely these things are not mutually exclusive? I think our parties need to know what choices are on the table.

'Nick, I have studied history. I approached Ming [Campbell] in 2007 on this. I know that the future of our country is a progressive alliance between two progressive political parties. The election has provided a moment of opportunity which will not return. We could miss this opportunity for ever. It is an opportunity. . .'

It sounded like a script that someone else had written. The great Labour tribalist was suddenly making a deathbed conversion to the benefits of co-operation with another party, towards which his usual stance was one of contempt. It was somehow not entirely convincing.

On and on he went: 'The possibility has eluded us before Nick, for various historic reasons' – he did not mention that his own determined opposition had been one of these – 'You would get electoral reform, it would be a pro-Europe government and we would have a progressive economic policy. There is a real prize here which we must not neglect.'

Nick was by now becoming a little frustrated by being lectured: 'Yes, I see the pot of gold at the end of the rainbow but—'

Gordon Brown cut in again: 'But I can deliver on this Nick. I can deliver my party, and a majority in the Commons and the constitutional change.'

Nick, increasingly exasperated, but trying not to show it, said: 'Yes, but Gordon, I just can't sit down to discuss this at 8am tomorrow morning. I have to meet my party. I have to talk to the Conservatives. I just can't do it. I hear the urgency. Maybe later tomorrow.'

'But Nick,' Mr Brown continued, 'There is a problem all over Europe. We will be hit too if we cannot deliver a stable government. Look, I am aware that I cannot control events. But I am anxious to meet. There are some things I cannot say on the phone. Let's try to fix a meeting via Peter Mandelson or Jeremy Heywood.'

Nick tried to sum up, 'I will go away and talk to my folk to see when we can discuss all this. Danny Alexander will fix it with Peter.'

Mr Brown made one last pitch: 'Don't be disappointed by your results, Nick. You have made a huge impact. The agenda of the future has been set by this election. We need to work closely. . .'

'Yes, yes, yes, that's very helpful,' Nick said.

There was a final exchange of pleasantries and then the phone call ended. It had been twenty-three minutes long – twice the length of the discussion with David Cameron.

Alison Suttie, who had been listening in, said: 'That sounded like a twenty-five minute lecture!'

'Well, it certainly wasn't much of a conversation,' said Nick. The Lib–Lab discussions had not got off to a good start.

Nick was not the only one who felt that Mr Brown's negotiating style lacked a certain subtlety and charm. Peter Mandelson was listening in on the conversation and in his memoirs he diplomatically records that, 'I was a little worried that Gordon might have come across a bit too heavily, telling Nick what he should think rather than asking him what he thought' (*The Third Man*, p. 545). Indeed.

That evening the talks with the Conservatives began. To my satisfaction, we weren't wasting any time. The negotiating team assembled – Danny, Chris, Andrew and me, along with Alison Suttie. We met first in the National Liberal Club, after we eventually succeeded in persuading a rather strict doorman that we could be trusted to use one of the gloomy meeting rooms down in the basement.

We met at 7pm and only had until 7.30pm to be around the corner in the Cabinet Office for our formal meeting with the Conservatives.

We agreed that we needed to highlight our four key manifesto pledges – on tax cuts, a pupil premium, political reform and a sustainable economy.

And we needed to convey very clearly the importance to us of a referendum on electoral reform, the least convincing part of David Cameron's afternoon statement.

Andrew was concerned that we should not rush our talks. He advised 'slowing things down'. Danny suggested we should plan to meet for about four hours each day, and that we should agree a future schedule of meetings now.

I would have been happy to meet throughout the day and night to make decent progress, but I was just relieved that the talks were starting fairly early. In Scotland, following the 1999 Scottish Parliamentary elections, it took until the Monday after polling day for serious talks to start, which I felt was much too late. We at least had sixty hours head start in comparison.

At 7.25pm we ended our preparations, left the National Liberal Club and made the short journey around the corner onto Whitehall, and over the road to the Cabinet Office, at 70 Whitehall. We had been informed before the election that, in the event of a hung parliament, a suite of offices and a conference room would be set aside for cross-party negotiations here in the Cabinet Office, just next door to Downing Street.

We arrived to be greeted by the Civil Service team who were there to support the negotiations.

Both the Civil Service and Buckingham Palace had been preparing for the possibilities of a hung parliament for many months. Nick Clegg and Danny Alexander had met Gus O'Donnell to talk over the various issues which would arise, and Danny had also spoken to the Queen's Private Secretary about the expectations of Buckingham Palace.

When we arrived we were led up a long and rather stark staircase and then taken to our 'Lib Dem' suite of offices, just down the corridor from those allocated to the Conservatives. We had two medium-sized rooms available to us – an outer office with three or four desks in it, and an inner office with a conference table and four armchairs.

We had a few minutes before the talks were due to begin. Chris Huhne sent out an early signal of his serious intentions by settling down in an armchair and leafing through a huge volume containing photographs of the government art collection, which is available to decorate the offices of Secretaries of State and other ministers. This was planning for coalition government in earnest!

The Conservative team arrived somewhat after us, but eventually we both got together in the large, light and rather grand conference room which had been allocated for our joint use.

We shook hands with each other in a friendly and expectant atmosphere. Both sides were aware that this was political history in the making.

The Conservative team of William Hague, as chair, George Osborne and Oliver Letwin sat along one side of a narrow conference table, with their backs to the main part of the room. On the other side of the table sat Danny Alexander, Chris Huhne, Andrew Stunell and me.

On the two ends of the table sat Ed Llewellyn, with his back to the window, and at the other end of the table was Alison Suttie.

It was good neutral ground for a meeting, and although the room was rather large the conference table was not, so there was a sense of intimacy rather than formality. The two teams were separated by a couple of feet at most. We were now to discover the dimensions of the political space that separated us.

We surveyed each other with the pleasant surprise of acquaintances who had known each other for years and suddenly found themselves at the altar, having never quite seen the possibility.

I weighed up the Conservative team opposite us, and in truth it was a good team to use to front a pitch to the Liberal Democrats – senior, serious but also courteous, open and direct.

I did not know William Hague and in fact I don't think that I had ever spoken to him before. But, he was friendly, warm, pragmatic, helpful and relaxed. He never pretended to be a liberal, and on issues such as Europe there was obviously quite a difference in approach between the two sides, but he was straightforward, respectful and businesslike.

George Osborne I knew far better. George had arrived in Parliament the same year as me, 2001. We had led for our respective parties on the Child Trust Fund Bill, where I had opposed the Labour government's legislation, while George had picked holes and prodded, but had avoided outright opposition. I think, in truth, that George would have happily opposed the whole Bill, but the Conservatives were a little nervous of blanket opposition, given that the first government trust fund cheques were due to be sent out very close to the likely general election date in 2005 – a remarkable coincidence, no doubt.

I learned while serving on that Bill committee that George was bright, sharp and amusing, with a mischievous sense of humour. He also has an extraordinary strategic and tactical understanding of British politics – not just Conservative politics, but that of the Labour and Liberal Democrat parties too. I never made the mistake of underestimating him, as some of my other colleagues did, and was not surprised when he turned out to be the first Conservative shadow Chancellor to get the measure of Gordon Brown, and to really get under his skin.

After the publication of the *Orange Book*, which I co-authored in 2004, there was increased speculation about the scope for co-operation between the Liberal Democrat and Conservative parties.

But I recall not long afterwards sitting in George's office in Portcullis House, warning him that if the Conservatives ever cherished the idea of forming a coalition with the Lib Dems then the price would be a referendum on electoral reform.

'You need to understand', I had told him, 'that this is not just about the views of the party leadership. In our party, you cannot go into coalition without taking the rest of the party with you. And the party would never, ever, allow us to go into a coalition at Westminster without some prospect of electoral reform.'

George must have decided that there were better ways of forging partnerships between us, because in the summer recess of 2006 he asked to see me in my office in Westminster, unexpectedly and at short notice.

I agreed, thinking that he probably wanted to discuss the scope for co-operation on developing a critique of some part of Gordon Brown's economic policy – perhaps on tax credits, where there were huge administrative problems.

George arrived in my office on the fifth floor of 1 Parliament Street, and with very little introduction plunged into his proposition: 'I have come here with David Cameron's agreement to say that if you will join the Conservative Party we would like to offer you a place in the shadow Cabinet, and then – when we win, which we will – the Cabinet.'

I was pretty stunned, but knew this was not an offer to leave hanging in the air.

'I am going to have to decline that, however flattering,' I said. 'The truth is that I am a liberal, not a Conservative. I believe passionately in creating a fairer country, but I happen to believe that this will be done through liberal means and not by big government solutions.'

George clearly thought I was stark raving mad. 'But don't you actually want to be in government doing something, rather than spending a lifetime in opposition?' he asked.

'I don't expect to spend a lifetime in opposition,' I said. 'I think that Labour will lose the next election, but I don't think you'll have enough seats to form a government. At that stage there may well be some sort of coalition.'

We had a long discussion on the difference between liberalism and Conservatism, and where we both saw the three political parties positioned. He gave no ground and neither did I. We both agreed to keep our discussions confidential and so they remained for a good six months, until the journalist Peter Oborne phoned me up one day to tell me he had heard the story from someone – I know not from which party – and that he was going to write it all up. By then, it didn't really matter.

Now, suddenly, the prospect of being in the same government as George, but representing different parties, seemed remarkably real. We must both have seen the irony of the situation, though neither of us mentioned it.

The third member of the Conservative team was Oliver Letwin, my next door parliamentary neighbour, the MP for West Dorset, whose house is a couple of villages away from mine. Oliver's national reputation used to be as an extreme right-winger and he was the Conservative who was chased around the countryside by the media during the 2001 general election, when he went beyond agreed Conservative policy to talk about the need for big public spending cuts of £20bn.

But I remember Paddy Ashdown telling me many years ago: 'Do not underestimate Oliver. He is not merely very charming, he is bright, decent and actually pretty liberal on many issues.' Paddy was right. Oliver did turn out to be warm, cheerful, honest, trustworthy and pretty liberal-minded. At times he almost seems too nice, too decent and too straightforward to be in politics, which I mean as a compliment.

Oliver does have very liberal instincts on many issues, and was frequently teased by William and George as being the secret liberal on their team.

Ed Llewellyn was the fourth member of the Conservative team. He was thoughtful, bright, low-key but highly perceptive. He had, for a time, been a member of Paddy Ashdown's staff while Paddy served as High Representative in Bosnia, so there was already a connection there with Liberal Democrats such as Paddy and Julian Astle (now of the liberal thinktank, CentreForum).

So this was a Conservative team that was not only very senior, and which clearly had the full confidence of David Cameron, but which also turned out to be able to engage in a sensible, mature and respectful way with our team. At the time, that did not seem too much to expect, but our negotiations with the Labour Party were later to show that these things cannot be taken for granted.

William Hague started off the meeting by assuring us of the Conservatives' serious intent.

'We sincerely want this to work,' he said, 'and we think each side needs to understand the other's internal processes.' I hardly dared say that I had been a Liberal Democrat for twenty-five years and was still struggling to understand our party's internal processes.

William Hague continued: 'We need to fix other meetings with each other, so we can bring the talks to a swift conclusion. Our team will be available twenty-four hours a day over this weekend. Our own internal processes are rather simpler than yours, I think. There is no "triple lock" on the Conservative leader!'

Danny explained our own procedures, including consultation with our shadow Cabinet, Parliamentary Party, Federal Executive and perhaps even a special conference. I groaned inwardly. William Hague listened carefully, and – although frowning a little – was clearly trying his best not to look too appalled. Danny also emphasised that we needed to take enough time to get the policy agreement right. 'We think that serious talks should therefore start on Sunday, after consultation and background work,' he said.

But Danny agreed with Oliver Letwin that in the meantime we could exchange papers on a range of policy issues, to get the preparatory work done. Oliver Letwin said: 'We understand that there are four key bottom-line issues for your party. We can draft our response on each of these and send over a paper for you to look at. This will help both sides to start to make progress.'

I replied: 'That would be really helpful. The key issues for us are delivering a £10,000 personal allowance, a properly funded pupil premium, a sustainable economy, as well as electoral and wider political reform.'

I expressed concerns about David Cameron's proposal, in his statement earlier in the day, of a committee to review electoral reform options. 'It all sounds pretty flaky to me,' I said. 'I have to be blunt, there is no way our party is going to buy this.'

George Osborne then responded: 'Look, let's start on the economy. We support raising the personal tax allowance. The issue is one of cost, and how much we can afford. But I am very happy to talk about that. But on tax, stopping some of Labour's planned increase in national insurance contributions next year is a bottom-line issue for us. We won the argument for this during the election campaign, and I think you also agreed in the election that if we can afford to, we need to stop these rises.'

'We also need to start cutting public spending in 2010. The Treasury has already identified the £6bn of cuts that I want. It can be done, and it isn't huge.'

Chris Huhne chipped in: '£6bn is less than 0.5% of Gross Domestic Product. Not huge.'

George continued: 'The debt crisis we have in the UK is a real problem and we have got to move swiftly to address it.'

I then intervened to say: 'And what about funding the Pupil Premium? This is a very important policy for us.'

George replied that the Conservatives supported the policy, and that he was happy to work with us to look at how it could be funded. 'This is a funding issue, not a policy issue,' said Oliver Letwin.

I then came to the potential big sticking point: 'Look, the one big problem here is voting reform. We believe in this strongly, but your review would just kick this into the long grass. No Lib Dem MP is ever going to support something as weak as you are proposing here.'

George Osborne paused and then said: 'Look, this is a subject of a lot of discussion in our party. Electoral reform is tough for us, but on the rest of the political reform agenda we are very open to your ideas. But I agree that this is the trickiest issue.'

William Hague now intervened: 'We have to start by recognising a big difference between our parties on this. It is a very difficult issue for Conservatives, most of whom support first-past-the-post. There isn't any support for proportional representation in the Conservative Party. You need to understand that.'

Chris Huhne responded robustly: 'We understand how this is difficult for you. But our party has been strung along before on PR – not least by Tony Blair in 1997. We don't want to repeat that experience. We don't want to repeat the whole Jenkins experience, of a review which leads nowhere. We must be able to make progress on a political reform package, including on the size of the House of Commons. Maybe we need to look at multi-member constituencies. But perhaps we need to park voting reform out of the talks for now. The leaders need to talk about it.'

William Hague replied: 'Well. We are prepared to reflect on it.'

We then discussed how Sunday's negotiations would proceed. It was agreed that we would each draft papers on particular policy issues, and that we would have major discussions on the four or five big policy areas, including the four key Lib Dem areas on tax, education funding, political reform and the economy.

William Hague also suggested dealing with the issue of forms of co-operation and 'red line' issues, but Danny said he was concerned we might be trying to cover too much in one day. I also said that we could give the Conservatives a copy of a draft confidence and supply agreement which we had prepared.

George Osborne said: 'Before we break up, a couple of points – David Cameron would really prefer the stability of a full coalition with Lib Dem ministers and so on. Ken Clarke, John Major and others also think that is what the country needs given the economic crisis. That is David Cameron's sincere view. But I accept that progress on policy will help determine the nature of our potential co-operation. I also want an early discussion on the economic situation. I am worried that the Greek crisis could spread to Spain and Portugal. And we don't want to get caught up in this in the UK, as a consequence of political uncertainty.'

We agreed that an early discussion of the economic challenges was essential, as well as political reform.

William Hague said he thought it might make sense to start on Sunday with the areas where policy agreement would be easiest. 'I think our discussions need to proceed in three stages,' he said. 'First, we should cover your core issues – your four key policy tests. Then we should look at what form co-operation between our two parties might take. Then we need to finish by looking at some of the "red line" issues, including those that are crucially important for our party.'

He continued, 'On Sunday I suggest we start by covering all of your four key areas, plus the deficit and civil liberties – six areas in total. We can start with some of the areas where there is agreement, for example on ID cards and a "Freedom Bill".'

But Andrew Stunell said he favoured starting with the controversial areas. I suspect Andrew was right, and this is what we agreed to do. So it was decided that we would start with the issues of political reform and the economy. This would at least mean that we could have something useful and reassuring to say on the economic issues before the markets opened on Monday morning.

We concluded the meeting with an agreement that William Hague and Danny would sort out the timing issues, and that policy papers would be prepared to facilitate discussion. George Osborne asked if it would be possible and sensible to discuss deficit reduction without Vince Cable being present.

Danny reassured him that we were in constant dialogue with Vince, and that we would ensure that he was content with whatever we agreed. We pointed out that we had a mandate to negotiate on behalf of the whole Lib Dem shadow Cabinet and Parliamentary Party.

At the end of the meeting, we shook hands and exchanged a few pleasantries. It had been a good start – open and constructive. The Conservative team left first by the front door. By now, a large group of reporters and camera crews were located outside the main exit onto Whitehall. We decided to dodge the waiting media by being shown out through a back exit. We were escorted through various corridors by the civil servants and out through a locked gate onto a deserted Horse Guards. We made our way back to Cowley Street without disturbance through a few crowds of German tourists.

Back in Cowley Street, we caught up on the media coverage of the day's events, and then reassembled in the same rather dingy first-floor conference room in which we had welcomed Nick Clegg back to London that morning.

We reported back to Nick on the relatively positive progress with the Conservatives, and stayed on with our team of policy experts to talk in more detail about how we would deal with the big issues that would dominate the negotiations over the next few days.

We were hugely assisted throughout the talks by a formidable team of policy advisers who had been working at full stretch during the general election, and who now also threw themselves into the detailed preparations for the negotiations. This team included Polly Mackenzie from Nick Clegg's own office, Christian Moon from the Lib Dem policy unit and our group of portfolio advisers – the excellent Chris Saunders and Will De Peyer (Treasury), James McGrory (Home Affairs), Sam Cannicott (Education), Katie Waring (Work and Pensions), and Ben Jones (Foreign Affairs and Defence). Many of this team were to become special advisers in the new government.

Earlier in the day, Paddy Ashdown had invited me over for a drink at his Kennington flat, once our work was concluded. By the time we left Cowley Street, it was about 11pm when I arrived at his house.

Paddy had no formal role in the negotiations, but anyone who thought that would stop him from trying to shape the future of British politics would soon discover how wrong they were. In any case, given Paddy's contacts within both of the other parties, he was working behind the scenes at Nick's request. Paddy is not a great spectator. He was a brilliant MP for Yeovil between 1983 and 2001, and I found that there was almost no aspect of constituency activities in which it was ever possible to exceed what he had achieved. He had only one blind spot as a 'local' MP, and that is he would never, ever, go along to watch and support one of our local sports teams, either Yeovil Town FC or the Ivel Barbarians rugby team. He is a man who has to be on the pitch himself, in the middle of the scrum or playing centre-forward. He is not a man for the touchlines of life.

From the very beginning, Paddy was one of Nick Clegg's strongest and most robust supporters, in fair weather and in foul. Indeed, Paddy was the first person to tell me about this bright young Lib Dem called Nick Clegg, then working in Brussels for Leon Brittan around a decade ago.

Paddy had urged Nick to stand for the leadership of the party in 2006, and he was one of his strongest supporters in 2007. Nick listened to Paddy, and Paddy in turn would speak to Nick on a regular basis.

Paddy and I sat down and opened a couple of beers. Paddy said that he was still of the view that any prospect of a deal with Labour was off the table because the parliamentary numbers simply didn't add up.

I could see the difficulties myself, but I was not quite so persuaded that this option could be ruled out categorically. But Paddy was, as ever, in no mood for such refinements. 'Look,' he said 'a "rainbow coalition" of parties would be the worst sort of advertisement for the politics of coalitions and partnerships, which must necessarily come with proportional representation. A weak coalition of this kind would kill stone dead the prospect of winning a referendum on voting reform, which would be crucial if such a coalition was to be formed.

'Can you imagine weeks of indecisive government, having to buy off the Irish, Welsh and Scottish on every single vote, and then after months of this you go to the people and say, "Please could you vote for AV or PR or whatever, so we can have much more of this type of government in the future?" It would be utterly dotty and it would kill PR stone dead for a generation. Look. A coalition with Labour is impossible. Doing nothing is impossible. That must point to a deal with the Conservatives.

'Don't you remember that bit from Sherlock Holmes? How does

it go? I think it is something like: "When you have eliminated the impossible, whatever remains, however improbable, must be the truth." Well, all the other options are clearly impossible.'

Although he was later to change his mind about the prospects of a deal with Labour, Paddy anticipated precisely how the Liberal Democrats would end up making the most difficult and important choice in their recent political history. Over the next few days we would gradually as a party eliminate the impossible options. We would be left with only one option still standing – an option which had for many years seemed as improbable for the Liberal Democrats as some of the solutions to the crimes which Mr Sherlock Holmes had to solve.

Consulting the party, 'listening' to Labour

I awoke on Saturday 8 May after very little sleep, and with a sense of impending gloom. Today was scheduled to be a day of 'consultation' in the Liberal Democrat Party. The Lib Dems love consultation and relish making life difficult for their leaders.

Telling the Liberal Democrat conference that a particular amendment has 'the total support of the leader and the Parliamentary Party' used to be an absolute assurance that it would go down to a crashing defeat.

And it is not only Lib Dem leaders who have found our party frustrating to deal with. Rhodri Morgan, when once Labour's leader in Wales, claimed that trying to get agreement amongst Liberal Democrats was like 'herding cats in a thunder storm'.

Lib Dem Parliamentary Party meetings with even a minimal timetable can often stretch on for hours, as every last MP determines to have his or her say. And the power of committees such as the Federal Executive or Federal Policy Committee is real and can be very destructive to a leader who cannot carry a majority there.

Moreover, I knew from my experiences in Scotland in 1999 and in Wales in 2000 that there are some Liberal Democrats who prefer the certainties and easy sound bites of opposition to the hard choices of government. Indeed, I was astonished in 1999 and 2000 at how many seemingly sensible people thought that our best strategy was to stay out of government no matter how much of our manifesto was going to be delivered into being through a coalition. For some people, avoiding the unpopularity that can come with responsibility seemed more important than making a difference.

I was under no illusion. Being in a coalition would almost certainly reduce the party's precious 'distinctiveness' and would, in at least the short term, reduce our opinion poll ratings. But what on the earth was the point of being in politics, if it was not to put your policies into practice?

Political popularity is not an ultimate objective to be carefully protected and conserved. It has to be used to make a real difference. And here was just that rare chance.

In addition, if we could secure the great prize of voting reform, this could help increase the chances that even more liberal policies would see the light of day in the future as well.

Of course, for me, coalition had a price. The other coalition partner had to concede enough on policy to make it worthwhile. And I was always willing to walk away if they did not. But I was under no illusion that being in government was better than the alternative, and that this should be our ultimate objective.

So a day of endless discussion with the whole Lib Dem shadow Cabinet, Parliamentary Party and Federal Executive did not seem like much to relish. It was, nonetheless, extremely important and, in spite of my frustrations about our internal processes, I was an advocate in these circumstances of holding such meetings early and often, in order to make sure people had their chance to be heard.

Taking a 'third party' into a coalition was bound to be a risky and controversial enterprise – not least when some Lib Dem MPs saw Labour as the greater threat and others the Conservatives. A leader who did not have the broad support of his or her party for a venture such as this would find proceeding into coalition to be difficult or impossible. In addition, delivering any sort of discipline in government would be almost impossible if people did not feel that they had had a chance to have their views heard, and that a majority had backed the decision.

So I did not expect reaching an agreement to be easy. From my previous experiences in Scotland and Wales I expected a sizeable minority of our party to oppose a coalition option under all conceivable circumstances. And the rest I expected to be split between those favouring Labour on 'progressive' grounds and those favouring the Conservatives on pragmatic ones.

I thought getting the party to a position of unity on any outcome would be very difficult. And the risk was that this would cause us to agree only to do nothing, to remain on the opposition benches. I was worried that we would only be able to unite around indecision, fudge and soft options.

Such an outcome, in my view, risked making us look unserious and unwilling to assume responsibility – in which case we would be the big losers from a second general election.

With such thoughts in my mind, I made my way over Lambeth Bridge and into Cowley Street for our 8am strategy meeting.

There we discovered that the first major scheduled Lib Dem meeting of the day, of our shadow Cabinet, was going to have to be delayed to allow Nick Clegg to go to the Cenotaph to lay a wreath to celebrate VE Day, along with Gordon Brown and David Cameron. This was at 11am.

Nick then returned to Local Government House in Smith Square, Westminster, for the Lib Dem shadow Cabinet meeting, which had been put back from 10am to around 12 noon. Every member of our shadow Cabinet was there and the room was packed with senior party staff.

Nick started with his assessment of the situation: 'Look, of course I am disappointed that the results weren't better. We had an excellent general election campaign, and everything was pointing to a real increase in seats. But although the results were not as good as the polls suggested, it is our job to keep up party morale. We have got to remind our members and supporters that our vote is up, and our vote share is up. And we are getting thousands more members joining – a huge surge in support. We have a responsibility as leaders of the party to rebuild morale and energy.'

'Where do we go next? Well, we clearly now have a hung parliament, and we have a big responsibility to the people of this country. I spoke to David Cameron yesterday afternoon, and our two negotiating teams met last night, just for preliminary talks.

'I said during the election that we would talk first to the party with most seats and votes, and I am going to keep that promise. We must play this with a completely straight bat. We will also negotiate on the basis of our manifesto pledges, and in particular our four key pledges on tax, schools, the economy and political reform.

'I have appointed a negotiating team of Danny Alexander, Chris Huhne, David Laws and Andrew Stunell. They will do all the negotiating, but will then report back to me and to the Parliamentary Party. They have already briefly met the Conservative team – last night – and Danny will report back to you on that in a minute. Let me be blunt. We need to move quickly. The markets will not like uncertainty, if the negotiations drag on. We have only two or three days to sort this out, or we will lose people's support and lose momentum.

'The choices we face are tough. The Conservatives would have to concede a lot to us on policy and electoral reform to make a deal possible. But a deal with Labour would also be very difficult. Gordon Brown phoned me yesterday too. We spoke – or rather he spoke – for almost half an hour. He was clearly desperate to do a deal. But there are big problems with a Labour deal. Firstly, I think Brown himself is pretty toxic politically. Secondly, Labour has clearly lost, and putting them back in power would not be popular. Thirdly, the parliamentary arithmetic means having a deal between four or five parties, and I just don't know if that would work.

'With the Conservatives the issue is one of substance – can we agree on the big policy issues? With Labour, we ought to be able to agree on most of the policy, but the politics of putting them back in power stinks and the politics of delivering a stable government is very tough. If we do not go into a full coalition with either party then the alternative is, bluntly, a minority Conservative government. If we get that, then frankly we can all go off and plan for a second general election this autumn.'

Danny then gave an update on the previous night's talks with the Conservatives and Nick opened the meeting up for comment.

There was a brief review of the election results, and congratulations to Nick Clegg for his performance during the campaign – not least in the televised leader debates.

Paul Burstow, the party's Chief Whip, said the great prize must be electoral reform. We had to focus on that. A number of MPs said that we needed to secure a fixed-term parliament to deliver stability and to avoid a second election. Tim Farron said that we mustn't look like we were worried about a second general election, but that we really don't want one – not least because party coffers are run down.

John Thurso said that the national interest really must come first: 'We will be written off if we don't act responsibly. Nick, your speech yesterday was just right. There are only three real options – a Conservative coalition, a Conservative minority government, or a national government.' Lorely Burt said that she did not think that putting Labour back in power was a serious prospect, and Jenny Willott told us she was against the rainbow coalition.

Chris Huhne, Tom McNally and Don Foster wanted to keep the rainbow coalition option in play. Steve Webb joked that he assumed that the rainbow coalition would consist of everybody except the Conservatives and Gordon Brown!

Most colleagues were guarded in their comments. But there was a clear consensus that the country would expect us to deliver a stable, decisive, government. And there was agreement that a second general election would be damaging if it was seen to arise from any reticence on our part to take up the responsibilities of government.

That was an important conclusion. It meant that we had started to eliminate the unacceptable options. We did not yet know it, but we were on the 'Sherlock Holmes track' towards coalition.

Essentially, we had four choices facing us. We could stay in opposition and offer little or no support to any minority government – beyond, perhaps, not opposing their first Queen's Speech. This would, in Nick's view and that of our negotiating team, lead inexorably to an autumn general election. That view was now endorsed by our shadow Cabinet.

The next possibility was that we could sign a confidence and supply agreement with the Conservatives, in which we could secure various policy concessions in exchange for supporting the Conservatives from the opposition benches on confidence motions and on key economic votes. In our pre-election analysis, we regarded the life of such a government as being of uncertain length, but with a bias towards shortness, given the tough economic decisions needing to be taken. Indeed, many of us thought that this, too, would be likely to lead to a second general election, in late 2010.

The third option was for a full scale coalition with the Conservatives. Finally, we could seek to form a coalition with the Labour Party, with 'side deals' with the smaller parties – this was the so-called rainbow coalition, already being dubbed by the media the 'coalition of the losers'.

We had already rejected the prospect of a confidence and supply arrangement with Labour, before the general election.

When the shadow Cabinet was over we had coffee and some rather dull sandwiches, and then all trudged down the corridor into a larger conference room for a meeting of the whole Parliamentary Party. We did not then know that within barely three days we would be returning to this same room to hear that Nick Clegg was to be the country's Deputy Prime Minister.

Nick led off the Parliamentary Party meeting by repeating the introductory comments which he had made to the shadow Cabinet, and by welcoming our newly elected MPs. He emphasised the need for party discipline and for speed in the negotiations.

The discussion which followed was very much along the lines of that at our shadow Cabinet and was remarkably harmonious (what had happened, I wondered, to my colleagues' reputations for truculence?). People also seemed to be very pragmatic and realistic. All of this meant that there was much more unity of view than I expected. Many MPs made clear that they did not want a weak minority government and felt that it would be bad for the country. Having just spent months getting elected, they also did not want a second general election! The national interest and the electoral interest of our MPs were in alignment – always a powerful combination.

So, without ever stating this explicitly, our Parliamentary Party had already taken one important decision: we had rejected the first of our four options. Doing nothing, sitting on the opposition benches without any responsibility, was off the table. There were now only three choices left.

Meanwhile, outside in Smith Square, a large demonstration had formed during our meeting in support of voting reform. I was a bit mystified about this. Why lobby Liberal Democrats about the benefits of electoral reform? It seemed like the equivalent of holding a public protest against the evils of the European Union outside the offices of the UK Independence Party. Why anyone would think we might renege on our commitment to voting reform, given that we had just been awarded a mere fifty-seven parliamentary seats for 23% of the national vote, is beyond me.

But Nick Clegg was able to go out to make this point at the end of our meeting, and he received a huge cheer for his efforts. It was then decided that I should make a short statement on the steps of Cowley Street, to announce the 'conclusions' of our meeting. Since we had made no particularly dramatic decisions, I didn't have anything very exciting to say. But the media appetite for a 'story' was so great that my platitudes – 'Parliamentary Party/shadow Cabinet have fully endorsed the position as set out by Nick Clegg', 'we will continue to put the national interest first', 'importance of economic stability', etc. – seemed to suffice. No doubt they were analysed at length for clues to our intentions by a media with a lot of broadcast time to fill.

Our main intention was to send out the clearest possible signal that we would support tough action to steady the financial markets. A financial market panic would not just be disastrous for the country, but would be the worst possible backdrop against which to make difficult decisions with big implications for the country and the party.

In my statement, I emphasised that we were negotiating with the Conservatives and would 'listen to Labour'. 'Listening' was meant to imply something rather distant and passive, but the truth was that we felt obliged to do a little more than that. Gordon Brown and Peter Mandelson had been pressing Nick very hard indeed for an early meeting of our teams, or for formal contact of some kind. It was vital that we kept our Labour options in play, not least because the Conservatives were not expected to offer any serious prospect of voting reform. And if the Labour option was not kept in play, Gordon Brown might simply resign, forcing the Queen to call David Cameron to form a government before our discussions had time to bear fruit.

Danny Alexander had agreed with Peter Mandelson that we would meet informally and secretly with Labour's team that afternoon. So as I left the Cowley Street scrum of reporters, I headed to the parliamentary estate, where the cameras could not follow us. Neither the press nor our own MPs were briefed about this meeting. The meeting was held on the third floor of Portcullis House, in a conference room (number 391) that was part of the Lib Dem allocation of parliamentary office space.

We had decided not to meet in the Cabinet Office for reasons both of secrecy and presentation. This was to be an 'unofficial' meeting of the two parties and their negotiators. The meeting started around 3pm. By the time I arrived, the Labour team of Peter Mandelson, Andrew Adonis, Ed Balls and Ed Miliband were seated on one side of the large hexagonal table, with Danny Alexander, Chris Huhne and Andrew Stunell on the other.

The discussions had already begun, and Peter Mandelson was setting out Labour's position. Although the conference room was considerably smaller than the huge, tennis court sized room in the Cabinet Office, the meeting was rather less intimate than that with the Conservative team, as the table was so vast and broad that we were sitting some distance away from each other.

Peter Mandelson sat in the middle of the Labour team. I had not met him before, but given his history of involvement in the 'Lib–Lab-bery' of the period from 1996 to 1999, when Paddy Ashdown and Tony Blair were contemplating some form of coalition government, I assumed that he would be a supporter of the talks.

I detected, however, a modest degree of detachment, scepticism even, from him. It was not that he was in any way dismissive or unfriendly; it was more an absence of conviction and enthusiasm than anything else, combined perhaps with a certain degree of lofty detachment.

Was it, I wondered, that he doubted the parliamentary arithmetic would support a Lib–Lab deal? Was it that he was struggling to come to terms with the end of the Blair–Brown era, or having to negotiate with the Liberal Democrats to stay in office?

I cannot say, except that the same sense of urgency and seriousness that was present during our talks with the Conservatives was never quite present during our discussions with the Labour team.

Andrew Adonis sat on Peter Mandelson's left. Andrew was earnest, serious and professional. It was clear that if anyone on the Labour side believed in this enterprise it was Andrew – and, I assume, Gordon Brown himself.

I had asked Andrew in a telephone conversation that morning whether Gordon Brown, no great lover of 'Liberals', as he called us, was really serious about the negotiations. 'Oh yes,' said Andrew. 'The thing to understand about Gordon is that he has these obsessions from time to time, when all his energy is absorbed by a particular project. This deal with your party is now Gordon's project and obsession. It is all he is thinking about for about twenty hours a day.'

The other members of the team were Ed Balls and Ed Miliband. When I first met these two, they were working together at the Treasury with Gordon Brown. Ed Balls was in those days very much the senior of the two – the chief economic adviser to the Treasury, who was widely regarded as the 'deputy Chancellor', if not more. Ed Miliband was in those days the slightly geeky sidekick.

Ed Balls was that rare combination of someone who was ferociously bright but also ferociously political. He was also confident, assured and not afraid to show it.

When I first met him in 1997, he at the Treasury and myself as director of policy for the Liberal Democrats, I was astonished when he told me openly how the Treasury had just 'shredded' Frank Field's welfare reform proposals. Frank was a Labour minister at the time, and I was an opposition party employee. So it struck me that this was a rather extraordinary confidence to share. If he talked in this way in front of someone from another party, what must he be like with people he trusts, I thought?

Although Ed Balls had long been a Brown loyalist, a degree of separation seemed to have grown up between them as Ed's own political career had developed. And I never doubted that while Ed was a loyal supporter of Gordon Brown, he would have his own opinions and would not be shy in putting these forward.

Ed Balls was, it had always seemed to me, tribally Labour and pretty contemptuous of the Liberal Democrats. While he knew me, he had never made any serious attempt to discuss the possibility of a Lib–Lab partnership, or to establish any relationship of trust or mutual interest, even when it was obvious that Labour was going to lose power.

I guessed that Ed would be willing to deal with the Lib Dems only if absolutely necessary, and while holding his nose. And I guessed that he would be difficult, perhaps even impossible, to work with in government – certainly if he was in any position of power, such as Chancellor.

With expectations of an impending Labour leadership election, there could be no doubt that Ed Balls would be a candidate and I suspected that he would want to keep his distance from the Lib Dems, given our unpopularity with many Labour members. There were already rumours from well-placed sources that Ed was fundamentally opposed to any coalition with the Lib Dems, and that he believed that Labour should return to opposition, leaving the Conservatives and Lib Dems to clean up the economic mess.

I had rather higher hopes of the fourth member of the Labour team, Ed Miliband. I had known Ed for just over a decade, not well, but firstly in his capacity as a Treasury special adviser, and later when he came into Parliament.

The striking thing about Ed was that while he was a member of the Brown inner team, he had somehow managed to remain courteous, civilised, unaggressive and thoughtful. Indeed, it seemed difficult to imagine how he had survived so long with Gordon, Charlie Whelan, Ed Balls and the rest of Gordon's rather brutal gang.

As a consequence of being decent, polite, reasonable and somewhat geekish, Ed had never seemed likely to rise to the very top of his party. His elbows did not seem nearly sharp enough.

But something odd had happened over the past couple of years. In a government of such thuggish brutality, Ed's very niceness seemed to have become a virtue, and he had clearly begun to carve out his own distinctive niche.

Ed Miliband's advantage in any leadership election was clear – he was not a Blairite, when that classification was out of favour with many in his party. And although he had worked with Gordon Brown, he was not as identified with the thuggish tendency around the Prime Minister as people such as Ed Balls.

Rumours circulated of his falling out with the ambitious Ed Balls, and one can well imagine that Ed Balls may have acquired Gordon's tendency to regard any potential alternative leadership candidate as a deadly enemy to be ruthlessly briefed against.

I held out the hope that Ed Miliband might be an ally in the event that a Lib–Lab partnership ever proved to be viable. He seemed like a person that it would be possible to do business with.

But, over time, I became a little more sceptical of the chances of this happening. Firstly, though Ed would often say in passing things like: 'We really must meet to discuss things. . .' nothing ever seemed to come of these suggestions.

And, secondly, although on the surface of things Ed Miliband seemed to be an archetypal moderate, the closer you looked the more you realised that he was actually quite a long way to the left in the Labour Party – certainly more so than his brother, but quite possibly more so than Ed Balls too.

I had heard from more than one 'New Labour' minister that 'when the chips are down, Ed is just an old-fashioned lefty'. It was also clear that within the Cabinet his very deliberate courting of the unions was causing some concern.

As it was almost certain that he would now be a candidate in a coming Labour leadership campaign, I wondered whether this would further affect his willingness to be seen to be supporting a deal with the Liberal Democrats.

Throughout the negotiations I felt that Ed Balls and Ed Miliband were eyeing each other carefully, as two fighters who expected soon to be in the ring together, and who were sizing up each other's strengths and weaknesses, not wanting to leave any hostages to fortune.

It has been suggested by Ed Balls and others that the Labour team came to the meeting with us with little preparation and no negotiating strategy. Indeed, he made clear on Nick Robinson's BBC documentary, that his 'preparation' for the first meeting was a brief discussion with Peter Mandelson over a coffee just before we met.

But, in fact, Labour did table a set of proposals which were presented as the basis for an agreement (see Appendix 4). This was in the form of a four-page note, typed in bold capital letters.

The paper contained forty policy bullet points, divided up into seven sections: 'Democratic and Constitutional Reform', 'Tax and Spending', 'Public Service Reform', 'Environment/Green Economy/Transport', 'Home Affairs/Civil Liberties', 'Housing' and 'Defence'.

This list included some pretty vague pledges, for example to 'develop a comprehensive empty homes strategy'. But it seemed at least to offer a starting point for negotiations and it touched upon what we had already decided were our four bottom-line negotiating issues: political reform (including voting reform), a Pupil Premium, tax cuts for those on low pay and action to restore the public finances and create a sustainable economy.

We talked through the electoral arithmetic with the Labour team and some of the key issues of importance to both sides. There was one uncomfortable point later on in the meeting when Chris Huhne took it on himself to raise the issue of Gordon Brown's future. 'We have yet to discuss,' he said, 'how we deal with the Gordon Brown problem.'

Peter Mandelson pretended to look surprised and taken aback, though he knew, of course, that for us this was already a key consideration. However, this was not the right environment to discuss such a sensitive issue. Peter Mandelson and Danny Alexander had already been in touch on this very point.

Danny intervened quickly to say: 'No Chris, that is not a matter that we are discussing,' which put an end to the conversation. Ed Balls and Ed Miliband grimaced.

The meeting only lasted an hour and we made clear that this could not be a formal negotiation, but was more of a 'listening' opportunity. We reported back to Nick Clegg and Vince Cable afterwards.

That night, at around 6.30pm, Nick also met with David Cameron at Admiralty House. This was supposed to be a private meeting, involving some nifty footwork to shake off the watching media. But some clever investigative work by Nick Robinson of the BBC meant that its existence was revealed on the evening television bulletins. This was a critical moment, a time when the two leaders could establish whether they could work together and trust each other. They met for an hour and fifteen minutes without anyone else present and eventually had to be interrupted by Alison Suttie, who reminded Nick that he was soon supposed to be talking to Gordon Brown.

And at 8.15pm Nick took another call from a hyperactive Gordon Brown, keen to push the negotiations forward.

Paddy Ashdown also phoned me in the evening to invite me to a dinner at his house in Kennington, with a group of Lib Dem MPs.

But I was unable to attend because of the ongoing planning work for the coalition talks, which went on well into the night. I finally got to bed at around 2am.

Sunday 9 May 2010

Talking to the Tories

I awoke early the next morning, after just four hours more sleep, and was contacted by Paddy Ashdown.

The last time I had spoken in detail with Paddy, he was dismissive of the prospects of any deal with Labour. But in the last twenty-four hours he had had a dramatic change of view. And Paddy does nothing by halves.

Paddy told me that the previous afternoon that he had received a call from Lord (Chris) Rennard, the party's former Chief Executive and campaigns expert. Chris and Paddy had come to the conclusion that a Lib–Lab deal was a more serious prospect than had previously been considered. This was because although the two parties could not command a majority of MPs in the House of Commons, they did have a clear majority over the Conservatives. Chris had pointed out that the other parties were unlikely – in his view – to vote with the Conservatives on key issues of confidence and supply. This issue was further discussed that evening at a dinner at Paddy's house, attended by MPs including Sir Menzies Campbell, Norman Lamb, Michael Moore, Jeremy Browne and Alistair Carmichael.

Paddy now told me that he was much more optimistic about the prospects of forming a coalition with Labour, and he felt that it was a genuine option which we needed to explore. He also said that it would strengthen our negotiating position to have more than one option.

He went over the arithmetic with me. Labour and the Liberal Democrats together had 315 seats – eleven short of an overall majority. But there was in addition: one Green MP (Caroline Lucas), three SDLP MPs, one Alliance MP, and an independent (Sylvia Hermon). If these could be coaxed into co-operation, that brought the numbers up to 321 MPs.

There were in addition eight Democratic Unionist MPs, and our Labour contacts were claiming that these MPs could be relied upon to support a Lib–Lab coalition and to oppose the Conservatives.

Finally, there were three Plaid Cymru MPs, who were said to be unlikely to want to support the Conservatives. There was also a larger group of SNP MPs, who everyone seemed to agree could be relied on for absolutely nothing, other to act with maximum opportunism.

The hope was that out of this grouping could be formed some sort of broad coalition – in Germany it has been called a 'traffic light' coalition, of 'red, yellow, green'.

I had always believed in exploring this option to the full; firstly, because I was concerned that the Conservatives would not offer us enough on policy, and secondly because it obviously strengthened our negotiating hand.

But the problem seemed to me that there would have to be rather a lot of different coloured bulbs in any traffic light coalition which we sought to form. And the chances therefore of securing a green light on any particularly controversial policy proposition seemed to me quite remote.

In essence what was being proposed was a Lib Dem–Labour coalition agreement, accompanied in all probability by a confidence and supply arrangement with the Democratic Unionists, supplemented by further understandings with up to five other groupings of MPs or individual MPs.

It seemed to me that such a coalition would be more 'car crash' than 'traffic light'.

Indeed, one did not need to be a master political tactician to see that holding together such a coalition, while implementing the necessary substantial and inevitably controversial spending cuts, would be extremely challenging. Every vote would be on a knife edge and the leverage of the very small parties would be enormous.

It was not only the smaller parties that might prove unreliable. A tiny number of Labour or Lib Dem rebels would regularly be able to hold the government to ransom.

Much as I wanted us to be able to explore this option in a serious way, it seemed to me that it would be next to impossible unless there was a clear and deliverable understanding with the DUP. And I had no idea if this was really possible.

Without such an understanding, a 'traffic light' deal would be seen by the markets as weak and incredible, which would be bad for Britain's economy. More importantly, such an arrangement was fraught with the risk that it would collapse in a mess within weeks or months – which would in all likelihood lead to a second general election, with the Conservatives being returned with a clear mandate.

However, Labour were insistent that the prospects of DUP co-operation were good, and it seemed to me foolish not to pursue the Labour coalition option in a serious way, to find out if it really could deliver. I was also doubtful that the Conservatives would concede the referendum on electoral reform without us securing more leverage in the talks.

In any case, it seemed clear that we would soon have two options in play, though the latter would also depend on whether Gordon Brown would step down as Labour leader. We were increasingly of the view that this was the minimum condition for serious Lib–Lab talks.

After talking on the phone to Paddy about these issues, I met up with our negotiating team at 8am to consider a pile of detailed papers that had been prepared to assist in our talks with the Conservatives. Some of these had been drafted before the general election, and some had been put together by our team of party researchers.

Danny and William Hague had agreed that the first substantive talks with the Conservative team would start this morning, at 11am, and run on well into the afternoon. So we discussed our negotiating positions on a range of issues, and went through everything we expected to come up in the talks.

At around 10.45am, we set off from our party headquarters at 4 Cowley Street for the Cabinet Office at 70 Whitehall. We considered walking the short distance across Parliament Square, but it soon became clear that the media 'scrum' would make this impossible. Helicopters circled overhead, media were camped out in front of Cowley Street and we were told that outside the Cabinet Office was a hoard of journalists that would make the rest of it look like a tea party.

So three black people carriers were arranged and, after ensuring that none of our paperwork could be seen by waiting camera crews, we left Cowley Street and headed off in convoy to the negotiations. We arrived in Whitehall and the cars pulled in twenty-five metres or so down the road from our meeting place, to give us a chance to get out away from the scrum of waiting reporters. We then walked off towards the Cabinet Office, our papers stuffed into large yellow folders, with one journalist cruelly suggesting they may have been left over from 1974 (when Jeremy Thorpe was called to discuss a coalition with Ted Heath).

We made our way through a hundred or so waiting journalists, camera crews and photographers. This was pleasantly different from the usual Lib Dem press call, where party staff were often dragged in to ensure that the turnout of journalists didn't look too meagre. We were again met in the entrance to 70 Whitehall by the Civil Service team, who led us up the long staircase to our suite of rooms. Chris Huhne was soon immersed again in the volume on the government art collection. I teased him and told him that for a Liberal Democrat he had an admirable seriousness about preparing for power.

Again, we were met by Gus O'Donnell and by the Queen's Private Secretary, Christopher Geidt. Both were clearly relieved to see that serious talks were finally to get underway. Both no doubt dreaded days of delay and uncertainty and both wanted a government.

The Conservative team arrived just after us, and the talks started in earnest just after 11am. Both teams made their way into the main conference room, where we took up the same places we had sat in the previous Friday.

Gus O'Donnell welcomed us and made some comments about the state of the markets and the importance of our work. He said that the Civil Service could offer advice on constitutional issues, budgetary and other matters. He then offered to have us briefed by the Governor of the Bank of England and a representative from the Joint Intelligence Committee, so that we could understand the 'seriousness of the economic environment' and other matters.

Both sides declined this opportunity. We Liberal Democrats suspected that we knew what both were likely to say, and we did not think it appropriate to have such a briefing at this stage in the negotiations. I suspect that the Governor of the Bank of England's intervention would be perceived to have been aimed more at us than at the Conservatives, and we didn't want to feel manoeuvred into policy positions that we weren't comfortable with by outside advice.

Later in the day, concerned that our rejection might be misinterpreted, we suggested that Vince Cable, our Treasury spokesman, might speak to the Governor instead.

Gus O'Donnell also suggested that our negotiations could be 'supported' by the Civil Service, who might sit in and take notes. Both sides looked at each other for a lead. Then we both simultaneously said 'No'. William Hague jokingly noted that he wasn't sure that he wanted our discussions to be written down and then to become open to freedom of information requests! Gus explained that these discussions might well be exempt from disclosure from Freedom of Information. We all laughed and felt we were already beginning to discover the secrets of Whitehall.

The Cabinet Secretary therefore left us to our negotiations, retreating through the door of our Conference Room like a latter-day Sir Humphrey Appleby, after being left out of some vital prime ministerial meeting.

We started our discussions by agreeing that there were a number of key issues that we needed to focus on if a coalition agreement was to be delivered. And it was on the basis of seeking this full and comprehensive agreement that we started our talks.

Danny suggested that we should begin by dealing with political reform and then break for a sandwich at around 1pm. Then in the afternoon we should discuss the economic issues.

William Hague agreed, and said that we could start by using the Conservative paper which had been tabled to cover the key policy issues (see Appendix 1). The Conservative team had sent us on 8 May a detailed paper setting out their positions on political reform: deficit reduction, public spending, taxation and banking reform. This included specific concessions on these issues which they were willing to make to us. This certainly facilitated the talks, as we used this and our own papers to structure the discussions. It was a far more professional and interactive approach to negotiation than we were to experience later with the Labour team.

At this meeting, the Conservatives also tabled two additional papers on 'The Green Economy' and 'Civil Liberties'.

The Conservative team were aware of our four main priorities, which we were determined to deliver on.

For us, significant progress on every one of these key issues was crucial if agreement was to be reached. We also had other priority issues such as the environment, civil liberties and restoring the earnings link to the state pension.

As agreed, we started our discussion with the issue of political reform, using the Conservative paper as the prompt for our discussions. We reached agreement relatively quickly on some issues, including Lords reform and decentralisation of powers to local government and the devolved administrations. We kicked other issues that were clearly contentious off into the long grass, for example, English-only voting in Westminster.

It was also clear that both sides wanted some part of the political reform package to build in stability for the coalition – not least given the tough economic decisions which needed taking. Chris Huhne mentioned the possibility of having a threshold of say two thirds of MPs needing to vote to trigger a dissolution of parliament, as in the Scottish system. Both William Hague and George Osborne indicated that we needed a mechanism to build confidence in each other, and that there was a clear argument for such a mechanism on constitutional reform grounds. That pointed to fixed-term parliaments, which was already one of our priorities.

Andrew Stunell pointed out that trust and confidence was very important to us, and that we wouldn't want to find the PM calling an election at a time that did not suit us. 'That works both ways!' said William Hague. We mentioned that our own policy was for four-year, fixed-term parliaments. George Osborne made the point that five-year parliaments were better, as they allowed governments to get into implementing their plans before having to start worrying about the timing of the electoral cycle. We made no objection to this, and Britain was on its way to five-year, fixed-term parliaments, for the first time in its history.

But voting reform for Westminster was always going to be the toughest issue to secure agreement on. In his statement on Friday 7 May, David Cameron had offered us 'an all-party inquiry on political and electoral reform'. It was the weakest part of the Conservative pitch, as David Cameron must have known.

There was simply no way that the Lib Dems would ever go into coalition on the basis of some vague and unbankable offer on fair voting. And as I had explained to George Osborne in his office four years before, voting reform becomes more important in coalition politics, where the junior party is on the whole more likely to be hit by the coalition's unpopularity and is less likely to gain from its successes.

At our first meeting on Friday 7 May, we had – of course – come to no agreements on fair votes. Instead the Conservative negotiating team had promised to go away and flesh out David Cameron's offer. The 'fleshed out' proposal was sent to us in the 8 May document (Appendix 1), but it was in truth still pretty hopeless from our perspective.

What it amounted to was a seven-person 'All-Party Inquiry', which would draw up a list of possible voting systems, without expressing any opinion on the merits of any one system. This full list of systems would then be voted on in the House of Commons, with a free vote being given to each MP and party.

In practice that meant, in our view, that it would be easy to assemble a 'coalition' of MPs against almost any real change in the voting system, which meant that a referendum on PR or AV would simply never materialise.

Such a proposal therefore had as much chance of being approved by Lib Dem MPs and the party's special conference as a plan to build 1,000 coal-fired power stations in south-west England. There wasn't the remotest chance of attracting the support of Lib Dem MPs for such a proposition, and nor should there have been.

David Cameron must have known that we could not agree to such a proposition. The issue now was could we break the logjam? And did the Conservatives want to break the logjam? Did they want a full coalition, or would they be happy to drive us into a short-lived arrangement that would make it look as if we were obsessed only with PR, therefore helping the Conservatives make the case for an overall majority in any second general election in the autumn?

Had we already encountered the Conservative bottom line on voting reform or should we expect that the Conservatives would be saving their real concessions until later, as would happen in most negotiations. In particular, I recalled again the negotiations in 1999 with Labour for the first coalition government in the new Scottish Parliament. The Labour team played incredibly hardball, conceding almost nothing of any importance on any issue for about four days, until it was clear that our team was simply not going to budge.

But in truth, we did not know the answer to these questions. However, we knew that there was no way that we could sell coalition to our party on the basis of such an offer, and we knew we had to make that clear today. Before the general election, I had proposed to Nick Clegg and the other Lib Dem negotiators that there was only one way of securing agreement on a voting system referendum from the Conservatives.

That was to push for a referendum on the most modest form of electoral reform – the Alternative Vote, which allowed candidates to be ranked in preference order and which required MPs to secure 50% of the vote to be elected – and to link this to Lib Dem support for the Conservatives' own reform plan, which was to reduce the number of parliamentary seats and to remove Labour over-representation.

It seemed to me that both proposals could be defended in their own right, that no one party could guarantee to push through either policy by itself and that linking boundary reform to AV would help to sell this to the Conservative Party. This is because we would be offering the Conservatives something which would be likely to offset any loss of seats that AV might deliver. In addition, from a Conservative perspective, a coalition with the Lib Dems might improve their chances of picking up Lib Dem second preference votes.

I suggested before our meeting on 9 May that this proposal should now be seriously tabled. Danny Alexander had half-jokingly suggested that we should seek to 'sell' AV to the Conservative team as just an 'enhanced' first-past-the-post system. Chris Huhne added that the Conservatives used an AV type system to elect their own leaders.

Now, in the actual talks, Danny set out just how important electoral reform is to the Lib Dems. He said: 'The bottom line is that we need a bankable commitment to change. Our MPs will expect that, if we are going to have a coalition. And they are mighty suspicious of "reviews" – we've been there before.'

Danny then said he had a proposal designed to break the impasse. William Hague and George Osborne listened carefully, realising that this was a key moment.

The Lib Dems, Danny said, accepted the Conservative criticism that the present unequal size of constituency electorates just wasn't fair. There was, therefore, a strong case for a boundary review, with fewer constituencies and a more equal number of voters in each constituency. Inevitably, this would help correct the current serious and unjustifiable bias in favour of Labour.

It would also help to deliver what both parties were committed to – fewer MPs.

'So what I am suggesting is this,' said Danny. 'We will support your proposals on redrawing the constituency boundaries, to make voting fairer. But in return, we want your support for a referendum on a reformed first-past-the-post system.'

George Osborne frowned and looked interested. 'What do you mean by a reformed first-past-the-post system?' Chris Huhne explained.

George thought for two seconds, smiled weakly, and then said: 'Oh! You mean AV don't you! No. That won't work for us. Good try though!' Danny said that this was key to securing the support of Lib Dem MPs, and that it could help usher in a new and more co-operative politics and a fairer voting system.

William Hague frowned, looked rather serious and leaned back. 'Look,' he said, 'you must accept that this is very difficult indeed for my party, as you already know. The Conservatives are opposed as a party to both the Alternative Vote and proportional representation. And calling AV "reformed first-past-the-post" won't change our people's minds! We are now offering a review, and some of my colleagues think this is already going too far. But we are willing to consider offering a free vote in the Commons on AV. Theoretically there would be a majority, because Labour is committed to AV in its manifesto.'

I smiled, and looked rather dubious. 'But I really don't think we can rely on Labour to stick to its manifesto commitments under these circumstances,' I said. 'We know many Labour MPs don't like AV, and it will be too tempting for Labour as a whole to act cynically and find a reason for voting against AV – perhaps on the basis of opposition to the planned boundary review. Look, surely most Conservative MPs are opposed to PR and not AV? AV is a far more incremental and modest change. And in a coalition, the old assumptions on how people use their second preferences could change. AV might not be bad for the Conservatives under those circumstances.'

Oliver Letwin insisted that if AV was a free vote issue, then Labour would feel able to support it in a vote. But I expressed serious doubts about that. 'I happen to know from a good Labour source,' I said, 'that there are many Labour MPs who are violently opposed to AV, even though it is a Labour manifesto commitment. We just cannot rely on Labour MPs to hold a Lib Dem–Conservative coalition together on this. It won't work.'

George Osborne looked troubled and thoughtful. He said that it would not be easy to sell any voting reform to Conservative MPs. 'Surely', said Chris Huhne, 'the Conservative leadership is sovereign on policy matters?'

William Hague intervened to say: 'Chris, you must understand that the Conservative Party is like an absolute monarchy, but this is qualified by regicide. If we take any form of PR back to our parliamentary colleagues, they will be looking for new leadership.'

George Osborne said that we needed a process whereby Parliament and the people took ownership of the issue. The best way the Lib Dems could make progress on AV was to accept the Conservative offer, he said. George also said that in his view Labour could not deliver AV because of the parliamentary arithmetic and opposition from senior people such as Alistair Darling. The present voting system, he continued, helped Labour, and their commitment to reform was skin-deep. 'Under the present system and boundaries,' said George, 'Labour could have the same vote share as us and they would have a majority of 200 MPs!'

As I pointed out, the problem with this line of argument was that it rather undermined the notion that we could hope to rely on Labour votes to get an AV referendum through the House of Commons. Danny also chipped in to say that Labour's defence of the existing first-past-the-post system was a very good reason to introduce PR, as a new system would clearly be fairer to both the Liberal Democrats and the Conservatives.

But George Osborne was unimpressed. 'We need to be clear,' he said, 'the best Conservative offer on this is going to be equalisation of seat size and a free vote in the Commons on an AV referendum.'

I came back to emphasise that this was also a crucial issue for the Lib Dems. 'George, we spoke about this four years ago in your office, and I predicted that the Lib Dems would never go into a coalition with anyone without bankable progress on electoral reform. That is still the case. We cannot persuade Lib Dem MPs to vote for a Lib Dem–Conservative coalition without this. We honestly can't.'

I knew that my strong statement on this would send an important message, as my image was undoubtedly as someone who was more 'right wing' and Conservative-friendly than most other Lib Dem MPs. I wanted the Conservatives to understand that this really was a bottom-line issue for us.

I did not see any point in fudging. I did not believe for one moment that the Lib Dem Parliamentary Party would agree to a coalition with the Conservatives without the chance of progress on voting reform.

There was silence in the room. It was difficult to know whether this was where the Conservative team wanted or expected to end up in the negotiations, or whether there was a genuine desire to secure a full coalition. But I detected in the silence a genuine frustration about this roadblock, not least because of our progress in other areas. I suspected that the Conservative team knew that our talks would founder on this particular rock, but I was not persuaded that this was their hope or their strategy. Nor could we assume that the Conservative leadership would relish the prospect of a second general election in just a few months, given their failure to secure an overall majority under circumstances which they must have considered to be unusually favourable.

George Osborne broke the silence by saying: 'I don't think we can move on this. There isn't any point in us discussing it further. David and Nick will need to think about this. We should look at other areas.'

William Hague said: 'The guarantee of a referendum really could be a breaking point for the Conservatives. We would have real problems instructing our MPs to vote in favour of a referendum.'

I took this to mean that the door was not completely closed to further movement on the issue. After all, we could hardly expect the Conservatives to move straight to their bottom-line negotiating position. How big the impediment was remained to be seen. We had reached an impasse. We looked at each other and knew that we could make no more progress on this issue. Danny suggested a five minute 'time-out' break. The Conservatives agreed, but as we concluded George repeated his view that the Conservative offer on AV was more likely to deliver a referendum than anything Labour could offer.

'Before we finish on this,' said George, 'let me make clear that what we are offering is a guaranteed free vote on a referendum on voting reform by the end of this year. I agree that AV and equalised boundaries would be the best way of securing support for a referendum.'

Our two teams split up and went back to our rooms. There we had some coffee and chatted about the progress of the talks so far. Danny said that we needed to push the issue back up to the two party leaders. The current Conservative offer was just unacceptable, but we needed to go on and discuss other crucial issues such as the economy. We certainly did not want the talks to collapse solely on the issue of voting reform.

He pointed out to us that he expected Labour would offer not just a referendum on AV but a two-question referendum. The first question would be change or no change. The second question would then give people a choice between AV and a more proportional system.

When the talks restarted, it was agreed that Nick Clegg and David Cameron should talk together about electoral reform later in the afternoon. William Hague said that we might want at this stage, and in advance of our economic discussions, to hear from the Governor of the Bank of England, Mervyn King, and perhaps even the permanent secretary to the Treasury, Nick Macpherson. But we declined – we didn't want to feel bounced on economic policy by what anyone else might say, and we felt we understood the issues. In addition, our view was that any such discussion really needed to involve Vince Cable, our shadow Chancellor.

Oliver Letwin proposed a short break for lunch. Chris Huhne suggested restarting for the economic policy discussion at 2.30pm. Everyone eagerly agreed. By now the conference room was insufferably hot, as the central heating seemed to be permanently jammed in an 'on' position and for some reason could not be turned off. A staff member had to be sent for to open up some of the windows – not a great example of environmental sustainability in government.

We broke for some rather uninspiring sandwiches of chicken, tuna, beef and cheese, and a few biscuits. The age of public sector austerity seemed already to have arrived. Over lunch we held another conference call with Nick Clegg. We reported back to him on progress at our meeting, including the expected blockage on voting reform.

I said that it would not be sensible to expect the Conservatives to table their bottom-line negotiating position on this issue so early in the talks, so I was personally unclear about whether or not to expect some further serious concessions.

Nick said that we should continue negotiations and keep open the possibility of a confidence and supply arrangement, in case the coalition option fell through.

Nick added that in talks with David Cameron he had made a strong case to the Conservative leader for allowing the British people their say on voting reform. He also said that his understanding was that the Blairites in the Labour Party were now working to persuade Gordon Brown to stand down, in order to clear the way for serious talks with the Lib Dems.

Nick rang off, and we then discussed our strategy for dealing with the economic policy issues, on which I was to lead. We then resumed our meeting with the Conservatives, and turned to the big issue of the economy, taxation and spending.

We all knew just how important our discussions on this issue were going to be.

The context, of course, was Britain's massive public sector deficit – one of the largest as a share of the economy in the developed world.

It would clearly have to be a priority to cut this deficit as soon as possible. If a new government failed to tackle the deficit, we were acutely conscious that there would be three adverse consequences.

First, there was a serious risk of a loss of confidence in the UK, which could manifest itself in real problems in selling British government bonds. At best, this would mean higher market interest rates. At worst, it could lead to a Greek-style financial meltdown.

Second, if we did not tighten fiscal policy, it was inevitable that the Bank of England would need to increase official interest rates sooner and by a greater degree. This would hit businesses, and hurt millions of people servicing mortgages and other debts.

Third, if we failed to act we would store up a huge short-, medium- and long-term debt servicing bill. More and more public spending would have to be used to pay interest on the national debt, instead of paying for priorities such as education and the NHS.

Before the general election, and in our manifesto, we had taken the clear view that the job of deficit reduction should start in earnest in 2011, by when the economic recovery was expected to be firmly grounded. We had gone into some detail on the spending cuts that we were proposing, but we were clear that these were only the first of many cuts which would be necessary.

We also made clear before the election that we did not believe that total government spending should be cut in 2010, because we were concerned not to depress economic activity before it was clear that a recovery had begun. Our manifesto was drafted early in 2010, when it was still unclear whether the UK had yet emerged from recession.

However, in our manifesto we did identify some spending cuts to be made in 2010/11, which we envisaged should be reinvested in projects that would help to boost the economy.

By contrast, the Conservatives had taken the view that spending cuts should start immediately, with £6bn of net cuts in 2010/11. These cuts, under Conservative plans, would be used to reduce the deficit in 2010/11, and in 2011/12 would help to avoid some of Labour's planned increase in national insurance contributions – the so-called 'tax on jobs'.

Needless to say, all parties made a great deal during and before the general election over the issue of whether early cuts in public spending, in 2010/11, would 'endanger' the economic recovery. This was clearly an important issue. But the truth was that the cuts being proposed by the Conservatives – £6bn – were pretty small in the context of total public spending, and even smaller in the context of the whole economy. It was difficult to argue convincingly before the general election that this scale of cuts would drive the economy into recession or indeed that they were essential. But the £6bn of cuts became totemic of the dividing line between those who wanted early spending cuts and those who did not.

In preparing our manifesto in late 2009 and early 2010, we were comfortable with our analysis and proposals on the deficit, but by April and May we began to realise that two developments might cause us to have to revisit our plans.

First, in our discussions about hung parliament scenarios, we became increasingly concerned that the financial markets would react badly if a strong government could not be established, which had the votes and market credibility to deal with the deficit. That would not be entirely in our hands to determine, but we were convinced that we needed to be in a position in a hung parliament scenario to send out a clear signal of our willingness to take tough action on the deficit.

Our manifesto therefore explicitly tied us to supporting an emergency budget soon after the election, and a credible deficit reduction plan. We realised that because of market scepticism over any partnership or coalition, there would under these circumstances almost certainly be a need to take credible, early, action of some kind, to reduce the future scale of the deficit.

In our view, even if this additional action was economically modest, it could have a disproportionate effect in restoring confidence. We envisaged, however, that this action would be focused on deficit reduction starting in 2011.

The second, crucial, development which began to influence our thinking during the general election itself was the crisis in Greece, which risked spreading to other high-deficit countries. Greek bond yields had soared to 12% from just 7% on the eve of the election. This showed what could happen when the markets lose confidence in a government's ability to control its deficit and service its debts. The UK was not initially in the markets' sights during this Greek crisis, but nobody doubted that we would be if the election resulted in a parliament which could not or would not put in place a credible deficit reduction plan.

With a UK deficit of around 12% of GDP, we knew that the economic fundamentals for the UK were pretty awful, and that British government bond prices were being held up only by the expectation that a new government would stop dithering and start taking action. This certainly began to influence our thinking in the final couple of weeks before the general election, as well as on the days after the election, when the risk of the crisis spreading seemed to be growing by the hour.

This was the spectre which loomed over our talks. This was the reason that the Governor of the Bank of England stood ready to brief us on his perspective on the risks to the UK. But neither we nor the

Conservatives needed this briefing. We understood the risks. We were determined that whatever the result of our talks, we would not expose the UK economy to a financial crisis.

Both parties knew that if a credible government with a credible deficit reduction package could not be agreed, there would be a major loss of confidence in UK financial assets – with plunging bond prices, rising interest rates, a falling pound and weak share markets. This would not merely be politically disastrous, but it would have a very real economic impact as well, putting recovery at risk.

Both parties were also agreed that the main burden of deficit reduction should be borne by spending constraint, not by higher taxes. Conservative plans relied on spending to bear 80% of the burden of deficit reduction. According to the Institute for Fiscal Studies, our plans implied 70% of the burden would fall on spending. We did not wish to be tied to some arbitrary figure in any agreement, but we were convinced that these were broadly the right orders of magnitude.

The Conservatives argued in our talks for an explicit commitment that the bulk of the structural deficit should be eliminated within five years, but we resisted agreeing to this on the basis that we did not want to hem in the new government until we had had a chance to 'look at the books'. We made clear that we were not against this in principle, but that this should be a matter to be investigated thoroughly before the first Budget Statement, in late June.

George Osborne had, in our first meeting on Friday 7 May, explained that his view was that the £6bn of in-year spending cuts proposed by the Conservatives would need to be delivered and that these were a key test for the markets of whether a Conservative/Liberal Democrat government was willing to carry out the necessary deficit reduction plan. The Conservatives claimed that the Bank of England and the Treasury shared this view.

We carefully considered George's proposals after the meeting on 7 May, and we were inclined to agree that the markets would be unimpressed if the coalition's first action on spending was to cancel relatively modest cuts which had been planned.

Both parties were already talking tough on deficit reduction. But we knew that the markets would be sceptical of warm words, and would judge the new government by its actions and not by good intentions.

There would be no clearer indication of the coalition's determination to reduce the deficit than an early package of spending cuts – and we considered that such a package could help to restore economic confidence and reduce market interest rates.

So we had decided before the meeting started that we would concede this point to the Conservatives. We knew that some people – not least in the Labour Party – would criticise us for an apparent change of position, but we regarded this as justified by the changed circumstances and right for the economy.

We knew that we could negotiate with the Conservatives, and that if we wanted to we could probably succeed in watering down the £6bn in various ways. But, bluntly, we thought that the signalling value of these limited cuts was important, and we were prepared to take the political pain in order to do the right thing for the economy.

My job was to lead on the economic issues, so I started by setting out our position on some of the key questions. 'We want to see the budget deficit being brought under control, so that confidence in the UK economy can be rebuilt. We agree that there should be an early Budget package.

'We understand that stopping the increase in national insurance contributions was important to the Conservative campaign. We would like to see the background work which has apparently been undertaken to show that the immediate cuts would be deliverable without damaging front-line public services.

'Our own view has been that the main public spending cuts and fiscal consolidation should begin in April 2011, after the recovery is more secure, but of course we did propose in our manifesto some spending cuts in 2010/11, with the money recycled into areas such as green jobs and investment spending, to underpin recovery. In our manifesto proposals we also had around 70% of deficit reduction coming through spending cuts, in contrast with 80% in the Conservative manifesto.'

Oliver Letwin chipped in to say: 'Well, we could just specify at this stage that the majority of the fiscal consolidation should be through spending cuts?' We agreed that specifying an exact figure wouldn't be sensible at this stage.

George Osborne then set out his position. 'Look, our view is that Labour's deficit reduction plans are just too weak, and we believe that the deficit should be sorted out by the end of a five-year parliament. It is very important for a new government to show that it is serious about deficit reduction, and that a coalition government or even a minority government is capable of making spending reductions. Without that assurance, financial markets may panic and interest rates would be driven up. That is why I am strongly in favour of some modest cuts this year, with the main action starting next year – as you suggest.

'I am also committed to more openness in fiscal policy, with an independent body looking at the government's growth and borrowing forecasts so that these cannot be fiddled by politicians. That is crucial.'

Danny mentioned that Vince Cable was going to be seeing Mervyn King, the Governor of the Bank of England, and Nick Macpherson, permanent secretary to the Treasury, later in the afternoon.

I continued by saying that it was essential that we did not tighten fiscal policy too rapidly, that the majority of the tightening should still be delayed until 2011. But I went on by acknowledging: 'We do understand that the financial market situation has become a lot worse over recent weeks, given the loss of confidence in Greece and the risk of this contagion spreading. We also agree that the markets will be looking for evidence that a hung parliament will not mean that tough choices are dodged. We need market confidence in the UK government in order to keep interest rates low.

'We accept that cuts of £6bn aren't huge in the context of the whole economy, but we need reassurance that they can be delivered and that at least some of the money can be ploughed back into investments which will help the economy.'

George replied: 'If we can deliver the £6bn of in-year cuts, that will send out a very powerful message. And I am happy to talk about reinvesting some of those cuts, as long as the bulk goes to deficit reduction. I will also get the figures to Vince for him to look at, and he will find that Mervyn and Nick are very supportive of what we want to do. Meanwhile, we will need work on a spending review over the summer, so we can set out the new spending plans from 2011 onwards in the autumn. If we have a coalition government then the Lib Dems will have a collective input and responsibility for spending decisions. But if we have a looser arrangement, there would be consultation but the Conservatives would have to take the decisions.'

I replied that we wanted an emergency budget by the end of June, and that this would have to demonstrate some progress on our key pledges, but that we fully agreed that the markets needed to see that the coalition was committed to deficit reduction and to an acceleration of existing plans to cut the deficit.

I also confirmed that we agreed to protect the NHS budget in real terms. To be honest, I had always been deeply sceptical that any government would be able to make real-terms cuts in NHS spending without seeing a big deterioration in the quality of this service. After all, real NHS spending had grown on average by around 3% each year under the government of Mrs Thatcher, which hardly had a reputation for profligacy in public spending.

Oliver Letwin summed up by saying that we agreed to make some cuts in spending in 2010, but some of the money would be reinvested to support recovery. We would accelerate the pace of deficit reduction from 2011 onwards, but we would not try to fix the detail of this now. That, clearly, should be an issue for a June emergency Budget.

We then had to take a break as a message came in that Vince Cable wanted to speak to us urgently on the phone. It turned out that Vince had had a conversation with Gordon Brown who seemed very disturbed that Vince was proposing to talk to Mervyn King and the Treasury. We assumed that this was vintage Brown – the control freak who wouldn't want us to be getting any advice that he would not find helpful. We then resumed our meeting and moved on to some of the key public spending and tax issues.

I pushed hard for a Conservative guarantee that our pupil premium – more money to fund the education of the most disadvantaged pupils – would be properly funded. I said that the pupil premium would not be deliverable if it was just moving money from one school to another. I pointed out that we were prepared to take some tough decisions on public spending, for example, cutting back tax credits for higher earners, in order to secure the money.

George Osborne said that he supported the principle of the pupil premium, but he needed to consider if he could find additional money. I said that this was a bottom-line issue for us that we could not concede on. I pointed out that it was one of our top four priorities. Extra money needed to be found outside the schools area. Our manifesto committed us to a £2.5bn pupil premium, and while I accepted that we could not pin down the precise numbers immediately, the premium needed to be real and significant in scale.

Danny and the other Lib Dem negotiators watched this tussle with amusement. They had heard me make the same arguments for extra money for the pupil premium to Nick Clegg and Vince Cable in my capacity as Lib Dem schools spokesman, before the election. I felt that I had helped ensure that this was a substantive pledge in our manifesto, and I was now determined that it would not be watered down in the coalition agreement. George promised to look further at the matter and at how far the Conservatives could go. He said he understood the importance of there being extra money in the schools budget.

I then raised a number of other issues with tax or spending implications which were important to us: 'We want to see the earnings link on the state pension restored by April 2011. We want to make rapid progress to a £10,000 personal allowance. We think savings can be made by reviewing areas such as Trident. And we need to sort out what we are doing on national insurance contributions.'

George replied: 'On the pensions issue, we are certainly agreed that the earnings link should be restored by 2012, but I need to look at the costs before committing to 2011 – but we will do that. On tax, we are very happy to make the £10,000 tax allowance a major tax priority, as our paper indicates. On inheritance tax, we won't make this a priority – the allowance will come first. The same will be true on the marriage tax proposals which we have, where we are happy also if you want to abstain. We will write that into any agreement. But the issue is how fast we can go on the £10,000 allowance. It will cost a lot. We need the Treasury's advice on what it will cost.'

Chris Huhne said: 'We really need to reach the £10,000 figure by the next general election.'

'Yes,' said Andrew Stunell, 'and there should be a rough timetable to show how we can get to that.'

George replied: 'The Treasury advice I am getting is that spending cuts alone won't be enough to deal with the deficit – that tax rises will be needed. So that will make it doubly difficult to pay for an increase in the allowance.'

Danny Alexander intervened: 'Yes, but this allowance will help those on lower incomes. It will encourage work, and it is much fairer. It will help cushion the blow of deficit reduction measures on those on more modest incomes. It is incredibly important to us.'

George Osborne replied: 'How about if we cap the benefit to just basic rate taxpayers? If we did that we would make it less expensive to introduce, and we would focus more of the cash on people on lower incomes. I might need to do that.'

Oliver Letwin chipped in to ask what wording we wanted on the allowance. 'Would it be enough to talk about a "significant movement towards a £10,000 personal allowance"?' he asked.

Chris Huhne suggested that the allowance should be delivered in full by the end of the parliament, with significant real progress towards the £10,000 being achieved in every year. That was agreed.

Chris asked whether a Mansion Tax could be introduced to pay for the higher allowance, but neither George nor Oliver were very keen – as the Conservative paper had already made clear. This was not a surprise to me, and I did not push the issue.

'I think we are already making quite a lot of concessions in this area,' said William Hague nervously.

George Osborne indicated that he was willing to be persuaded to accept Lib Dem proposals to curb the costs of tax credits for higher earners and to shut down the Child Trust Fund.

The insistence by each party of holding to its 'bottom line' policy commitments soon became a real strength in the negotiations with the Conservatives. Instead of the negotiations leading to 'lowest common denominator' compromises, what actually happened was that on the whole we made a choice to include either the Lib Dem or Conservative position, more or less in its entirety. This created a sense that we were picking the best of the policies of each party, and it soon became a standing joke amongst the negotiating teams as each side agreed to drop its least favoured policies while embracing the better alternatives presented by the other party. No doubt some in both our parties would have been horrified to hear cherished policies being so happily cast onto the coalition bonfire.

Mindful of the need to demonstrate that we Liberal Democrats were also capable of supporting action to limit spending, we insisted on explicit agreement on controlling public sector pay and pension costs, while protecting accrued rights.

We also insisted on drafting in an important line about protecting those on lower incomes from the spending cuts which would need to be made. This was to become a crucial principle of the coalition's approach to deficit reduction.

On banking reform, there was a reasonable degree of consensus, and we went through the various issues agreeing forms of words that we could both sign up to.

We paused briefly to consider the issue of what we should say about Britain joining the euro. 'It will not surprise you to know that we are opposed to this,' said George Osborne. Chris Huhne, a former

MEP and euro enthusiast smiled, and said, 'Well. We have met none of the criteria for convergence, so this is not really an issue.' I shouted out 'Hurrah!', as I have never been a big fan of Britain joining the euro, and have never thought that there was the slightest chance of the British people supporting the euro in a referendum. Andrew Stunell lent forward and said to the Conservative team: 'I hope you realise that this is a very big Lib Dem concession!' We all laughed.

We next came on to the environment, a key area for us and one where the Conservatives had also come armed with a long list of policies which had a very high Lib Dem appeal. It did not take long to agree this section. The Conservatives objected to a Lib Dem proposal for road pricing and it was agreed that this would be restricted to foreign lorries only.

But on nuclear power we came to an area of obvious disagreement. Oliver Letwin said: 'Look, there is a genuine disagreement here. But this need not be an area of confidence. We can agree that the Lib Dems do not need to support nuclear power.'

Chris Huhne responded that the issue was one of public subsidy, 'Can we agree that there should be no public subsidy for nuclear power? It is incredibly expensive.'

Oliver replied: 'Yes, there will be no direct public subsidy. But as we push the carbon price up, that will obviously favour non-carbon generating technologies.'

We agreed a form of words on this, and then moved on to the issue of civil liberties, where again both sides had a long list of rather similar proposals. Oliver Letwin led on this for the Conservatives. 'Oliver is, of course, a closet Lib Dem,' said William Hague. And this was certainly not an area in which it was difficult to agree.

Our talks eventually concluded at around 5.30pm. We had made a good deal of progress on all issues, except for the crucial issue of voting reform. William Hague suggested returning later in the evening to continue the negotiations. 'Coming back tonight would send out a very positive message,' said Ed Llewellyn.

Danny was cautious about this: 'Well, we now need to report back to Nick Clegg and Vince Cable to brief them on all of this. And there is clearly more work which both of us need to do.' It was agreed that we would therefore meet again on Monday morning, and in the meantime both delegations would leave the Cabinet Office separately, with Danny and William Hague making short, positive, but otherwise rather bland, statements on the Cabinet Office steps.

Before we left, Danny had a brief chat with Gus O'Donnell.

Gus was still nervous about the economic environment and asked whether we thought the negotiations would be finalised before the markets opened on Monday morning. Gus clearly needed an additional briefing on the workings of the Liberal Democrat 'triple lock' and our requirements for party consultation!

Danny replied: 'Look, we understand the need for speed, but it is also crucial for us to get the agreement right. This is going to take a bit more time.'

We made our way back down the staircase at 70 Whitehall, and outside to a huge gathering of UK and international media. Danny made his short statement, and we plunged into the crowd and made our way back up Whitehall in the middle of a media circus.

Our Lib Dem strategy team met again in Cowley Street at around 6.15pm, including Nick Clegg, the negotiating team, Jonny Oates, Chris Saunders and Polly MacKenzie.

We started by briefing Nick on the talks with the Conservatives. Danny Alexander summed up the position by saying that with the exception of voting reform it looked possible that we could agree sensible positions with the Conservatives on most issues.

Nick said he was happy with what we had agreed, including on the economic issues.

Nick said that he wanted to update us on discussions which he had held earlier in the day with Gordon Brown. Nick Clegg and the Labour leader had met in the mid-afternoon in the Foreign Office. Nick said: 'It was pretty striking stuff. They are obviously desperate. Brown says he will do anything we want to secure a coalition, including standing down as Labour leader. He also claims that we could sort out the parliamentary arithmetic with the minority parties.

'He is talking about a jumbo referendum on constitutional reform in the autumn of 2010. He says he would legislate for AV, and claimed he would also deliver on no person earning under £10,000 paying any net income tax, though the details on that were a bit unclear.

'He was up for extra taxes on aviation and a Mansion Tax, and says he will agree to sixteen of the twenty items which we want in a Freedom Bill. He even said he would agree to speeding up the pace of deficit reduction.

'He accepts that we would need to think carefully about the public reaction to all this. He made clear that he would be willing to stand down as Labour leader in order to clear the way for a Lib Dem–Labour coalition. He said he would go whenever the timing was right. In the meantime, he said I could make all the announcements on new policy so that the government has a new "feel" to it!

'Clearly we need to consider all this, and if Gordon Brown goes then we may be able to talk formally to Labour, though the parliamentary arithmetic still looks tough to me. However, this is too big a chance to ignore. So we need to think this through; decide on our terms, and then put these to Mandelson.'

Chris Huhne said that maybe Labour would consider immediate action to deliver AV, with a referendum on proportional representation on the general election day in May 2014. The alternative could be a multiple choice referendum, with a first question on the issue of change and the second question being on what type of change.

Andrew Stunell said he was pretty sceptical that a coalition with Labour would work. He thought Labour was tired, and still very unpopular with the public. 'Look at the figures,' he said. '258 Labour. Fifty-seven Lib Dem. This will still look like a discredited Labour government, and it would tarnish our image and Nick's. This could be our one chance as a party to deliver real change – we cannot afford to blow it.'

Danny said he agreed that a Lib–Lab government could be very difficult given the parliamentary arithmetic. He thought the press would attack it relentlessly and that it would be a major challenge to make the government look in any way 'new'.

Chris Huhne, however, argued that the AV prize was worth taking a risk for: 'Remember, if we secure AV, this will be a dramatic breakthrough in the history of our party.'

Jonny Oates looked tired and deeply sceptical: 'This would still be a "coalition of the losers" wouldn't it? And can AV be delivered in the Lords? We need a government with the strength to last. We won't fix the economy in just two years.'

There was a discussion over how long any deal could last. Chris Huhne pointed out that the economy would take years to 'fix', which meant that any deal would have to last for at least four years.

I responded: 'Look, the choices we face range between the unpalatable and the disastrous. There is no easy choice. We need to explore both options seriously and see which is better for the country and which is more likely to deliver on our priorities.'

Nick summed up by saying that we needed to maximise our leverage with both sides.

He reported that he and Danny would be meeting Gordon Brown and Peter Mandelson again that evening for further talks.

Nick clearly felt that these developments opened up a real prospect of meaningful Lib–Lab talks, but when he spoke to Gordon Brown again in the evening at 9.30pm in the Prime Minister's House of Commons office (along with Peter Mandelson and Danny Alexander) the Labour leader had changed his tune and was now talking about going 'sometime later in the parliament'.

Gordon Brown was still talking about Nick being the public face of the coalition, but with Brown staying on as interim Prime Minister, for an unspecified period of time.

Nick eventually told Brown: 'Please understand that I have no personal animosity, but a Lib–Lab coalition will not be sellable unless you move on swiftly, in a dignified way.'

The Prime Minister replied: 'Look, if I stay on I can help with the referendum campaign on AV'.

An exasperated Danny Alexander said: 'But we will never win a referendum with you in charge!' Gordon Brown looked rather taken aback.

'Gordon is just impossible to deal with,' a frustrated Nick Clegg told us later that evening. 'Earlier today he seemed to get it. Now he is going back on all his undertakings and talking about staying on for some unspecified period. That will never work.'

Meanwhile, Nick and David Cameron had further discussions to explore the potential for movement on voting reform. The two leaders met at 7.45pm one-to-one in Room 391 of Portcullis House, spoke on the phone at 9.15pm, and then again at 10.55pm.

The Lib Dem Reference Group (a wider team established by Nick to advise him on these issues) returned for a final meeting of the day in Cowley Street at 11.15pm. This time we were joined by Vince Cable and by the Chief Whip, Paul Burstow. Nick started with his assessment of our position, following all of the day's meetings.

'I want to tell you where I think we are. I really feel that we must reach a conclusion on all of this tomorrow. At present, we are between a rock and a hard place – our choices are a minority Conservative government with some informal Lib Dem support, or a coalition with Labour and various other parties.

'I am really worried about the economy, and having a government that can deliver stability and confidence. Neither of these two options will deliver that. At our latest meeting, Gordon Brown seemed to go back on the timing of his departure. Now he is talking about the autumn, or maybe next year – after "steering us through to recovery" That is just not workable.'

I said that I felt that we needed to be clearer about what was on offer from Labour:

'When will Brown actually go? We cannot risk him being there for month after month! What will happen on the PR referendum, can it get through? Will the government be able to govern? We need to test these things out. We need to explore both the Tory and Labour options.'

Danny said that it would simply be impossible to work with Gordon Brown for any length of time. Danny said that he would go back to Peter Mandelson and make it clear that Gordon Brown would have to be gone by the summer parliamentary recess at the latest, and that we would want a two-question referendum – change or no change, combined with a variety of different 'change' options.

Andrew Stunell remained sceptical over a deal with Labour: 'I am going to repeat what I said earlier. There are so many problems – legitimacy, deliverability, credibility. I doubt we could win a referendum if Gordon Brown was anything to do with it, and it would damage our party's brand to put back in a defeated Labour Party.'

We agreed to continue to explore both paths, and to report back to the Parliamentary Party the next day. As for the idea of Gordon Brown staying on to steer the country through the economic recovery, and an AV referendum, none of us thought that was very attractive or realistic. After this possible strategy was later trailed in the newspapers by Labour spin doctors, a Conservative MP said of it: 'It is like Neville Chamberlain saying in 1940 I intend resigning, but not until after the autumn party conference because I am the best man to deal with this rather large German offensive coming through the Low Countries' (Keith Simpson, quoted in the *Guardian*, 10/5/2010). Indeed.

Monday 10 May 2010

An offer spurned, a leader resigns, Labour talks fail

After further discussions with our negotiating team and advisers that evening, I finally left for home just after midnight.

I did not then know that Monday 10 May was to be one of the most dramatic and important days in recent British politics, as well as being the crucial day of the post-election talks.

At sunrise there was all to play for. By sundown the die was cast.

But the day started not with some much needed sleep, but with more coalition discussions.

Paddy Ashdown had phoned on Sunday afternoon and insisted that I call at his house in Kennington on the way home 'regardless of what time it is.' I took Paddy at his word, and arrived at his house at around 1am. I think he had long given up on me and gone to bed, but he eventually emerged, opened the front door, and invited me in for a chat and a late-night whisky.

I briefed Paddy on the day's events. By now, he was strongly of the view that the Lib–Lab option needed to be our first priority, and that it was a real opportunity. Paddy had last spoken to Nick Clegg earlier in the day, when Gordon Brown was offering a swift resignation and departure. Now I had to tell Paddy that in later conversations Gordon Brown was talking about hanging on for many more months.

'God, the man is impossible,' said Paddy. 'Why is he doing this? Doesn't he understand that this is completely terminal for any deal? We have to sort this out. I will call Mandelson or Andrew Adonis. They have to get Gordon to see sense.' With that, Paddy phoned 'switch', the Downing Street switchboard, which can famously track down ministers and senior politicians anywhere in the world. Paddy asked to be put through first to Peter Mandelson and then to Lord Adonis.

Their phones rang and rang. Neither could be reached, which was not surprising as by then it was around 1.30am. I was beginning to feel a little tired myself, and thought that would be the end of our late night lobbying. But Paddy was not to be deterred by the minor issue of people's need for sleep. 'I will call Blair,' he said suddenly. 'It really is crucial that we make Brown see sense.'

Paddy then called Tony Blair's home, waking Cherie, who told him that Tony was somewhere in the Middle East, where it must have been 3am or 4am. After a couple of calls, a sleepy Tony Blair finally came onto the phone. 'You won't believe what Gordon is up to,' said Paddy. 'First he promised to stand down immediately as leader, then a few hours later he said he wanted to stay on for up to an extra year.' I could hear Tony Blair chuckling at the other end of the phone. He could doubtless see the irony of Gordon Brown being pressed for an early exit date!

Although uncertain of whether a Lib–Lab deal could work, Mr Blair promised to phone Gordon Brown to do his best. He chortled at Paddy's description of how difficult it was to deal with Mr Brown. He had his own scars to prove just that.

I left for home at around 2.45am, with strict instructions from Paddy to leave my mobile phone on 'in case he needed to speak urgently'. What could possibly be urgent at 2.45am wasn't clear to me. So as soon as I got home, and having averaged only three hours sleep for the last five nights, I switched off my phone only to be woken half an hour later by Paddy who, having failed to get through on my mobile, had managed to track down my pager number instead. I cannot remember what he said to me at 3.15am, but I have the distinct recollection of thinking that it could have waited until a more civilised hour.

Across London, a few hours later, another Lib Dem was receiving an early morning telephone call. This time it was Vince Cable, who was woken by Gordon Brown on the telephone at 6am. It would, perhaps, have been more productive if Paddy and Gordon had been speaking to each other directly. Although totally different characters they both have an unquenchable appetite for hard work and long hours.

A sleepy Vince nevertheless managed to focus enough to spell out to Gordon Brown that the price of a Lib–Lab deal was likely to be his immediate resignation. As Vince and Gordon Brown knew each other well, that would have made an important impact on the Labour leader.

News of the Lib Dem–Conservative stalemate over voting reform must have been communicated to Labour's high command, who knew that if they were to make a breakthrough in the talks, then Monday 10 May was to be the crucial day. By mid-morning, media rumours emerged that senior Labour figures had visited 10 Downing Street to call on Mr Brown to stand down.

The messages seemed finally to be getting through, because at our Cowley Street HQ, a morning phone call between Peter Mandelson and Danny Alexander finally confirmed agreement by Labour to the Lib Dem requirement for Gordon Brown to announce his resignation if serious Lib–Lab discussions were to start.

Meanwhile, at just after 10am, the Lib Dem negotiating team returned to 70 Whitehall to continue our negotiations with the Conservative team. At the same time, just down the road in the Palace of Westminster, Nick Clegg and Gordon Brown were meeting again in the PM's office to discuss the future both of the Prime Minister and the government itself.

Our meeting with the Conservative team eventually started at around 10.15am, in the same large conference room at 70 Whitehall in which our earlier discussions had been held. Each party was represented by the same teams – William Hague, George Osborne, Oliver Letwin and Ed Llewellyn for the Conservatives, and Danny Alexander, Chris Huhne, Andrew Stunell and me for the Liberal Democrats.

The atmosphere was again positive, but William Hague started the meeting by saying that no further concessions were possible on voting reform, so the Conservatives were now making 'an offer' to the Liberal Democrats of a confidence and supply agreement to support a Conservative minority administration. The coalition option was now clearly on the back-burner.

William Hague opened by saying: 'This would be a new politics. The idea would be to make it difficult for either side to break the agreement without legitimate cause.'

A four-page draft agreement was tabled by the Conservatives, and we spent the morning amending this (Appendix 2). This agreement would require Lib Dem support on confidence and money votes, in exchange for a package of economic, political and green policies.

Oliver Letwin introduced the document. Included in the pledges was action to increase the income tax allowance, a free vote in the House of Commons on an AV referendum, a pupil premium for disadvantaged pupils and action on the 'green economy' – in other words, progress on at least three of our four key election pledges. There was also a substantial package on civil liberties and the environment.

On the economy there was to be 'formal participation by Liberal Democrat representatives in a financial stability council that will be consulted on the allocation of spending reductions between departments.'

The original draft concluded by expressing the hope that the agreement would lead the two parties 'in due course, to agree a closer collaboration'. But this was struck out of the final agreement, at our suggestion. It seemed to us that it was either coalition or confidence and supply. We weren't convinced that one would lead in government to the other, and we did not wish to set hares running.

Essentially, what was being offered was most of what had been agreed between the teams to date, but without a coalition, without direct Lib Dem involvement or influence in government, and without any pledge to deliver an AV referendum.

Oliver Letwin explained that we would be expected to support the Conservatives on issues of confidence and supply, but there would be no requirement to support the government on individual pieces of legislation. Andrew Stunell replied: 'That is good, because the overall idea must be to create a stable administration. This will not mean that we will support every bit of legislation – so each defeat of the government must not be seen as a crisis.'

George Osborne looked a little dubious and said that there would need to be close co-ordination, communication and co-operation: 'This will never work if it is just "death by a thousand defeats",' he said. 'It will need a real measure of trust and co-operation.'

Chris Huhne suggested that the two party leaders would have to work closely together and each Cabinet minister would need to work with his or her Lib Dem opposite number. 'I would certainly want to consult the Lib Dem Foreign Affairs Team,' said William Hague. 'But confidentiality will be key.'

The two negotiating teams discussed and amended the document. The agreement was now to be in the context of making provision for four-year, fixed-term parliaments, in order to seek to give extra durability to the arrangements.

The section on deficit reduction was brought to the beginning of the document, to reflect its importance, and the financial stability council's remit was widened to include consultation on Budget issues as well as on spending plans. It was also agreed that there needed to be an 'Operational Annex' to set down in detail how the two parties would work together.

'Well, we have made good progress,' said William Hague. 'Our shadow Cabinet meets at 4pm this afternoon, and our Parliamentary Party meets at 6pm. We will then consider this document in detail at those meetings.'

Oliver Letwin added: 'If necessary, we can meet again between 2pm and 4pm to make further changes.' George Osborne said: 'I know your Parliamentary Party is meeting earlier, at 1pm. I am a bit worried about leaks, which could be destabilising if my colleagues learn about this from the media.'

Danny said that he understood this, and we would not circulate copies of the draft agreement at our meeting for this reason. Oliver Letwin added, 'It would be very helpful if we could have a read-out of your meeting before our shadow Cabinet discussions. Could we have this by 3.30pm?' Danny agreed to this.

We had put the finishing touches to a draft confidence and supply agreement. But there was, certainly for our Lib Dem team, no sense of celebration, finality or conclusion.

Our team knew by then that the Labour option was highly likely to be brought into play later in the day. We did not think that a confidence and supply agreement was the best outcome for us. And we did not know if we had really hit the Conservative bottom line on voting reform. Were the Conservatives really planning to take this back to their party with a recommendation to press ahead on this basis? Or were they merely testing whether we would blink first, and agree to a coalition without a referendum guarantee on voting reform? Could we expect the Conservatives to offer something better of their own accord later on?

These were difficult questions to answer. My guess was that this Conservative team was genuinely disappointed not to have been able to pursue the coalition option with us, but that they were preparing to sign off on the confidence and supply agreement if we stuck to our guns on voting reform. It seemed likely, therefore, that the two teams left the Cabinet Office with rather different assumptions about what the next few hours would bring. Our talks ended at around 11.45am, and after a brief statement to the media we left to update Nick Clegg on progress.

When we arrived in Nick's office in the Palace of Westminster, Nick was still meeting with David Cameron – the two leaders had opened discussions again in Portcullis House (Room 391) at around midday.

When he returned, Nick reported back to us on his discussions with Gordon Brown, earlier that morning. Mr Brown had promised that he would announce later in the day that he would step down as Labour leader to facilitate Lib–Lab discussions.

We then moved on to brief Nick on the confidence and supply agreement that we had just finished negotiating with the Conservatives. From our perspective this was a good version of such an agreement, which is all we ever expected to be able to agree if the Conservatives were the only party which we could do business with.

However, there still seemed a possibility either that the deal with Labour could get off the ground (with a more bankable guarantee on voting reform), or that David Cameron would have to up his offer. We certainly did not expect the Conservatives to move straight to their bottom line on voting reform, but we did not now expect any movement from them on this issue unless we could bring Labour into play as a serious alternative.

It is unclear whether the Conservative team thought that they had a deal which we were bound to recommend to our own Parliamentary Party, but we certainly thought that any such recommendation would be premature. So we prepared to brief the Parliamentary Party on progress to date, without feeling that we had got to a point where we wanted to recommend one course of action.

Some commentators have suggested that Nick and key members of the negotiating team went to the Parliamentary Party meeting determined to sell the confidence and supply agreement to the party. This was untrue. We regarded the confidence and supply arrangement as a second best solution, and we were far from sure that it would last much beyond six months. Our view all along was that we wanted to be part of a government that was strong and stable, that could deliver on the economy, that would implement key Lib Dem priorities and that would give a real chance of delivering voting reform. Nick, and each of us on the negotiating team, was committed to those end objectives – not to doing deals with any one particular political party.

The Lib Dem Parliamentary Party met at around 1.30pm in the Grand Committee Room off Westminster Hall. MPs were in a remark- ably good heart in the light of the general tendency of Lib Dems to be suspicious of their leaders, and given the understandable concerns about how high the stakes were. By now, Nick knew that Gordon Brown would soon be announcing his resignation. But this was not news which could be shared with a hundred Lib Dem MPs and peers.

The meeting began slightly late, and we updated our colleagues on our talks with the Conservatives over the last two days. There was a good reception for the concessions that we had secured, but there was obvious disappointment that these did not include progress on voting reform. To my surprise, given my previous experiences, there was a strong view that both the country and the Lib Dems would be better off with a coalition than some loose form of confidence and supply agreement.

Speaker after speaker argued for a full coalition with one of the other parties, rather than a confidence and supply arrangement – and this represented a spread of opinion across the whole party. This conviction about the merits of a coalition was far stronger than any view that this partnership should be with either the Conservatives or Labour – on that issue MPs had different views or were open-minded.

At the Parliamentary Party's meeting on 8 May the first crucial decision had been taken: not to simply stand back from the responsibilities of governing. Now the second key decision was taken: our preferred outcome was to be coalition, not some more distant arrangement.

This was the second, crucial, step in the 'Sherlock Holmes strategy' of eliminating the impossible options. Our MPs and peers did not believe that a looser agreement could deliver the stability that the country needed, and they believed that it presented a high risk of a second election. They also took the view put forcibly by Chris Huhne before the election, namely that a confidence and supply arrangement would offer us all the downside of a coalition in terms of responsibility, while offering none of the upsides in terms of power and influence.

However, MPs and peers also took the view that coalition was unacceptable without voting reform.

There was an appetite for responsibility and power which I had not expected to be so strong. So, if the Conservatives would not budge on voting reform, all of this pointed to the Labour option becoming a more serious possibility.

Then, halfway through the meeting, Nick Harvey, our MP for North Devon, handed me a note with some useful intelligence on it – a journalist had told him that the Conservative whips were asking their own MPs whether they would be willing to accept a referendum on the Alternative Vote as the price of a coalition with the Lib Dems.

This was helpful confirmation, and the first that I was aware of, that the ice on the Conservative side was thawing on voting reform, and I immediately reported this to Nick Clegg. It bolstered our willingness to put the Conservatives on the spot. By the end of the meeting, it was clearly decided that we would pursue a full coalition option. We would enter talks with Labour if Gordon Brown announced he was standing down. In addition, Nick would go back to David Cameron to tell him that we were no longer interested in confidence and supply, only in a full coalition, and only on the condition that Conservative MPs would back a referendum on AV.

After the meeting, at around 4pm, I made a suitably vague announcement of the conclusions we had reached to the press who were waiting in Westminster Hall. The key to my statement was talk of seeking 'clarification' from the Conservatives on a number of issues, including on political reform and schools funding. I also talked of our decision to pursue strong and stable government.

What this all meant in plain English was that we wanted a coalition, but that the Conservatives would have to move on electoral reform before they were players in that game. It also signalled discretely that we were about to open up talks with Labour, if Gordon Brown delivered on a clear commitment to stand down.

Others have already put a different gloss on what had happened. According to Steve Richards, in his book *Whatever It Takes* (2010):

> The meeting broke up with an announcement that the negotiating team would seek 'clarification' on some issues with their Conservative counterparts. The term was a euphemism that allowed the two wings of the Liberal Democrats to play for time. As far as David Laws was concerned, clarification related to a few minor details in relation to the pupil premium. . . The social democratic wing had growing hopes that in the space still left a deal could be reached with Labour.

This was untrue. There was never any 'plot' by me, Nick Clegg or any other Liberal Democrat to go into coalition with the Conservatives come what may. There was instead a hard-nosed appreciation of the electoral arithmetic in the House of Commons, a strong desire to maximise our negotiating leverage in order to deliver as much Liberal Democrat policy as possible, and an appreciation of the national interest in having a strong and stable government able to deal in particular with the economic challenges. These three factors were our guiding lights throughout the days of negotiation.

While I made my statement in Westminster Hall, Nick Clegg slipped away from the meeting, avoiding the waiting press by descending in a lift, and returned to his office. Nick then telephoned David Cameron to tell him the conclusions from our meeting. The phone call took place at around 4pm: Nick said: 'I want to update you on the meeting which I have had with my Parliamentary Party. There is overwhelming support for a full-blown coalition of some kind. And I have to be blunt and say that there is not much support for a confidence and supply agreement. People just don't think it will last.

'I will be quite candid with you. My colleagues are divided about who they want to be in coalition with, but a lot of people want me to explore the Labour option to the full. I have been clear just how much your party has been willing to concede, and people are really pleased about that. We have travelled a long way with your people in the talks. But what we also really need is progress on the Alternative Vote – not just a guaranteed referendum, but legislation now.

'This is crucial because smaller parties usually see their support squeezed if they go into coalitions, so that makes a fairer electoral system even more important to us. And there is a growing clamour for electoral reform in the country, as people see just how unfair the first-past-the-post system is. I don't see why AV is so difficult for your party – you already use it for some of your own internal, party, elections.

'So, confidence and supply is now off the table. We want to look at coalition options. But a coalition with the Conservatives means you will need to move on AV.'

David Cameron listened. 'OK. I understand. We will get back to you on this.'

This was the crucial stage of the negotiation for us, where our leverage was at its maximum. As the news of the Lib Dem insistence on AV got out, alongside speculation that Gordon Brown's resignation would open the way for Lib Dem–Labour talks, an unnamed Conservative MP, with a sense of humour, reported that: 'We feel the hand of history on our gonads, squeezing very hard.'

An hour after our meeting broke up, at 5.05pm, Gordon Brown stepped outside into Downing Street to announce that he would resign to clear the way for full Lib–Lab talks. The stalemate with the Conservatives on the AV referendum, combined with Gordon Brown's decision to stand down, had for the first time opened up the real prospect of a Lib Dem–Labour coalition.

Paddy Ashdown took a copy of Brown's statement to a meeting of the Lib Dem peers at 5pm. They were delighted with the announcement. For many of them it marked the culmination of years, decades even, of hopes that a 'progressive alliance' of Liberal Democrats and the Labour Party could be established, based on electoral reform. This was the big prize that Liberal, Alliance and Lib Dem leaders had all worked for, particularly in the thirty years from the establishment of the Lib–Lab pact in 1977, right up until the election of Nick Clegg as leader in 2007.

David Steel, Roy Jenkins, Paddy Ashdown, Charles Kennedy and Menzies Campbell were all instinctively politicians of the centre-left, as were many Liberal Party members and those who had joined the SDP in exasperation with an increasingly extreme Labour Party in the early 1980s. Moreover, many MPs, peers and party members had had their politics defined in opposition to Mrs Thatcher's government and the Conservative administrations of 1979 to 1997. In addition, almost all Lib Dem seats, up until around 2005, were held against the Conservatives, with Labour trailing far behind.

This meant that for many years a large number of leading Lib Dems had dreamed of a hung parliament and some sort of centre-left coalition, alongside electoral reform. After the election of Tony Blair as Labour leader in 1994, this dream seemed for a while close to becoming a reality, but the scale of Tony Blair's majority, his instinctive suspicion of PR and the compromises he felt it would require, plus strong resistance from "tribal Labour", meant that the opportunity had been lost.

Although Gordon Brown was one of those who resisted PR and Lib–Labbery in the 1994–2007 period, after Paddy Ashdown's departure as leader in 1999 it had always seemed to me that the Lib Dems were more likely to secure PR with Gordon Brown as PM than with Tony Blair.

This is because it seemed to me much less likely that Gordon Brown would be able to hold together the huge coalition of support for Labour that Tony Blair had assembled, at least until the Iraq war. It seemed inevitable to me that eventually Gordon Brown, in spite of his tribalism, would see his and Labour's self-interest in creating a Lib–Lab alliance of some sort. Indeed I put this theory to two of Gordon Brown's special advisers – Ed Balls and Ed Miliband – in an informal meeting back in the Treasury in 2004. Neither responded – perhaps not desiring to acknowledge that 'their man' would be a less popular PM than Mr Blair.

But in spite of one early and ham-fisted attempt to bring senior Lib Dems into his government in 2007, an attempt which only succeeded in undermining the authority of his friend and Lib Dem party leader, Menzies Campbell, Gordon Brown failed to act to establish either a partnership or the basis for one. And then, in 2007, the Lib Dems elected a new leader in Nick Clegg, a leader from a new generation, and an individual who was close neither to the Conservatives nor Labour.

Much as Nick was doubtful about Conservative social policies and their attitude to Europe, he was deeply distrustful of Labour's lack of respect for civil liberties, their top-down approach to governing and of Gordon Brown himself. Indeed Nick, like many senior Labour Cabinet members, found Gordon Brown almost impossible to deal with. This was not the best basis for a coalition which needs to be founded on trust and mutual respect.

The philosophical basis for a more 'liberal' Liberal democracy had already been created in 2004, with the publication of the *Orange Book*, which was edited by Paul Marshall and me. This challenged the notion that liberalism could only be delivered by 'big government' solutions, and it led to more emphasis on policies such as cutting tax for lower earners, reforming the delivery of public services, raising money for social investment through cuts to lower priority programmes rather than higher taxes and privatising the Royal Mail. It sought to explain how 'social liberal' ends could be delivered by 'economically liberal' means.

In spite of the sharp reaction of many in the party towards these ideas (I was almost lynched during a two-hour-long inquisition of the Lib Dem Parliamentary Party in October 2004), this volume helped shift the centre of gravity of the party to a more liberal and less statist location, and it created stronger links between a group of Lib Dem MPs who were ambitious about the party but had been concerned about its previous policy positions. This included Nick Clegg himself, Vince Cable, Norman Lamb, Ed Davey, myself, and (after the 2005 election) Jeremy Browne and Danny Alexander. Chris Huhne was an economic 'dry', who also contributed to the *Orange Book*, but he was notably more cautious about public service reform, believing essentially in devolving power from Whitehall to Town Hall, but not to individuals themselves.

As well as the repositioning of Lib Dem policy on more equidistant ground, it was also the case that from 2002 onwards, as Labour's support began to fade, the Lib Dems started to make major gains against Labour in many parts of the country – not least in former Labour 'heartland' areas such as Liverpool, Newcastle, Sheffield and Hull. This meant that the natural 'anti Tory' fit between the Lib Dems and Labour faded somewhat, and many Labour MPs and activists came to see the Lib Dems as their 'real' enemies on the ground.

Despite these developments, most Lib Dems – including all of our negotiating team – welcomed the prospects of real negotiations with Labour. We were concerned that the Conservatives wouldn't budge on electoral reform, and felt that it should still be easier to construct a good policy agreement with the Labour Party.

We trusted people such as Andrew Adonis and – with perhaps some greater caution – Peter Mandelson, who had long been advocates of Lib–Lab co-operation, and we were persuaded by Andrew and others that Gordon Brown was now, finally, fully committed to delivering a Lib–Lab coalition as part of his political legacy.

And although there would be questions about the 'legitimacy' of any arrangement that kept a defeated Labour Party in power, the plain fact was that a Lib–Lab arrangement would represent some 52% of the electorate, against the 36% secured by the Conservatives on 6 May.

Nick Clegg therefore welcomed Gordon Brown's announcement, and plans were made for the two negotiating teams to assemble again that evening, after a meeting of the Cabinet. Even though the talks with Labour had now moved on to a 'formal' status, the decision was taken to continue to use the Lib Dem meeting room on the third floor of Portcullis House, rather than the facilities at the Cabinet Office. We realised that talking to both the Conservatives and Labour at the same time created some interesting presentational challenges, and we did not want the negotiations to begin to look too chaotic or promiscuous. We therefore decided to keep the two locations separate. This also had the considerable advantage of us not having to march through vast ranks of the world's media to go in for our talks.

Danny Alexander, Chris Huhne, Andrew Stunell and I therefore gathered in Room 391 in Portcullis House at around 7.30pm, for a meeting with Labour which was moved back to 7.45pm because of the Cabinet meeting, which had been called to hear from Gordon Brown.

While we waited for the Labour team, rumours swirled around Westminster that the Conservatives were to make a new offer to us to hold a whipped vote in the House of Commons on an AV referendum, in return for a full coalition. This was confirmed later in the evening. The Conservatives had moved swiftly and decisively to issue 'a bankable offer' on a referendum on AV (see Appendix 3).

Quarter to eight came and went and there was no sign of the Labour negotiating team. We wondered if there had been some problem at the Cabinet meeting. Eventually, at around 8pm, the door to the conference room opened, and in stepped Peter Mandelson, Andrew Adonis, Ed Balls and Ed Miliband, joined on this occasion by Harriet Harman. Again, we sat around the huge hexagonal table – the Lib Dems on one side and the Labour team on the side nearest the door.

Peter Mandelson sat in the middle of the Labour team with Andrew Adonis seated to his left, and Ed Balls to his far left. On Lord Mandelson's right were Ed Miliband and then Harriet Harman.

This time Gus O'Donnell was also present at the beginning of the meeting. He explained that Civil Service support was available, on the same basis as offered for our talks with the Conservatives. Once again, this external support was declined. This was all very different from the coalition negotiations in Scotland in 1999, after the first elections for the Scottish Parliament. Those negotiations were actively facilitated by the Civil Service, which worked with representatives of the Lib Dems and Labour to produce drafts of the coalition agreement, which were then sent to the main negotiating teams for amendment. A problem in Scotland was that we felt that some of the civil servants were inclined to see Labour – the larger party – as their political 'bosses'. This led to one or two rows, including one occasion when I insisted on a civil servant being removed from the team which was working with us. But on this occasion we were once again meeting politician to politician.

Peter Mandelson led off the talks, referring to Gordon Brown's resignation and what a significant moment it was for the Labour Party, and apologising for the team being late. 'I hope you will understand', he said, 'that the Cabinet wanted to pay tribute to Gordon for his contribution to the Labour Party over many years. For that reason, our meeting did overrun a little.

'Let me start by saying that we are approaching these talks', he said rather grandly, 'as the Labour Party and not as the government. If we are to be successful in this process, we need to form a "new" government with a new programme.

'We will only gain legitimacy if we have an exciting, inspiring programme, not just a continuation of the existing government. We understand that we need to make sure that what we offer is enough to overcome public scepticism. It must offer something for ordinary families and for the country.

'Sometimes we will have to listen to your ideas, reflect and come back with new policies. Of course, Alistair Darling will have views on all of this and so will Vince Cable. We do not presume to know Alistair's views. Perhaps he and Vince Cable should talk some time.'

Peter Mandelson then talked about the parliamentary arithmetic, recognising that a coalition would not be easy to manage, but referring to the prospects of securing the active support or at least co-operation of the SDLP, the DUP and others.

It was interesting to watch the body language of the Labour team, and this was something that all of us on the Lib Dem side of the table were conscious of.

Peter Mandelson was engaged and serious, but I thought I detected an element of distance. Was it, as his memoirs suggest, that he wasn't convinced that the coalition 'plane' could really get off the ground? In *The Third Man* he presents himself as a loyal but sceptical supporter of the coalition talks which he was leading. But, according to these memoirs (p. 544) he considered that 'a deal between us and the Lib Dems was highly unlikely'.

Or was it the arrogance of thirteen years of power that made it awkward and uncomfortable to have to sit down and negotiate as equals with four Lib Dem MPs?

Andrew Adonis was, as we expected, committed, professional and thoughtful. There could be no doubt that he was 100% signed up to achieve a deal. Between these two, however, and the three other members of the team there was a wide gulf of attitude, expression and enthusiasm, which one did not need to be a mind reader to detect.

As the talks proceeded, we realised that we appeared to be negotiating with two separate Labour teams, with their own distinct policy and political agendas. One team wanted a deal. The other didn't. One team said that it was concerned about the scale of our spending commitments. The other said that it was worried that we were too hawkish on the deficit. One team seemed to be signed up to electoral reform. The other team was lukewarm at best.

Ed Balls was already rumoured to be committed to taking Labour into opposition. He had never been a supporter of Lib–Lab links and, like Gordon Brown, he found it difficult enough to compromise within his own party, let alone with another. Ed stared off into the distance while Peter Mandelson talked, and occasionally winced or frowned at comments from either side that displeased him.

I had expected Ed Miliband to be far more constructive, as he had often stopped me in corridors to talk about the importance of keeping the door open to Lib–Lab co-operation. Was it now, though, that he intended to be a candidate in a Labour leadership election that he could see the value in a sharper opposition to the Liberal Democrats? His body language was as cool as that of his namesake, and he gave the impression of being at best indifferent to the success of the talks.

Harriet Harman, too, was clearly not an enthusiast. She said little, but wore a smile that was simultaneously pained, patronising and sceptical. When talking to Chris Huhne, our Home Affairs spokesman, on some point of policy detail about ID cards she said: 'Look, Alan Johnson really needs to talk this through with whoever the Lib Dem Home Affairs spokesman is.' 'That would be Chris,' Danny retorted. It was perhaps a minor slip rather than a calculated snub, but it suggested a level of preparation and focus that was not cheering.

On the table in front of us was a new policy paper which Labour had tabled that morning (see Appendix 5). This second paper was a longer and amended version of the first Labour paper which was tabled on 8 May. It converted the previous short bullet-point paper into a detailed twelve-page document, divided into four major headings – on 'The Economy', 'Political Reform', 'Wider Social, Environmental and Public Service Reform', and 'Britain in the World'. Our team also tabled its own 'Heads of Agreement' paper on 9 May.

The Labour paper contained some important policy changes – for example, it was notably tougher on deficit reduction, and we hoped that changes of this kind might indicate a greater willingness to compromise.

Danny responded to Peter Mandelson's opening gambit. 'Peter, we quite understand why you are late, and that you all wanted to be at the Cabinet to pay tribute to Gordon Brown. We appreciate this is a difficult time for you. We echo what you have said – we are trying to create a new government here. We have looked at your policy document, and there is clearly quite a lot of common ground here. We have also updated our own policy paper, which we will now give you copies of.

'We are particularly keen to talk about economic and political reform tonight. By the way, we are mandated to negotiate for our party. We assume you are too. We do not need separate talks between Vince and Alistair, as we are constantly in touch with Vince, and his views are reflected in our positions. Can we start our discussion on the economy area, where David Laws is going to lead?'

I started to set out our position, including commenting on Labour's negotiating document.

I was aware that Labour's new proposals did reflect significant movement on the issue of the deficit. This followed Gordon Brown's own comments to Nick Clegg that Labour was prepared to go further in accelerating deficit reduction. Instead of implying that the existing Labour debt reduction plan was sufficient, Labour's new document said that: 'In light of market concerns, tough action will be taken to reduce the deficit.' This, and a commitment to an economic statement to be made after the Queen's Speech, seemed to go some way to meet our requirement of holding an Emergency Budget by the end of June, with cuts to the projected deficit figures for the period 2011–15.

But the new Labour offer document went further still. While the previous paper pledged 'not to cut public spending overall in 2010/11', the new paper proposed to 'reallocate a proportion of any identified in year 2010/11 savings to the promotion of growth and jobs'. That gave both a green light to tougher spending action in 2010/11, while implying that some proportion of the spending cuts in 2010/11 might be allocated to deficit reduction rather than to new spending.

But on this point there seemed to be a serious division on the Labour side.

Ed Balls appeared to be leading on the economic issues, in the absence of Alistair Darling, though it did not appear that he had been given a formal mandate to do so.

In spite of Gordon Brown's comments to Nick Clegg, and the wording in the new Labour paper, Ed Balls stuck to the line that the deficit could not be reduced any faster than existing plans. I was confused by this, as it was clearly not what the document said, and it suggested that the divisions within Labour in government on the issue of deficit reduction, were now being played out in the cross-party negotiations. (In the Labour leadership election which followed the establishment of the coalition government, Ed Balls expressed his opposition to even Alistair Darling's deficit reduction plans – so clearly the divisions that we perceived were very real.)

This opposition to credible action on the deficit raised serious concerns in our mind. If we had a new government, with no clear majority and no credible deficit reduction plan, there was a high risk that the markets would react very badly – with a major loss of confidence in the United Kingdom. Market interest rates would undoubtedly have risen sharply, and with them not only mortgage rates but the costs of servicing the UK's huge public sector deficits. This could have made it difficult to raise the amounts of borrowing needed in the markets, and could have squeezed real spending on front-line public services, by having to fund even higher public spending on debt interest payments.

It was only too clear to us that there was now a real likelihood that a Lib–Lab coalition government would have no credible, agreed, deficit reduction strategy, and would in any case have an almost impossible job assembling a majority in the House of Commons for the many unpopular decisions a new government would need to take.

I continued our discussion by trying to address these issues: 'There is, of course, a lot of common ground here but also some issues where more work is needed. It looks as if you are now happy to have a substantive economic statement, essentially a mini-Budget, early on. However, we need to make progress on deficit reduction, and your paper is a bit unclear on how this will be delivered. We think that deficit reduction needs speeding up, not least from 2011 onwards. Your latest paper is helpful in that it talks about tough action on the deficit, and some cuts in 2010/11. This will be really important, because frankly the markets are going to be very sceptical on whether this coalition, without a Commons majority, can actually deliver.

'If savings in non-front-line public services can be made in 2010, some of this should go back into investment in the economy, but some could go on deficit reduction – which would reassure the markets. The markets will need convincing that this coalition can take these tough decisions. Credible action will be highly desirable given the big deterioration in the markets because of loss of confidence in Greece and some of the southern European countries.

'We also want to see a much higher personal tax allowance to help those on middle and lower incomes. All your paper offers is an increase to £10,000 in the allowance for pensioners, but I think that will look like we are pulling a fast one, because the pensioner allowance is almost £10,000 now anyway! That is not much of a concession!

'We also want a properly funded pupil premium, and the restoration of the pension earnings link. Set against this we have plans for specific savings, for example, on tax credits and on public sector pensions. We really need movement from you on these key issues. Without going into too much detail about our other talks, the Conservatives have already offered us much more on tax cuts for those on low pay, and on the pupil premium, and it would look very odd if we settled with you for a lot less than they have already offered us.

'Hmmm,' said Peter Mandelson. 'Well we need to think about all that, and maybe get Alistair and Vince together?'

Danny said: 'We understand that you want Alistair Darling's views on this, but can you not give us a sense of your own perspective and attitude?' I agreed, 'Surely we do not need to rely on input from Alistair? After all you are the negotiating team.'

'Ed, what is your view on this?' asked Peter Mandelson.

'Well,' said Ed Balls. 'The key issue here is credibility, and a £10,000 personal allowance will cost an awful lot of money. People will want to know if we can deliver what we promise. It is not enough to talk tough on the deficit, we need to show how we would deliver.'

'We agree,' I said, but Ed was in full flow.

'We have all these expensive Lib Dem pledges,' he went on, 'but how do we fund them, and cut the deficit? It doesn't add up.'

I responded by saying: 'Look, Ed, as you know we are proposing that the higher personal allowance is funded by progressive tax reforms of the type I would have thought Labour would support – higher capital gains tax, a new Mansion Tax, and reform of pensions taxation.'

At this, Peter Mandelson frowned: 'Surely the rich have suffered enough?' The others said nothing, but looked rather mystified. It was clear that they did not share his view.

All this was in rather marked contrast to the much more positive tone of the Conservative–Lib Dem talks, and indeed the conversations between Gordon Brown and Nick Clegg.

Ed Balls went on: 'Is faster deficit reduction really sensible, either tax increases or spending cuts? I don't think we can make undertakings without Alistair's say-so.'

This was baffling as it seemed to contradict Labour's own document, and Gordon Brown's offer to Nick Clegg that Labour would go further on deficit reduction.

Andrew Adonis chipped in: 'Perhaps Vince and Alistair can meet tomorrow?'

Danny pointed out yet again that we were able to negotiate on these issues, and we assumed that the Labour team was empowered to as well. Chris Huhne interrupted to say: 'I agree we need action and not just words. That is what we are proposing. We need to be frank that at present a Lib Dem–Labour government will not be as trusted by the markets as a credible alternative, so we have to show by our early actions that we can take tough decisions.'

Ed Balls said: 'Look, I just think that a faster rate of deficit reduction would be very difficult.' 'But Ed,' argued Chris Huhne, 'the UK is starting with a worse deficit position than almost any other country. A Lib–Lab government would be distrusted by the markets, and it would be vital to show we could deliver on deficit reduction.'

I said that there were some clear ways in which we could demonstrate credibility, for example, we could establish a commission to review the affordability and fairness of public sector pensions. Danny said that this could be established on similar lines to Adair Turner's very successful commission on the state pension reforms.

Peter Mandelson and Lord Adonis looked sympathetic, enthusiastic even. But Ed Balls, Ed Miliband and Harriet Harman recoiled in horror, and competed to look shocked, horrified, and as if a rather unpleasant odour had assaulted their senses.

Not only was the Labour team clearly divided in its attitude to talks, but some interesting old/new Labour divisions were emerging during the policy discussions too.

Peter Mandelson clearly seemed to favour early action on the deficit, but Ed Balls and Ed Miliband did not. Peter Mandelson favoured action on public sector pensions, but the two Eds did not. Peter wanted to protect the rich from further tax hikes, but this was obviously not the view of the others. The Labour team could clearly have benefited from a little more preparation before coming to talk with us. If they were to negotiate an agreement with us, they first needed to agree amongst themselves.

What was also undoubtedly different in these negotiations compared with those with the Conservatives was any sense of respect or equality. The Conservatives had treated us as another opposition party on an equal footing, one that needed to be negotiated with.

The Labour team, and certainly the two Eds and Harriet, treated us to policy lectures from people who had been used to power for too long. Ed Balls told me that our proposals on the tax allowance and the pupil premium were simply unaffordable.

Yet on taxation, the Conservatives had already agreed in principle to seek to deliver our £10,000 personal allowance over the course of a parliament, with this policy given priority over other tax pledges. That was a very significant Conservative concession, and an important policy gain for the Lib Dems.

Labour's paper promised only to increase the allowance to £10,000 for people over the age of sixty-five, whose allowance was already close to this level. When I raised this with Ed Balls he looked slightly shamefaced that this trick had been spotted, but he said that no further concessions could be made without the permission of the Chancellor, Alistair Darling.

What was odd was that the negotiating team did not seem to have the authority to speak for the Labour Party on tax and spending issues. This was in contrast to our own situation, where Vince Cable was closely consulted and involved so that the Lib Dem negotiating team could speak for our whole party.

What was on offer on the key issue of the Pupil Premium was just as vague.

Labour had already announced its own 'Local Pupil Premium', but this was to be paid for out of existing funding, and not delivered fully for three years. In addition, there would be top-down control so that the money had to be spent on the Secretary of State's latest wheeze, regardless of what the schools wanted to do with the money. That was exactly the type of top-down 'command and control' in the public services that we so badly wanted to escape from.

On the economy, Labour was also opposed to a unilateral banking levy. There were also some big differences of position on the environment, with Labour insisting on a third runway for Heathrow and opposing more ambitious renewable energy targets.

Ed Miliband said that it was impossible to stop climate change without relying on nuclear power, and he rubbished our proposal to increase the renewables' share of energy production to 40% by 2020. 'There is no way we can deliver on our climate change targets without relying on nuclear power,' he said. 'And all this stuff about getting 40% of energy production from renewables by 2020 is just pie in the sky. We are already a leader in offshore wind technology, but we can never reach that sort of level.'

On civil liberties, we could not agree on our proposals to scrap ID cards in full, or to end the National Identity Register and the Contact Point Database.

If all of these impediments to an agreement were not enough, the discussion on political reform made clear that a Lib–Lab alliance was not going to work. Chris Huhne started off by saying that he assumed that Labour would be willing to introduce the 'Wright proposals' on reforming the House of Commons, including giving backbenchers more power. Harriet Harman looked sceptical: 'Well, we wouldn't want to throw everything into chaos.'

Chris Huhne said: 'But we are supposed to be giving the House of Commons more power. I thought Labour said it believed in giving power away?' Andrew Stunell added: 'Harriet, your reaction is that of an outgoing government. This is now a hung parliament. We must have a fresh approach on this.'

On House of Lords reform, Peter Mandelson and Andrew Adonis both said that this should be put on the back-burner in order to get the issue of AV through. Chris Huhne said: 'If we no longer have to deal with an endless supply of new Home Office Bills, there will be a lot more time for other legislation!'

Then we turned to voting reform. Chris Huhne said that AV was in reality a very modest reform. He argued that AV could be introduced immediately, including for by-elections, with a referendum later with a choice of the status quo, AV or a fully proportional system. Andrew Adonis said that any voting reform would need a referendum first. He added: 'We also need to discuss whether it is sensible to have more than one reform option. Most Labour MPs will support AV but vote against proportional representation. Would it matter if our two parties were split on this, and we were pushing for different options?'

Danny said: 'We understand that. But our view is that the referendum should have two questions. The first question should be change or no change. The second question should give people a say over AV versus other proportionate systems'

Harriet Harman said that it would not be easy to get an AV referendum through, 'Most Labour MPs will grit their teeth and vote for AV, but let's be clear that many of my colleagues are not exactly champing at the bit!' Chris and Danny continued to argue for a referendum which would include options – either AV or full PR. Andrew Adonis said that Labour would only support an AV referendum. But it was when we tested the commitment on AV that further cracks opened up.

We knew that many Labour MPs were not in favour of AV and we asked whether any would oppose legislation, knowing that assembling a majority for change would already be tough. Danny asked: 'Can we rely on Labour MPs supporting an AV referendum?'

'That is what is guaranteed in our manifesto,' said Peter Mandelson. 'So we can certainly get it through,' added Lord Adonis.

There was silence, and then Ed Balls intervened to say: 'Look, even AV would not be at all straightforward. In fairness, the Chief Whip thinks it could be difficult to get the AV referendum through. Many of our colleagues are opposed to it. It cannot be guaranteed.'

It was a deadly intervention and, I felt, a calculated wrecking device. If a hotch-potch, glued together deal with Labour and various other parties could not deliver on our policy prospectus, on economic stability or even on the most modest form of electoral reform legislation, what on earth was the point of it? How could we go into coalition with a Labour Party that could not even guarantee to deliver a referendum on AV, the most modest form of electoral reform, that it had promised in its own manifesto?

And how could we contemplate signing a deal with Labour which would not only deliver less stable government, but which would also deliver notably less on key Lib Dem manifesto commitments, on tax, schools funding and pensions?

It would then be open for the Conservatives to publish details of our own talks with them, and it would be obvious that on key policies such as the £10,000 allowance, civil liberties and even the environment, we had signed up with Labour to weaker commitments than would be available from a Lib Dem–Conservative coalition government. We would look foolish in the extreme.

The meeting had lasted a couple of hours. It was clear that not much more progress could be made. Danny explained that we had to brief Nick and then attend a meeting of our Parliamentary Party. In our first substantive meeting with Labour we had not even agreed or drafted one single line of a possible coalition agreement.

The talks broke up with Peter Mandelson suggesting further discussions the next day. We did not demur. We agreed to meet at 10am.

Before we finished, Andrew Stunell interrupted to say: 'If this is going to work we have to address the issues of legitimacy, credibility and workability. None of this is going to be easy. Not least creating the impression of a genuinely new government. How does Labour see this possible partnership and the feasibility of delivering?'

Peter Mandelson looked somewhat blank: 'What, do you mean in the Commons?'

Danny replied: 'Yes. Could this be delivered? Are the votes there, given that we would need the Unionists, nationalists and so on?'

Andrew Adonis intervened: 'Look, we would be absolutely bound in by coalition. But nobody is saying it would be easy. The AV referendum would help, though. It would be a force for cohesion.' Ed

Balls and Ed Miliband said nothing, but looked, sceptically, into the middle distance.

There was a pause. Then Danny said: 'Well. That was a very useful meeting. Thank you for your time – not least on a difficult day for your party, with Gordon Brown's resignation.' Peter Mandelson said: 'We need to work through all this quickly, but thoroughly. We don't have much time. The press will be very sceptical, and create problems. Let's meet again tomorrow morning.'

I do not know how the Labour Party negotiating team think the meeting went, but if they think it went well it can only say something about the way in which they are used to treating other groupings – and probably each other.

And if there was a desire for speed, it seemed odd that we had failed to agree even one line of a draft agreement. In any case, I believe that Ed Balls, Ed Miliband and Harriet Harman achieved what they set out to deliver – the planting of significant doubts in our mind about the likelihood of securing a Lib–Lab coalition.

When the Labour team had left our conference room, there were a few moments of silence, while we glanced around at each other. Before the meeting began we had expected a 'charm offensive'. But the charm had been in distinctly short supply.

Chris Huhne sighed and smiled. Andrew Stunell drily commented, 'that was interesting'. Danny Alexander turned to us and said: 'Well I don't know what you thought of that but I was pretty disappointed.' One by one we went around the table and recounted our conclusions. We were all agreed. The Labour Party was clearly split, and many senior figures were opposed to a coalition – even those on their own negotiating team. Gordon Brown's departure had opened the way to talks, but it had also shattered any remaining semblance of Labour Party unity.

Trying to do a deal with such an entity – tired, split, divided, and desperate for a return to opportunistic opposition – when there would in any case be no governing majority, would be a disaster. It was clear that if we went into coalition with Labour, we would not be establishing a new government, we would be chaining ourselves to a decaying corpse.

We made a list of the areas of major policy disagreement: increasing the personal tax allowance to £10,000, properly funding the pupil premium, restoring the pension earnings link in April 2011, the pace of deficit reduction, reforming public sector pensions and making savings in areas such as the Child Trust Fund and tax credits for higher earners, introducing a UK Bank Levy, targets for renewable energy, axing the third runway at Heathrow, identity cards, reforms of business practices in the Commons, Lords reform and second stage electoral reform.

That was without even taking account of areas such as Trident renewal, nuclear power and tuition fees, where we knew that there were disagreements with both other parties. It was a very long list and looked like being a great enough impediment to any agreement even on policy grounds.

We all agreed to report back to Nick and recommend against any prospect of a Lib–Lab coalition or a Lib–Lab deal of any kind. This was a crucial moment in our work. We had reached that final 'Sherlock Holmes' moment. Three impossible options had been ruled out. Only one possibility now remained.

This had been a historic meeting. But instead of ushering in the long anticipated Lib–Lab partnership, it had buried thirty years of Lib–Lab dreams. A Lib Dem–Conservative coalition was now the only door we could go through. And as we made our way back over to

Nick Clegg's office in the House of Commons, we heard the confirmation that David Cameron had now made a 'Bankable Offer from the Conservatives on Voting Reform' (Appendix 3). This provided the key to the last door that we could go through.

We did not then know it, but as our meeting with Labour came to an end, David Cameron was heading home to tell his wife that he considered that the premiership was slipping away from him, following Gordon Brown's bold gamble.

But in Westminster, we were returning to Nick Clegg's office in Parliament to tell Nick that in our view we had only one serious option left – a coalition with the Conservatives.

Back in Nick's office, at 10pm, we reported back on the meeting with the Labour team. Vince Cable, Jim Wallace, Paul Burstow and Ros Scott were also present.

Andrew Stunell started off: 'I thought the meeting went badly and I am concerned about the deliverability of any agreement, given the parliamentary arithmetic. The Labour team's body language was awful, and they seemed to have little understanding of our policy positions, and not much willingness to compromise. I don't think this will work.'

Chris Huhne said: 'Andrew Adonis and Peter Mandelson are clearly quite serious about this, but I don't believe that Ed Balls, Ed Miliband and Harriet Harman are committed to it at all. Ed Balls and Ed Miliband seem to me to have decided that it is better to go into opposition than to stay in government.'

I then gave my assessment: 'There were too many disagreements, and no effort by Labour to make concessions. Mandelson and Andrew Adonis are serious, but the other three are not. We have made little or no progress on huge issues such as raising the tax allowance, delivering a pupil premium, and deficit reduction. I am also very worried about AV. Peter Mandelson and Andrew Adonis claimed that we would get the support of Labour MPs on this, but Ed Balls made clear that he thought we might not. We are in danger of shackling ourselves to a decaying corpse. It would also be very tough to sell this as a "new" government, and I am not confident we would be able to command a majority in the House on crucial issues – including on AV.'

Danny said that he shared our analysis: 'There is now only one serious deal on the table – with the Conservatives. We must now go for this.'

'Is this really the view of all of you?' said Nick, somewhat taken aback by the strength and unanimity of our conclusion. 'God, this is going to make life very tough indeed. I have just had Paddy Ashdown, Ming Campbell and Charles Kennedy all talking to me separately and all wanting us to support the possibility of a deal with Labour.'

I added: 'This may be tough, but there is only one serious option open to us. And it would not be rational to just walk away from that.'

Chris Huhne intervened again: 'The "traffic light coalition" will clearly fall apart if we try it. Our historic mission is to create a British Liberal party whose influence will be embedded in our politics through a reformed voting system – a Liberal party capable of dealing with both other parties. Only a Conservative coalition now offers that prize, the prize of a guaranteed place in British politics for a strong liberal force. And only this agreement can now deliver economic stability for the country.'

Paul Burstow added: 'Yes, and this is not 1997. It would be very difficult to persuade the country that we should deal with Labour. How would we sell a traffic light coalition, with no clear majority? I think we need to give a clear recommendation to the Parliamentary

Party.' Ros Scott, as Party President, said that she thought that the Federal Executive was being very calm and rational about the whole process, and was persuadable over a Conservative coalition.

Vince Cable then intervened: 'Look, I have thought a lot about this and I am happy to speak up for the Conservative option. I can see that too many Labour people are just not interested in making a deal with us work. I may be viewed as being one of the "old guard" on the Lib–Lab stuff, but I can see that the opportunities of going in with the Conservatives in a stable coalition are immense. We will at last have a serious role in government – like the German liberal party, the FDP.'

'A big FDP!' said Chris Huhne. Jim Wallace also agreed that a Labour deal lacked legitimacy – 'The Tories have a greater moral mandate,' he said.

But Nick was clearly still worried about the party reaction: 'There is a real risk that we are going to have an almighty row and an almighty split over this. You will have to report back on this to the joint Lords/ Commons meeting in about half an hour, so that people understand just how difficult Labour is being. And – whatever your own views – I am going to have to insist that you meet the Labour team tomorrow morning to see if you can sort things out with them. Maybe they were just tired and grumpy after having to see their party leader resign? We need to check if things really are that bad with Labour. And if they are, at least we will then be seen to have gone the extra mile to secure an agreement. That will be vital if we are to win the support of the Parliamentary Party for a deal with the Conservatives.'

The four of us all groaned, like a group of children being asked to spend not only Christmas Day, but Boxing Day too, with a particularly disagreeable aunt. 'Do we really have to?' was the nature of our response, and a measure of how gloomy we were about the meeting with Labour. But Nick insisted that we would need to meet the Labour team again the next morning at around 10am.

'Right. That's it,' said Nick. 'But this is going to be bloody. We need to show our Parliamentary Party that we have gone the extra mile to really try with Labour. You will have to meet them again tomorrow morning. Now we need to be at the Parliamentary Party meeting! Danny, I will ask you to give a graphic account of the talks with Labour. But we have to get moving. We need this sorting tomorrow at the latest.'

'Agreed,' said Danny. 'Our aim must be a coalition government by the end of tomorrow.'

We finished our conversation with Nick, and then had to set off for yet another meeting of the Lib Dem Parliamentary Party – this time a joint meeting with our Lords colleagues, starting at around 10.30pm. We trudged down the staircase from Nick's office, across Members' Lobby, and down the stairs to Westminster Hall.

The great historic hall, the earliest parts of which date from the eleventh century, was quiet and in near darkness, but in the far corner was a dedicated huddle of journalists waiting to report the latest morsel of news from our negotiations. We bounded swiftly past them and up the steps into the Grand Committee Room, in which we had met only a few hours earlier that same day.

The room was jam-packed with Lib Dem MPs, peers, and senior staff. There was a feeling of excitement, even elation, at the events of the day, including Gordon Brown's resignation and the movement by the Conservatives on voting reform.

There was a feeling that the negotiation was moving our way, and that we were making progress on our key negotiating aims.

As Nick came in to the room there was a spontaneous burst of applause, while he made his way to the platform at the front. But Nick then had to deliver a dose of reality when he updated the meeting on the Labour negotiations. 'It went very badly, I'm afraid,' he told the meeting. There were some long faces, not least amongst our peers.

'You will hear from our negotiators in a moment, but the truth is that the Labour team seemed to be split, and it is very clear that many in the Labour Party are actively opposing a coalition. Labour failed to make serious policy concessions in most of the key areas, and – bluntly – they also failed to convince us that they could deliver an AV referendum.'

There were groans of disappointment, scepticism even, from some in the room who were deeply committed to a deal with Labour. Danny Alexander was asked to report back on behalf of the negotiators, and he fleshed out Nick's summary of the meeting.

But after he had finished, one MP shouted out 'I want to hear from the other negotiators', and so – one by one – we each gave our account of the meeting with Labour. Andrew Stunell went next, then Chris Huhne and then me.

By the time the four of us had finished speaking, people understood that there was a real problem with Labour. The four negotiators had been picked to reflect a broad sweep of opinion in the Parliamentary Party, so people knew that our appraisal was an honest one rather than a partial perspective designed to tilt the odds back in favour of a deal with the Tories.

First Norman Baker, and then Don Foster and others, spoke out to say that we had no choice but to strike a deal with the Conservatives – a view expressed by a wide swathe of party opinion. Crucially, Vince Cable also spoke out to say that he now thought that an arrangement with the Conservatives was the only viable option.

But others, not least from the House of Lords, spoke out strongly for a second round of negotiations with Labour the next day – which Nick Clegg confirmed was now planned. Some held out the hope that Labour would prove to be more flexible at a second formal meeting, and suggested that we should apply pressure overnight to get a more pragmatic approach. Paddy Ashdown asked me for a list of the key areas of policy differences that needed to be resolved at Tuesday morning's planned meeting.

After a long discussion, the meeting concluded just after midnight. The press were again waiting in Westminster Hall for an assessment of what conclusions we had reached, and I was again asked to make a brief statement to them. Since there was nothing much that we were willing to report, I stuck by the usual line about the importance of our Parliamentary Party fully endorsing Nick Clegg's strategy, and of any agreement delivering 'economic stability and a credible deficit reduction plan'. All I could offer in acknowledgement of their growing frustrations was that the party agreed that 'current negotiations need to be concluded rapidly'.

The more I said, the more disappointed the exhausted and sceptical media looked. I could see that they did not think that my meagre words were much of a return for two hours camped out in Westminster Hall at midnight on a Monday. Perhaps they thought that we were never going to make our minds up. There were one or two cynical groans for the first time since election day, and I made a swift exit out of Westminster Hall before I could be pressed any further.

I left with the firm view that the patience of the press and public was likely to be tested if the negotiations stretched out much longer. My sound bites were beginning to bore me, and if that were so they would certainly be beginning to bore others.

My view – formed well before the general election – that we should seek to conclude negotiations no later than the Tuesday after the election, felt right and I was determined we should do everything possible to strike a deal within twenty-four hours. That would be very fast by the standards of other European countries, but it would be what the media and markets pressed for, and what the British public expected.

So, I set off for home knowing that Tuesday 11 May was 'make your mind up time' for the Liberal Democrats. If we could not make a decision by the end of this day the media story would become one of 'dither and delay', and it was obvious to me that the Liberal Democrats would shoulder the blame for this. Tuesday 11 May would be a crucial day in the party's history, and a crucial day for the country too.

'Make your mind up time'

I was up again early on Tuesday, and our negotiating team and staff met in Cowley Street at around 8am to consider our strategy. On the morning media, George Osborne had described the Conservative concession on the Alternative Vote as a 'final' offer. Meanwhile, senior Labour MPs were beginning to rubbish the idea of a Lib–Lab coalition. It was clear to everyone that we were now into the 'endgame'.

Our first meeting, as agreed, was to be with the Labour team. We decided that at the beginning of the meeting we really needed to clear the air, and be blunt that yesterday's negotiation had not gone well and that we expected a more positive approach from today's talks. 'Who would like to deliver that message to the Labour team?' asked Danny. 'I think that Andrew would do a good job!' said Chris Huhne, glancing at Andrew Stunell. 'Fine,' said Andrew calmly, and we discussed how he would lay down the line to Messrs Mandelson, Balls and co.

Even with the benefit of a stern lecture from Andrew, we were not optimistic that the talks would succeed. But we were convinced that the Labour team would today be on better behaviour, not least because we knew that the Lib Dem/Labour hotlines would have been buzzing overnight with tales of bad body language and talks on a knife-edge.

We were also sure that if we did go into a coalition with the Conservatives, the Labour team – not least Ed Balls and Ed Miliband – would try to blame us for being determined to go in with the Tories, come what may.

We therefore expected that the 'truculent trio' – Ed Balls, Ed Miliband and Harriet Harman – would be on better behaviour.

Our fear was that the Labour team would do just enough to seem reasonable, but not enough to assure us on key issues such as tax, education funding and AV. This would make it more difficult for us to give Nick Clegg and our colleagues a clear recommendation, without which a final, decisive, verdict amongst our Parliamentary Party would prove difficult.

So we drew up a detailed list of the eighteen issues on which we still had important disagreements with Labour, and prepared to set off again for room 391 in Portcullis House. We knew that some of these eighteen issues could be resolved, but on some of the most important we still seemed far apart.

Before we could leave for the talks, we received a message that Gordon Brown was now asking all Labour Cabinet ministers to contact their Lib Dem opposite numbers to discuss agreement on policy issues. 'This is absolutely barmy,' said Danny. 'How can we conduct a serious negotiation in this way? What on earth is Gordon Brown up to?' The whole thing seemed bizarre and chaotic, and we quickly paged senior colleagues to warn them not to get involved.

The next call was more extraordinary still. It was from Vince Cable who told us that he understood that Alistair Darling's chauffeur-driven government car was on the way to Twickenham to collect him to take him to the Treasury for talks with the Chancellor. This seemed like yet another Gordon Brown wheeze to muddy the waters. Danny

Alexander asked that a clear message be sent immediately to Vince, saying that he should send Alistair Darling's car back to the Treasury.

Feeling distinctly underwhelmed by Labour's approach to negotiation, our team once again set out for Portcullis House. We arrived in our usual room and the Labour team trooped in, on time on this occasion. Someone suggested that we needed some refreshments, and Ed Miliband stumped up the money to pay for teas, coffees and pastries from one of the restaurants on the ground floor of Portcullis House. It was about the first financial concession that the Labour team had made to us, but we were far too polite to make this point.

Peter Mandelson moved to begin the talks, at just after 10am. 'I think we can leave the economic issues to one side,' he said, 'for Vince and Alistair to sort out during their meeting at the Treasury.'

Danny swiftly interrupted: 'Vince has cancelled the meeting with Alistair. There must be only one set of negotiations – the ones in this room. We will get in a complete muddle if we start having bilaterals all over the place. Our negotiating team has a full mandate from the leader and Parliamentary Party to discuss all relevant issues.'

At this stage, and after Danny's message instructing Vince to send the Chancellor's car back to the Treasury, we believed that the Cable–Darling discussions had been cancelled. But we later discovered that although Vince had sent the chauffeur-driven car back, he had decided to go by rail instead to see Alistair Darling in the Treasury! Vince later told us that he thought the objection was to the ministerial car and not to the meeting.

Vince was apparently extremely concerned that different Labour ministers seemed to be sending out different messages on the coalition issue, and he was determined to find out where the Chancellor himself stood. But when he met Alistair Darling at the Treasury, they both agreed that there was not much they could do to influence the outcome of the talks, and after a cup of tea and a brief discussion the meeting came to an end.

This was not known to us at the time, so Danny continued on the same basis: 'We are very keen to take forward yesterday's discussions. We have a couple of hours now, and then we need to go back and brief our leaders on progress. Can you say more about the Labour Party's internal procedures for agreeing any deal that is struck?'

Peter Mandelson said: 'Well, the Cabinet is obviously very important. The issue for them is how we can provide stable, strong, radical government. And a key issue for the Cabinet is whether we can get the parliamentary arithmetic to add up, and whether we can sell to the country what the new government is there to deliver.

'We believe that the numbers do stack up. The key is Labour, plus the Lib Dems, plus the Irish parties. There is no sign at all of the DUP going soft on the possibility of a supply and confidence agreement, with a Lib–Lab coalition. We have had no contacts at all with Plaid or the SNP. But Gordon does not believe that the SNP would want to side with the Conservatives. As for our internal processes, the NEC is giving the green light for this process, and our Parliamentary Party will meet tomorrow to discuss all of this. I have no doubt people will judge this by the strength of any programme we come up with. But this is primarily a decision for the Cabinet.'

Harriet Harman then intervened to say: 'Well, the Cabinet, the NEC and the Parliamentary Labour Party, Peter. They must all be convinced by any programme. The issues of "process" will not butter many parsnips – it will come down to what we are saying on policies.'

At this stage, and as planned, Andrew Stunell interrupted. Danny, Chris and I knew what was coming next, but the Labour team did not.

Andrew was very calm and very measured, and he began to lecture the Labour team on our concerns about the previous days' talks, and what we were expecting from the day to come.

Peter Mandelson looked surprised and a little shaken. The others listened quietly. Andrew had the air of a disappointed deputy head teacher who was ticking off a group of underperforming sixth-formers. 'Look, we felt that yesterday's talks were not as productive as they should have been. We aren't clear how committed you all are. We need to reach an outcome very quickly indeed, and we need a strong, radical, positive programme. Let's be clear. At present, we have a better deal on the table from the Conservatives. So you are going to need to do better than yesterday if we are to secure an agreement. There is a long way to go before we get a deal from you that we can live with. So let's get on with things in a positive way. This needs to be the framework for our discussions.'

Peter Mandelson seemed taken aback and the rest of the Labour team did their best to look shocked and hurt. 'Look,' said Mandelson, 'I have heard all this about body language and so forth, but I don't recognise this and I ask you to accept that we are serious about these talks. And you say the Tories will support an AV referendum, but will they actually deliver on this in the House of Commons?'

'We know all about non-delivery,' I said, 'because we were let down by Labour in 1997 and 1998 after the Jenkins Report on PR.'

'There are risks with both Labour and the Conservatives,' said Andrew Stunell. 'But you are not offering enough, and we don't know whether you are serious.'

There was a brief, uncomfortable, silence. Then Peter Mandelson began again. He said there were clearly three main issues to consider. 'The first is whether a Lib–Lab coalition could have political legitimacy. In my view it could because our two parties would represent a much larger segment of voters than the Conservatives. Secondly, can we reach a policy agreement? Again, this is not simple, but Gordon and I believe it could be achieved. Finally, deliverability. Could the coalition govern? I accept that this is not straightforward, but a Lib–Lab coalition could enter into some sort of confidence and supply arrangement with the DUP, as well as having support from the SDLP.' He went on to say that if there was agreement between us, this would need to be taken to the Cabinet, then the NEC, and then the Parliamentary Labour Party.

Andrew Adonis then intervened to say that perhaps it was now time to discuss some policy issues, starting with political reform. Chris Huhne began the discussion: 'The key issue for us is a post-legislative referendum on the Alternative Vote, which should also include an option for full proportional representation, with the Single Transferable Vote.'

Danny's phone signalled that he had received a text message. He glanced down to discover that it was from Peter Mandelson, twelve feet away on the other side of the table. It read: 'We need to get a more positive atmosphere if these talks are to be worthwhile.'. Danny acknowledged the point across the table.

Meanwhile, Andrew Adonis was replying to Chris Huhne: 'Look, this is not a simple piece of legislation, but it would clearly be a confidence issue for the government. But there would have to be agreement in a referendum before the legislation took effect. However we could certainly agree to a post-legislative referendum on AV.' Danny said we agreed with this.

Andrew Adonis continued: 'But if you put STV or AV-plus into the Bill, it becomes a big undertaking, and I do not think we could get it through by next May. And the more this is delayed, the harder it could be to get through. Also, it would surely be bad politics to have two coalition partners fighting over whether to support AV or STV? Labour would support AV but we would have to oppose PR.'

Peter Mandelson said that he agreed with Andrew: 'It could be an option on the ballot paper, but I do wonder about dividing the coalition on this. We need to unite over AV, where there is agreement. What are the best circumstances to get the best result? It must be to have a united campaign on AV.'

Ed Balls then chipped in, once again throwing cold water over the plans: 'Getting our people to support AV is going to be quite hard. There are a lot of Labour MPs who are opposed. If there are any other difficult issues it could be tough to get this one through.'

Andrew Adonis said: 'Well I don't think we could do both AV and Lords Reform in the first session – it just would not be credible.'

'Yes, but Lords reform has slipped out of the Labour programme for the last three parliaments. That just cannot go on,' replied Andrew Stunell.

Ed Miliband suggested a pre-legislative referendum on both AV and Lords Reform. 'What is the point of that?' said Andrew Stunell? 'Lords Reform is in the Labour manifesto – and ours!'

'Well, it would give more public legitimacy,' replied Ed Miliband.

'Surely there would be time for both?' said Chris Huhne. 'If you stop clogging up parliament with Criminal Justice Bills we would have plenty of time.'

'But these would be two huge constitutional bills,' said Andrew Adonis. 'The Lords would want to take a lot of time on them.'

On the Wright committee proposals, Harriet Harman said that she had looked into the matter and the government was ready to go to implement all the main proposals as soon as possible. 'We are not a roadblock to reform,' she insisted. I asked why in the previous day's talks Harriet had said that the proposals would 'create a rod for our own backs', if they were so supportive. Peter Mandelson intervened: 'We are committed to implementing this in full.'

On civil liberties, Andrew Adonis said that Labour would agree to scrap the National Identity Register, but not biometric passports. And on Contact Point, the massive new children's database, Ed Balls said that his department would not be happy to axe this, as we had proposed.

Peter Mandelson suggested that the Contact Point database should be 'reviewed after its first year'. That sounded like a very obvious fudge, though this was hardly a bottom-line issue, so we moved on.

Andrew Adonis then broke in and said that he had some progress to report on issues which we had raised the previous day. In particular, he was now willing to scrap plans for a third runway for Heathrow airport. For Andrew, as Transport Secretary, this was a big concession – something he had fought hard for and clearly believed in.

Ed Miliband then chipped in to say that when he expressed doubt the previous day on renewable targets it was not that he was not committed on the environment, but he doubted higher targets were the way forward. Chris Huhne said that we did not want to see public subsidies go into nuclear power. 'But Chris, the public subsidies on renewables are far higher,' said Ed. 'And there has never been a nuclear accident in the UK. We must have more nuclear power to meet our climate change targets.'

Chris Huhne suggested that there needed to be much greater ambition on carbon reduction and renewables, 'Until recently, Labour just hasn't done enough on this.'

'Well, both of our manifestos are more ambitious than that of the Tories,' said Ed.

We then moved on to some of the economic issues. I made the case for our pupil premium, with £2.5bn extra going into the schools' budget, to target the one million most disadvantaged pupils. This must be real extra cash, not just recycled money, I said. And schools must not be micro-managed in spending it.

Ed Balls, the Children's Secretary, responded: 'Look, I am sympathetic to this. But we would need to speak to Alistair Darling to get him to agree. This won't be easy to afford financially. But we are not against this in principle.' Danny said: 'But have you got a concrete proposal to make on this yet?' Ed Miliband replied, 'Well, we would need to come back with a proposal.' Ed Balls said: 'We might need a detailed paper to see if this is all viable.'

This was very disappointing. It represented no movement at all on one of our bottom-line issues, in spite of this having been discussed on two separate occasions. It seemed as if Labour had made no effort at all to offer us anything on this. What on earth had Labour been discussing overnight, if it was not how to deliver on what they knew were our four key pledges? And why did the Labour team not have a mandate to negotiate on behalf of their whole party? Was the invisible Alistair Darling a roadblock to agreement? What were his own views on the prospects of a coalition? And did the uncertainty within the Labour team on economic policy hint at some of the divisions within Labour's own team on the issues of tax, spending and the deficit? If we had known that Vince Cable was at this very moment in the Treasury, talking to Alistair Darling, we could perhaps have phoned him to ask. As it was, we were left entirely in the dark by the Labour team's extraordinary approach to negotiations.

Ed Balls and I then discussed the other economic issues. Yet again, and in spite of their known centrality to our negotiating bottom line,

Ed still said that he could not offer much on the £10,000 tax allowance. 'I can only say that this is a matter for the Chancellor,' said Ed. 'Our view is that we are not ruling it out, and we are open to persuasion.' That, frankly, was not of much value to us. We were in the endgame of the negotiations, and it was time for Labour to put its cards on the table and not play games. Danny asked, 'Is there really no further offer or progress to make on this?'

Ed Miliband answered, 'We do have a worry about this. This is an issue of credibility, not desirability. It is a feasibility issue.' 'We really need to have the Chancellor at these discussions,' said Harriet Harman. 'Yes, you're right,' said Ed Balls.

It was clear that nobody on the Labour side seemed empowered or even willing to make any commitments on two of the most important, bottom-line, Lib Dem requirements – on the £10,000 tax allowance and on the pupil premium. It was difficult to regard the negotiations as entirely serious while this remained the case.

'Look,' I said. 'We have the Labour MP with more knowledge than any other about economic issues in this room, surely we can make some progress on this?' Peter Mandelson looked quizzical. 'I am talking about Ed Balls,' I said. 'Well, this is really a matter for Alistair,' said Peter Mandelson. We were making little progress, and time was fast running out.

The same problem arose again when it came to the issue of restoring the pension earnings link in April 2011 – no guarantees could be given.

I then came on to deficit reduction. 'We need to make some tough decisions, and in our view that must include speeding up deficit reduction. We want a budget within fifty days of a coalition being established, and we need to show we are serious about deficit reduction. This should include introducing a banking levy. Look,' I said, 'there is no clearer sign that we can give of economic credibility than an early budget which takes some tough decisions.'

'Well, you are pushing at an open door there,' said Peter Mandelson. 'We could sit down together and agree greater deficit reduction in this year. Of course, a banking levy wouldn't take effect until next year. But cuts are important – but they would be a hard thing to deliver, requiring tough choices.'

'I think this is very important,' I said. 'You know during the election we have taken the same position as you on not cutting spending in 2010/11, or at least the cuts we were proposing would have gone back into green jobs schemes, extra training etc. But since then the financial markets have turned dramatically for the worse, and this coalition would not start with much economic credibility. We would need to be able to show the markets that we could make a difference.'

Peter Mandelson nodded. I continued: 'We still believe that most of the cuts should come after April 2011, by when the economy should be recovering, but a small reduction in non-front-line public spending now could be very important in keeping interest rates down and stabilising the markets.'

Chris Huhne said: 'This is important. We really need some credibility if we are to calm the markets. The international situation is very worrying.'

Peter Mandelson looked on approvingly, and I thought that we were making some progress, but then Ed Balls broke in: 'Macho speak does not deliver credibility. How are we going to be able to raise the personal allowance, fund the pupil premium, and cut spending? We can't deliver cuts. And it would be bad for credibility if we tried and failed. The £6bn of cuts that the Tories are talking about are just not deliverable.'

Ed Miliband also looked doubtful: 'This is the hardest thing for us – public spending cuts,' he said. 'We have already set down very tough spending plans. I am not sure that we can go further than this.'

Chris Huhne broke in: 'Six billion pounds of in-year cuts is surely credible. The Treasury has told us that it has already identified these cuts. And we would use some of the money to invest in recovery.' I asked: 'Look, I am confused. Is the door open or closed on this? Peter Mandelson is saying "yes", as does your written agreement.'

Ed Miliband asked: 'What is the bottom line here?'

'Credibility,' I said. 'We need to move further and faster to reduce the deficit. And we can make a start this year that will boost credibility without undermining growth or front-line services. We need a Budget this June. It can take action on fairer taxes and some action on spending. We then need a spending review for next April onwards.'

Ed Balls muttered: 'This would be very bad for credibility, because we couldn't do it.' Harriet Harman said: 'What if we fail to convince the markets, while panicking our people on public services?'

'Look, these are only the first tough decisions we are going to have to take to reduce the deficit – even on your spending plans,' I said. 'We are going to have to take action in areas such as public sector pensions reform, too.'

Ed Miliband looked horrified: 'Oh no,' he said. 'We cannot go further than our existing agreements with the unions.'

'That sounds like a line from your Labour leadership campaign!' joked Danny. Ed Miliband tried to look mystified.

There was a long pause. Ed Balls looked determinedly grumpy. Peter Mandelson looked a little confused. I felt that we were getting a glimpse not merely of the differences of view between Labour and the Liberal Democrats, but of some of the deep-seated divisions over spending, taxation and the deficit within the Labour Party.

Andrew Adonis filled the void: 'Well, it is fair to say that there is a lot more work to do on the economy, tax and spending. But on most other areas there is a large measure of agreement.'

Andrew's assessment was, perhaps, accurate. But the problem was that the economy is rather an important area in policy terms. To me, for whom these issues were of central importance, it seemed rather like telling a chef that his food was shockingly bad but that the tablecloth was beautifully ironed.

The truth was that we had no agreement on delivering a £10,000 personal tax allowance. We had no agreement on funding the pupil premium. We had no agreement on a banking levy, or on public sector pensions reform, or on restoring the pension earnings link. We had no agreement on a strategy for deficit reduction, and no agreement on spending. All of that meant that we were nowhere near being able to conclude a coalition agreement.

Meanwhile, we could not know if a Lib–Lab minority coalition could command the support to survive in the House of Commons, or even deliver the Labour votes necessary to push through a referendum on AV.

Our meeting had been better natured than Monday's, as we had expected. But on substance there was still no decisive breakthrough.

The parliamentary arithmetic was never going to be easy, but there was a lot more that Labour could have done to give the talks a real chance of success. Ed Miliband and Ed Balls finished the meeting by proclaiming their seriousness about securing a progressive coalition. But their actions seemed to speak louder than their words. Neither wanted to be blamed for the failure of the talks. But neither seemed to be willing to go the extra mile to give the talks a real chance.

We finished the meeting after around one and a half hours, with a promise to stay in touch. But neither side can have considered that enough progress had been made. After Labour left the room we said little but prepared to brief Nick Clegg on the meeting. We knew that the recommendation which we were about to make would be decisive in determining the future government of the country, and the future of our party.

We strolled back in silence across Portcullis House, and went down the escalator that connects with the main Palace of Westminster. We turned right before reaching the Terrace of the House of Commons, and then right again to the lifts to take us up to the first floor of Parliament.

The lift door opened and out came Susan Kramer, the former Lib Dem MP for Richmond, who had just lost her seat in a long and tough battle with Conservative Zac Goldsmith. Susan was struggling with four or five bags worth of books and other belongings, which she was removing from her rooms in Parliament. Susan was a very able MP, and it was a sad moment. We said hello briefly, but I suspect that none of those involved were in the mood for more than pleasantries, and we got inside the lift and headed up to see Nick Clegg.

Before speaking to Nick, we briefly agreed on our understanding of the meeting. A better atmosphere than Monday evening's meeting for sure. And clearly Andrew Adonis and Peter Mandelson were making a real effort to enable a coalition to go ahead. But there was still too little agreement on major policy issues, and no guarantee that Labour could deliver its promised AV referendum. Moreover, whether a strong enough position in Parliament could be guaranteed to take the tough decisions necessary on the economy seemed highly doubtful. This was particularly the case given the divisions on strategy in Labour ranks, which were becoming more obvious by the hour.

That morning David Blunkett had gone on the radio to suggest that a Lib–Lab coalition would spell electoral disaster for Labour, and John Reid was now joining the chorus of criticism. Jack Straw was rumoured to be drafting a newspaper article, criticising the idea of a Lib–Lab coalition, and even Andy Burnham had tiptoed out and given a radio interview to the same effect.

The splits in Labour ranks were not just on strategy, but they were also clearly policy based. After the coalition had eventually been formed we found that Peter Mandelson sought to blame our '£20 billion of unfunded spending commitments' for the breakdown, while Ed Balls claimed that it was our desire for early action to tackle the deficit which made it impossible for Labour to negotiate seriously with us. It is difficult to sensibly reconcile these claims.

Early in the day, Paddy Ashdown had again telephoned Tony Blair, urging him to secure David Miliband's public backing for a coalition. But this was snubbed by Mr Miliband himself, who wanted to keep his head down. Support for a deal with the Lib Dems now seemed to be in danger of becoming a contested issue in the forthcoming Labour leadership contest. Meanwhile, the semi-invisible Chancellor, Alistair Darling, was also said to be strongly opposed to a coalition.

Gordon Brown's departure had paved the way not merely for talks with the Lib Dems but for a total breakdown in discipline within the Labour Party. Indeed, other than Gordon Brown, Peter Mandelson, and Andrew Adonis it was not clear to us which other senior Labour politicians actually wanted to stay in office.

Labour was heading into opposition, not on the basis of some stitch up by right-wing Lib Dems and the Cameron Tories, but because it no longer had the will to be in office, the desire to make the compromises necessary to form a Lib–Lab coalition, or the guarantee of votes in the House of Commons.

As far as our negotiating team were all concerned, the prospects of a coalition with Labour were now dead and buried.

Nevertheless, in the early afternoon, at around 1.15pm, Gordon Brown met Nick Clegg again in his offices in the House of Commons. Nick reported back our view of Monday's talks, and was pessimistic about the prospects of a coalition.

Gordon Brown seemed absolutely desperate that the coalition should go ahead, and he pleaded with Nick to think again. 'It was quite embarrassing actually,' Nick reported to us later. 'I was very uncomfortable. He was very passionate about the whole thing, and seemed to be pleading with me.'

In turn, we reported back to Nick on our talks with Labour – we told him that we had made progress on some of the smaller issues such as the Wright committee reforms and axing of the third Heathrow runway, but no progress on taxation, spending, education funding, the deficit, and the banking levy. And we could have no guarantee that all Labour MPs would support AV in a Commons vote.

'Well, that's it,' said Nick. 'We need to move on with the talks with the Conservatives, and finish those as soon as we can. We must get on with all this, because there has to be an agreement today. And as soon as I tell Brown that a deal with Labour is off, he may just go to the Palace and resign.'

We now had only one option left on the table. It was time to conclude our talks with the Conservatives.

At around 2pm that afternoon, the negotiations with the Conservative team resumed. It was to be our last experience of arriving at 70 Whitehall and battling through the hordes of journalists who were encamped on the pavement.

Outside our meeting room, Gus O'Donnell and his Civil Service team, and the Queen's Private Secretary, looked nervously at their watches.

As we waited for the Conservatives to arrive, Chris Huhne filled the time by flicking through the large volume on the Government Art Collection, one last time, and then we all trooped off into our usual conference room.

When the talks opened, we did not discuss our meeting with Labour, but Nick Clegg and David Cameron had spoken in the morning. There can be little doubt that both sides now knew that we were into the end game, with a Conservative–Lib Dem coalition the almost certain outcome.

The atmosphere was still friendly, but I thought a little more business like than before. I got the distinct impression that the Conservative team felt that they had now conceded all they were willing to, and with the effective end of our talks with Labour our leverage was in its declining phase. It was rather as if we had gone from viewing a house to having signed contracts and paid the deposit. A point of no return had been passed, and the initiative had moved subtly but surely to the Conservatives.

There was still a great deal of work to be done if the coalition agreement was to be finished in the timescales now needed. But the Conservative and Lib Dem parliamentary parties were put on standby to meet separately that evening, with the assumption now being that this would be for the final time, to approve the detailed agreement reached.

There seemed a high probability that Gordon Brown would resign as soon as he concluded that the Lib–Lab talks were effectively over. We knew that as soon as this happened, the Queen would be obliged to send for David Cameron to ask him to form a government. Buckingham Palace had always made clear that they wanted the parties to have sorted out the nature of the new government before the Queen had to call for a new Prime Minister, and so the pressure was on to deliver as quickly as possible.

Throughout the afternoon, while we talked to the Conservative team, Nick interspersed serious discussions with David Cameron with brief telephone chats with an increasingly frustrated Gordon Brown. Everyone wanted Brown to hang on until a deal had been agreed. Britain was not supposed to be left without a government.

This led to increasingly strained conversations between Nick and Gordon Brown as the one tried to persuade the other that the prospect of a deal was still alive. The truth is that by 1pm the chances of a Lib–Lab deal were over. But the Civil Service, the Palace, the Lib Dems and the Conservatives all wanted Gordon Brown to remain in place so as to ensure that the handover of power happened seamlessly. It just about worked.

The document which was now in front of the two negotiating teams set out our agreements to date on most of the major issues of tax, deficit reduction and spending. But there were still some important issues to resolve.

In our meetings early that morning, our Liberal Democrat team had already identified fourteen issues that needed resolving in the areas of deficit reduction, taxation, spending, banking reform and political reform. In addition, the draft document which we had so far completed had nothing whatsoever to say on major issues such as immigration, welfare policy, schools and higher education, and relations with the EU.

We knew that we had only around five hours at most to cover all of these issues.

William Hague kicked off. We laughed as he told us: 'By the way,

I am informed by the Civil Service that they have started receiving Freedom of Information requests for the minutes of our talks, so I rather feel we were right to exclude officials!'

He continued, 'Anyway, we have a document in front of us with the agreements we have reached, but there is more work to do. And some of my party's "red line issues" must be reflected in the final agreement – I mean on issues such as Europe, immigration and Trident.'

We started on the economy, and George Osborne secured our agreement to a new Office of Budget Responsibility, to oversee the growth and borrowing forecasts.

He also emphasised how important he thought the £6bn of cuts were in 2010 – as they would be an early test of the economic credibility of the coalition.

We repeated that we were agreed to cuts on this scale in 2010/11, provided that other spending cuts were delayed until 2011, and on condition that a portion of the monies saved in 2010 were reinvested in measures to stimulate recovery.

In the section on public spending, we negotiated a line which made clear that we would look at the scope for cost savings in relation to Trident renewal. This was agreed to include the issue of whether three or four boats would be needed.

The Conservatives, after receiving a costings note from HM Treasury officials, agreed to our proposal to restore the earnings link for the basic state pension from April 2011 – with pensions then subject to a 'triple guarantee' that they would rise each year by the highest of prices, earnings or 2.5%. Over time, this 'triple guarantee' would have a major impact on delivering a decent basic state pension.

The Conservatives had also carefully researched our plan to increase the personal income tax allowance. George Osborne's economic adviser Rupert Harrison (who would later join George as a special adviser at the Treasury) suggested that there should be a £1,000 increase in the allowance in the very first Emergency Budget in June. This would be made affordable by concentrating the gains from increasing the allowance on those on middle and lower incomes.

We then discussed making similarly large steps in each future budget until, by the end of the parliament, the £10,000 sum had been delivered. We did not write this detailed understanding into the agreement so as to give the Chancellor some flexibility in the light of economic circumstances. Nevertheless, the Conservatives' willingness to investigate and discuss the details of delivering this objective, and the constructive proposals made at their own initiative, were in sharp contrast to Labour's unwillingness to make more than a token gesture on this key policy.

We were pleased with this progress, but also asked our own Treasury adviser, Chris Saunders, to agree the final wording with Vince Cable.

We then moved on to the issue of political reform. Chris Huhne emphasised that there could be no question of having any sort of threshold of support on the AV Referendum bill. A simple majority would be all that would suffice. Oliver Letwin joked: 'Yes, we will be absolutely straightforward with you on this. Then we will beat you in the actual referendum!' and he chuckled away in a very Oliver-ish way.

There was a debate for thirty minutes or so on arrangements for dissolving a parliament before the end of its five-year term. This was an issue which we raised, but William Hague soon realised that the main risk lay with the Conservatives. Without a super-majority for dissolution being required, the smaller party could leave the coalition and dissolve parliament almost at will.

Chris Huhne originally suggested that there should be a 66% threshold for dissolving parliament before its full term was up, in line with the situation in Scotland. George Osborne said he thought that 66% was rather high and that 55% or 60% would be closer to the mark. After some work on Ed Llewelyn's calculator, and consideration of by-election risks, it was decided that a 55% vote of MPs would be required to provide for a dissolution. This was just greater than the combined opposition and Lib Dem parliamentary parties, thereby safeguarding the Conservative position. No one could pretend it was a scientific process, but it would seek to deliver the stability and responsibility which both sides considered so important, and from which the country itself should gain.

Having completed these existing sections of the document, we had to work hard to draft from scratch new sections on immigration, pensions and welfare, education, and relations with the EU.

On welfare, we agreed to look at bringing the increase in the state pension age to sixty-six forward, and to take action to help those people who could work back into employment.

The Conservatives made clear that an immigration cap for non-EU migrants was a bottomline issue for them, as were certain elements of the EU section. David Cameron and Nick Clegg had already had a discussion between themselves on these two sensitive areas, and that allowed our talks to proceed with greater speed than would otherwise be the case. We agreed the annual limit on non-EU migrants, but insisted on a guarantee of ending the detention of children for immigration purposes.

On the EU, George Osborne said: 'Europe is important for the Conservative Party. The wording on this is crucial. There must be no further EU integration. And there must be a referendum lock on any future transfers of power.'

The EU section was at first rather negative and was also the final section in this draft of the agreement. I did not want this to be the last section which our MPs, and particularly our strongly pro-EU peers, would read before deciding whether they wanted to support the coalition, so I suggested moving the EU section further up the document and ending on two strong sections on civil liberties and the environment. These would warm the hearts of almost any Lib Dem, or certainly those who make up the bulk of our parliamentary parties.

We also managed to insert an opening line in the EU section about the British government being a 'positive participant in the EU', and linking this to action on poverty and global warming. Finally, we turned to the issue of education. Oliver Letwin and I had a brief debate about the mechanics of schools reform and market mechanisms, which left other members of the team impatient for us to conclude.

We agreed to new providers entering the state school system, and inserted some guarantees in relation to curriculum freedom and accountability. I felt that we had secured a good agreement on the pupil premium and this had been our top priority on education.

Higher education was clearly going to be a much more difficult issue. David Cameron and Nick Clegg had already spoken about this particular issue themselves. But we agreed a form of words which set out principles rather than policies, and which left the key decisions to the Browne report, which Labour and the Conservatives had established before the election. We also made provision for Lib Dem MPs to abstain if the Browne report came up with proposals that the Lib Dems could not accept.

In truth, I felt that our own policy on abolishing tuition fees was simply not the right priority in the current economic environment, and I had personally pressed hard for changing the policy before the election – without success. Even the National Union of Students was now campaigning for a graduate tax, rather than the complete abolition of fees. But Labour's tuition fees system had all the unfairness of the 'poll tax' that it essentially was, and I was sure we could do much better than that.

In any case, it was now clear, with the huge spending cuts that would be required under any government, that abolishing tuition fees without creating some other revenue stream would not be realistic.

As we pressed on with our talks, we were coming closer and closer to a final agreement.

But as the afternoon ticked by, Gus O'Donnell became more and more agitated by the time it was taking us to complete the agreement.

During one break in the talks he came in to the Lib Dem office and said quietly: 'How long is this all going to take? I have got a very unhappy Prime Minister in 10 Downing Street, who is desperate to resign. I really don't think I can hold on to him much longer, but I don't want him going until I know we have an alternative government!'

We could only point out that we were going as fast as we possibly could. Meanwhile, Nick Clegg was also on the phone to Gordon Brown, urging him to remain in place until the position of the talks was clear. But Nick was only too aware that Gordon Brown knew that the prospects of a Lib Dem–Labour deal had gone, and that he wanted to resign as soon as possible.

Our tables were covered in drafts and re-drafts of the coalition agreement. The final, crucial, touches were being made. Just before 7pm, we heard that a press conference by Gordon Brown was likely at any minute. We were going as fast as we could to incorporate the changes agreed in our new draft document, but we had to sign it off completely before we could finish the talks.

Then, at around 7.15pm, Gordon Brown emerged into Downing Street to make a statement. We broke off the talks and switched on a television, which was located on the other side of our main conference room.

As the final drafts of our agreed text were coming off the Cabinet Office printers, we stood before the television to see Gordon Brown make a brief, dignified and emotional statement. His wife, Sarah, stood beside him, also looking close to tears.

And then, statement complete, the former Prime Minister and his wife opened the door to Downing Street to collect their two young boys, who had rarely been seen publicly before. We were immediately struck by how carefully Gordon Brown and his wife had guarded their sons' privacy over his time as Prime Minister.

Whether friend or foe, it is always an emotional moment for those of us who care about politics when a Prime Minister leaves office, and when a political era ends. I felt sad rather than elated, but tried not to show it.

I felt that I had shadowed Gordon Brown for most of my active political life. When I had left the City to become the Liberal Democrat economics researcher in 1994, Gordon Brown was Labour shadow Chancellor, and Ed Balls had just joined him from the *Financial Times* as his economics adviser.

By then, the Conservatives in government were essentially a spent force, their economic credibility having been destroyed when Britain fell out of the Exchange Rate Mechanism of the European Monetary System on 'Black Wednesday' in September 1992.

So, even though Labour was another opposition party, I suppose I spent more time watching the development of their economic policy than tracking the fortunes of the crumbling Conservative government.

And when Labour finally came to power, the Conservatives were neither qualified in terms of morale or policy to oppose Labour effectively, so I worked to support our Treasury spokesman, Malcolm Bruce MP, in holding Labour to account.

We worked well as a team, and it was we rather than the Conservatives who highlighted first the 'black hole' in Labour's spending plans, and then the huge 'War Chest' of monies which Gordon Brown built up while Tony Blair's government was still committed to Conservative spending plans.

Gordon Brown did not appreciate the scrutiny of his policies, and it made him even less enthusiastic than he already was about the 'project' of Tony Blair and Paddy Ashdown to bring the Lib Dems and Labour closer together.

There were one or two meetings arranged at the Treasury in 1997 and 1998 to get the Lib Dem economic team together with its Labour counterparts, but Gordon Brown made only brief appearances at these, and left Ed Balls to chair them – even though on one occasion Paddy Ashdown himself attended the meeting.

With Gordon Brown there had never been any real affection or respect for the Liberal Democrats, and when he did ask to see us it was usually in the hope of smothering our criticisms of his policies or our identity as a party.

In 2007, for example, he complained to Menzies [Ming] Campbell, then party leader, about my attacks on the shambolic administration of his tax credits system. Ming quite rightly refused to muzzle me, but suggested instead that Vince Cable and I should go to see him in the Treasury to discuss our concerns about the way his policies were working.

We went to see the then Chancellor in his small office in the Treasury, with a detailed paper making serious proposals to reduce the vast scale of tax credit overpayments, which were pushing many people on low incomes into debt.

But we found a Chancellor in denial, who was not interested in talking sensibly about how the system could be improved, but who wanted instead to bludgeon us into silence. For an hour we argued. And I suspect Mr Brown wasn't used to people answering back. When Vince and I left, we agreed that it was a depressing meeting, and not a good omen for any future Lib–Lab co-operation. Afterwards, I wrote to Gordon Brown to suggest further work to improve the tax credits system. I never heard back.

Yet here was one of the biggest political figures of the decade, and one of the architects of New Labour. For years, he crushed his Conservative opponents, and his Budgets won plaudits from across the political spectrum. This was a man who was probably right to keep Britain out of the euro, a man whose interest in and influence over economic and social policy was probably unmatched by any previous Chancellor, and someone who seemed to care deeply about delivering a better deal for some of the poorest people in the world – in sub-Saharan Africa and elsewhere.

How was it possible that this was also the person who was regarded as one of the most brutal and aggressive political operators of his age, a man who would scythe down opponents and plot against colleagues and indeed his own Prime Minister?

Who was the real Gordon Brown: the street-fighting, political thug or the idealistic visionary who wanted to rebuild society at home and abroad in a more caring and Christian image? I could never really make up my mind.

For most of the time between 1994 and 2010 I wanted to believe that when you stripped off all of the outer layers of Gordon Brown, there was a good man, a good political leader inside. But it was sometimes very difficult to be sure. Many of his colleagues seemed to have the same doubts.

But in this moment of disappointment and defeat for him, after an extraordinary twenty years at the very top of British politics, it was difficult not to feel sorry for him, and to want to wish him and his family well. After extracting his two boys from inside Downing Street, he holding one by the hand and Sarah Brown the other, he then climbed into his waiting car to make the short journey to Buckingham Palace.

George Osborne and I watched all this on television, while hearing the helicopter overhead of us whose pictures we could see broadcast back on the television.

George reached out and slapped me on the back in friendly alliance and celebration.

It was an important moment in his life, as he was now almost certain to be Chancellor of the Exchequer at the remarkably early age of just thirty-eight, while his close friend David Cameron was now certain to be Prime Minister. I should have been more generous in my congratulations, but Gordon Brown's departure had left me rather subdued, feeling for those few moments the significance of the decisions we were making in that suite of offices in 70 Whitehall.

Were they the right decisions for our country and our party? Would our Parliamentary Party even approve the agreement which we had struck? If so, how would history judge us? I had never expected a full Lib Dem–Conservative coalition to be the outcome of the election, and suddenly had a brief moment of doubt over whether things were going to work out all right.

The doubts, however, did not last long. As Gordon Brown reached Buckingham Palace, the final drafts of our coalition agreement were brought in to us. Although barely seven sides of A4 paper in length, the document included many of the policies we had long fought for, and had given priority to in the general election.

And it was a model coalition agreement in its clarity and in its unwillingness to fudge. Where the parties had differed, we had generally decided on one policy or the other. Few serious issues had been kicked into the long grass or fudged. Arguably, both parties had agreed a common platform which was more powerful and convincing than their individual manifestos. Both parties had, in truth, used the coalition to jettison one or two commitments which might not be much missed by the British public.

Certainly, I felt that the country was getting a government whose policies would chime with the overwhelming majority of people in the country, and which would be able to deliver the strong and stable government that we particularly needed at that time. I also believed that a Lib Dem–Conservative coalition could be capable of delivering the 'tough but tender' economics which I had long believed in, and which would be essential in dealing with the budget deficit.

Were there risks for the Liberal Democrats? Of course there were. But for a third party, there are always risks. The biggest risk would have been to do nothing, and then be flattened in a subsequent general election. And the second biggest risk would have been to have constructed a multicoloured 'traffic-light coalition', which would in reality have been a 'car-crash coalition' unable to deliver on economic policy or on political reform.

Instead, the Liberal Democrats were on the verge of exercising real power in government for the first time since the Second World War. It was an exciting prospect.

So we gathered our paperwork together and prepared to leave 70

Whitehall for the last time. We thanked Gus O'Donnell and his team, and shook hands with the Conservative negotiators.

Our Lib Dem team left the building first, just after 7.30pm, after another marathon five and a half hours of negotiations. But we could report nothing of substance to the awaiting journalists. We were merely the negotiators. Our leader and Parliamentary Parties, along with the party's Federal Executive, would have the final say.

Danny Alexander faced the waiting press and uttered a few bland phrases on our behalf, the last such utterances that would be necessary after five days of talking in code. And we then made our way back through the usual mob of chasing cameramen and reporters and into the Palace of Westminster complex, via the Derby Gate entrance.

Three minutes later, the Conservative team left 70 Whitehall, and made the same brief statement outside the Cabinet Office doors. Barely ten minutes later, at 7.43pm, Gordon Brown and his wife Sarah left Buckingham Palace, Gordon having resigned as Prime Minister.

As we headed for Nick Clegg's office, David Cameron was on his way to Buckingham Palace, to become the youngest Prime Minister for 198 years. He arrived just after 8pm, less than half an hour after Gordon Brown's departure, in spite of his car being held up behind a learner driver for part of the journey. Mr Cameron accepted the offer from the Queen to establish a new government. But, as yet, neither he nor we could be sure that this government would be a coalition.

By 8.40pm, Mr Cameron was moving into Downing Street – just one hour and twenty minutes after Gordon Brown's departure. Waiting civil servants were able to congratulate themselves on delivering a smooth transfer of power, in spite of the unprecedented circumstances of coalition negotiations.

Half an hour later, and at the age of just thirty-eight, George

Osborne, was confirmed as the new Chancellor of the Exchequer – the youngest for more than a century. And half an hour after this, at 9.05pm, William Hague was confirmed as the new Foreign Secretary.

When we finally made our way through an empty Palace of Westminster, Nick's office was strangely quiet, when I expected it to be a hive of activity. Evidently he had been following the detailed negotiations closely, and was already happy with the final agreement which we had reached.

Our 'report back' was unnecessary. Our work was over. The momentum of events was moving ahead without us.

We got a snack to eat and I re-read the coalition agreement that I was increasingly proud of. At 9.30pm we headed over to Local Government House in Smith Square, for a joint meeting of our shadow Cabinet, MPs and Federal Executive. (A meeting of Conservative MPs had been set for the same time.) The meeting started at around 10pm.

When I came in to the room it was packed and the mood was one of elation. My fears that a Lib Dem–Conservative coalition might split the party seemed unfounded.

I sat down in the room about halfway back to await Nick Clegg, choosing a seat next to my old friend and our former leader, Ming Campbell.

Ming is an individual who I hugely admire, who is respected way beyond the usual political boundaries, who took over the leadership of the party under incredibly difficult circumstances and who has always been a true friend to me in the most testing of times. Indeed, I remember him taking me for dinner back in 2004 to nurse my wounds after a two-hour savaging at the Lib Dem Parliamentary Party meeting after the *Orange Book* was published.

Ming was also a friend of Gordon Brown and the late Donald

Dewar, and believed strongly in the possibility of a Lib–Lab alliance
– indeed, he had worked for this for many years.

I knew that Ming would be disappointed that the prospect of a
coalition with Labour was over, but I did not realise just how angry
and upset he was until I sat down next to him. Ming and I are friends,
and he has on many occasions come to speak to my constituency party
in Somerset. But on this occasion he was in no mood to talk, and I
was relieved when I was eventually asked to come to the front of the
room to join the other negotiators, and Vince Cable, who were seated
in the front row.

Nick came in to a standing ovation, cheers and applause, and it
was immediately obvious that what we had expected for months to be
a difficult final meeting was actually going to be a formality.

Nick was joined by Danny Alexander on the platform at the front
of the room, and the meeting was chaired by Ros Scott, the party's
president.

Nick gave a summary of the days' events, and said that he was
recommending acceptance of the deal negotiated with the Conservatives. He then paid tribute to the negotiating team, and there was
another long burst of raucous applause.

I would never have anticipated being cheered by Lib Dem MPs
for helping to negotiate a coalition with the Conservatives. But that
is what happened.

Nick explained that there would be Lib Dem ministers in the
government at all levels. 'What job will you have?' someone shouted
from the back. Nick looked up and with an interesting combination
of pride, modesty and shock said: 'If this goes ahead, I will be the
Deputy Prime Minister.' There was, again, a most un-Liberal Democrat round of applause and cheers of support. Someone at the back of

the room shouted: 'So you will be doing Prime Minister's Questions when Cameron is away?' 'I guess so,' said Nick modestly. Few people in the room ever expected a Lib Dem to be crafting the answers at Prime Minister's Questions.

Liberal Democrats usually assume that when their leaders are about to assume high office a sell-out of some sort must be on the cards. But on this occasion there was genuine pleasure and celebration.

I turned to Vince Cable, who was sitting on my left in the front row, and asked him if he knew yet which job he would be getting. 'Business Secretary,' he said, with the same combination of modesty and pleasure that Nick had just manifested. This was what I expected Vince to be given, as it was clear that George Osborne would be Chancellor of the Exchequer, and I could not see Vince working as his deputy, given Vince's seniority in the Lib Dems. Vince really needed a department of his own and Business was the only real alternative on offer.

I confess also to have felt a certain self-interested pleasure in knowing that this meant that the post of Chief Secretary to the Treasury was still vacant. This was the job that, more than any other, I wanted. Of course, I had no idea whether I would be given this job or any other, as we had never discussed ministerial posts during the coalition negotiations. Quite rightly, this was left to Nick Clegg to discuss with David Cameron. Nor had I had any discussions at all with Nick Clegg about the issue, as to do so during the general election campaign and the exhausting negotiations which followed would have seemed self-absorbed and self-indulgent.

Nick asked for copies of the final coalition agreement to be circulated, and he allowed time for this to be read by all present. The document was not a long one, so it took people only ten minutes or so to read. We then moved to a question and answer session, which turned out to be a mix of praise for the document, combined with some practical questions, combined with a few typically Liberal Democrat points of immense detail and seemingly relatively little consequence.

Sometimes the amount of time spent in political meetings on certain topics is not proportionate to their significance to the public. Indeed, I remember a Lib Dem meeting of MPs to approve our 1997 general election manifesto, where about five minutes was spent discussing economic policy and about half an hour on the pros and cons of pet passports. I suspect that this is something which is common to all political parties.

Ros Scott pointed out gently that the media would eventually be expecting a conclusion from the meeting, and that we didn't want to go on all night.

At that stage there was a very unusual outbreak of demands that the meeting and discussion should be cut short. In sixteen years of Lib Dem meetings, I cannot ever remember such suggestions being made, and certainty not at such a crucial meeting.

There were cries of 'Let's just get on with it,' 'Let's vote now,' and 'What are we waiting for?'

In any other party meeting this might seem normal, but in a Lib Dem Party meeting this is so unusual that it is more or less the equivalent of hearing calls for compulsory repatriation or capital punishment. Predictably, and rightly, the decision was to allow more time, but only a limited amount of extra time (another forty-five minutes), for questions. Paddy Ashdown and others also pressed for time to be allowed for comments on the overall strategy rather than the coalition document itself.

Most MPs and peers spoke strongly in favour of the document and for the establishment of a Lib Dem–Conservative coalition. Even those on the more 'radical' wing of the party, such as Federal Executive member Duncan Brack, seemed pleased with the agreement. But when Paddy Ashdown spoke there was a hushed silence and some nervousness, as it was clear that those with the greatest doubts were the former party leaders, combined with many of those in the Lords who had started their careers in the Labour Party and who had then moved to establish the SDP–Liberal alliance.

Nick looked down nervously from the platform. Paddy said that he found it difficult to support an arrangement which would mean abandoning his great dream of a realignment of the left. He said that he feared that there were considerable risks for the party. He said that his inclination was to throw in his involvement in politics and go back to his garden and his grandchildren.

It threatened to be a huge blow to the coalition, before its very launch. Paddy may have been only one voice in a room of one hundred and twenty people, but he was and is one of the most loved and respected members of the party. His opposition would be a huge blow to morale, and knowledge of it would leave major doubts in the wider party membership about the wisdom of a deal.

I had wondered whether Paddy would ultimately be willing to oppose the deal, because he is both a realist and also the strongest supporter of Nick Clegg bar none. And he is also, at heart, a deeply loyal person without any 'grandstanding' instincts.

There was no doubt that his opening words were a blow. But then it got better. 'However, after telling Nick my decision earlier today, I took the time to actually read the document which you have negotiated. I have to say that it is magnificent. Amazing. F*** it. How can I stay out of this fight? You know that I cannot resist a battle, not least in the company of my friends.' There was huge relief and then applause.

From the platform, Nick Clegg looked down and smiled, nodding to Paddy.

He knew then that resistance to the coalition was over, and that the agreement was going to be accepted. We were as good as in the co-alition. Within hours Nick would be Deputy Prime Minister of Great Britain and Northern Ireland, and Lord President of the Council.

Not long afterwards, we moved to a formal vote on whether to accept the agreement. There were three separate votes. MPs voted by fifty votes to nil in favour of coalition. The Lords voted thirty-one to nil in favour. Then the party's sovereign decision-making body, the Federal Executive, had to vote. This is made up not just of MPs and peers, but of councillors, MEPs and party activists. The result was an overwhelming twenty-seven votes to one in favour of the agreement. Only the former MP for Newbury, David Rendel, had voted against.

It was a quite extraordinary result. In Scotland, after the first Scottish Parliamentary elections in 1999, up to a third of the Executive and a quarter of MSPs had opposed the agreement with Labour, in spite of it being – at least to me – the only obvious course of action. In Wales, I had sat in meetings where party members were so opposed to sharing power that even when Labour offered to implement our entire manifesto, a significant minority of people wanted to stay in opposition.

And in Wales in 2000, Alun Michael suffered the indignity during late-night negotiations with the Lib Dem assembly members of sending up to them a list of major concessions only to be told that our team had left the building to go for pizzas!

Yet here in the UK elections, we had managed to go within weeks from a position where almost no Liberal Democrat in Parliament thought that a coalition deal could be struck with the Conservatives to a situation where a deal was agreed almost unanimously.

Such a result could only be explained by a coming together of a range of factors.

First, Lib Dem MPs made clear right from the very beginning that they did not want a second general election. They understood that unless we were seen to have genuinely sought a stable, strong government it would damage the Lib Dems electorally in the short term, as well as discrediting PR and 'partnership politics' in the future. And they concluded that a confidence and supply agreement offered responsibility without power.

Second, the electoral result gave us just enough possibility of forming a coalition with Labour as to give ourselves real negotiating clout. The Conservatives had to assume that there was a real risk of them staying in opposition if they failed to concede an AV referendum. Without an AV referendum, the Lib Dems would almost certainly have refused a coalition with the Conservatives. This meant that our original assumption that we could not get the Conservatives to concede in this area turned out to be wrong. Just as importantly, the negotiation had extracted a very good deal on many other Lib Dem key pledges. Indeed, we had probably secured a better deal than would have been available from Labour.

Third, Nick Clegg and Danny Alexander had managed the negotiation process superbly, not just after 6 May but before the election. Our four key manifesto pledges were not only good policies but they were deliverable. If we had instead made one of our pledges, for example, to abolish tuition fees that would almost certainly not have been deliverable. So we did not create hostages to fortune which would prevent us from agreeing a common platform with either of the other two parties. Our manifesto gave us a serious agenda for power, not an unachievable Lib Dem wish-list.

Detailed preparations for the negotiations had been made, while being kept well under wraps. In addition, Nick's superb performance during the election (even though this was not converted into parliamentary seats) had given him the respect of his colleagues and a strong position in the party. Indeed, Nick probably led a more united and disciplined Lib Dem force in Parliament than for any time in living memory.

Finally, David Cameron and his senior team seemed to have decided that a coalition agreement was not merely something that they wished to be seen to be trying to secure; it was something that they actually wanted to secure. This may have been because of doubts about how easy it would be to fight and win the second election, which we all felt was inevitable if a coalition agreement could not be struck. But there were also, surely, major advantages of a coalition from both a national and a Conservative Party perspective. The coalition gave the Conservatives the votes to govern strongly and to push through tough measures on the economy, while getting another political party to share the pain. And the boldness of the coalition and the concessions on policy might act as a huge 'detoxifier' of a Conservative brand which had still not quite been 'cleansed' by the Cameron team. Moreover, the position of the right wing of the Conservative Party would be notably weakened – they would no longer enjoy a blocking minority.

There were therefore powerful forces pointing to a coalition for the Liberal Democrats and the Conservatives. But surely the biggest winner was the country, which got what it appeared to want – Labour out, a stable government, but a pragmatic and constructive arrangement between the Conservatives and the Lib Dems.

The coalition meant dropping some Lib Dem policies which perhaps were not popular with the public – the euro and the amnesty for illegal migrants being two examples. But it also meant a more progressive agenda, with tax cuts for those on lower incomes taking priority over inheritance tax cuts, and with additional investment in a pupil premium and early restoration of the pension earnings link.

These were my reflections as our private Lib Dem meeting ended. The waiting press were then let in to hear Nick Clegg announce the conclusions of our meeting.

Afterwards, various groups of MPs and peers were drifting off home or to go for drinks.

It was around midnight, and I went back to Cowley Street briefly to have a chat with the staff and to recover my recharging mobile phone, and then left for home.

It had been an historic day. We had formed the coalition. I knew that the next day David Cameron and Nick Clegg would be forming the government.

Wednesday 12 May 2010

A coalition formed, a Cabinet joined

Later that night, I discovered a message on my mobile phone from Nick Clegg, asking me to call him. However, by the time I picked up the message and phoned back, Nick appeared quite sensibly to have gone to bed.

I woke up early on 12 May and switched on the radio to hear the back-to-back coverage of the formation of the coalition. On the whole, the media reception seemed to be very positive. There was a mood for change and for trying something new, which the coalition undoubtedly represented.

I doubt that the formation of a 'traffic-light' coalition with Labour would have met the same positive response. Instead, the markets would have given us a very swift thumbs down, and the speculation would all have been about how long such an arrangement could last.

I had to leave home early again, to appear on the *Today* programme, from Millbank.

But I had slept a little longer that night than for about a week – perhaps five hours in total – and the excitement of events meant that the many missing hours of recent sleep had yet to make any impact on me.

After the *Today* programme, I then headed for the green in front of Parliament, where there was a veritable feeding frenzy of press. Politicians and commentators were hopping from camera crew to camera crew, giving their analysis of political developments and their forecasts of what would happen next. Needless to say, speculation was already moving on to who would be in the Cabinet.

With William Hague now confirmed as Foreign Secretary, George Osborne as Chancellor, and Nick Clegg as the new Deputy Prime Minister, the shape of the government was already becoming clear. Vince Cable was already hotly tipped as Business Secretary, which I knew to be accurate from my discussion with him the previous evening. Chris Huhne was rumoured to be the government's Climate Change Secretary. That seemed an obvious choice, the environment being a key Lib Dem priority, and Chris being both a former environment spokesman and one of the more obvious Lib Dem choices for membership of the Cabinet.

Danny Alexander was expected to be the new Secretary of State for Scotland, which would be a suitable reward for his hard work in putting together the coalition, and which would give him a place in government to continue to work closely alongside Nick Clegg, as he had done most effectively ever since Nick became party leader.

According to the newspapers, I was to become Education Secretary. This was the portfolio which I was currently shadowing, and my Conservative opposite number, Michael Gove, had fuelled speculation that I might take over this role by giving an interview in which he said that he would be willing to give up his portfolio to me in the event of a coalition.

I was dubious, however, about these predictions. Michael Gove is one of David Cameron's most trusted allies and there was no way he was going to be demoted. Therefore, unless he was to be promoted to a role such as Home Secretary, it seemed to me likely that he would be kept on at Education. It also seemed to me that David Cameron would want Michael Gove to see through one of the most radical Conservative policies, of allowing 'free schools' to be established within the state system. The Lib Dems and Conservatives had some distinct common ground on schools policy, but we had some areas of difference, too. Our Lib Dem party members, including our strong local government base, were cautious or even antagonistic towards the idea of free schools.

During my time as Education spokesman I had coaxed the party towards what I considered to be a more liberal education policy, including allowing for 'sponsor-managed schools' within the state system. I am also a supporter of free schools, as I do not see why there should be a state monopoly of state-funded education provision. And, in practice, most of the concerns about how free schools might operate had been overcome in places such as Sweden, where they are now accepted by every party – other than the communists – as a legitimate part of state education.

But outright support for free schools seemed to be a bridge too far for our party members, and for our Federal Policy Committee. They wanted local authorities to be commissioners of all state education provision. I saw an important role for local authorities, but more in terms of local accountability and support, rather than monopoly commissioning. It would therefore have been difficult for a Lib Dem Secretary of State to lead in this area.

In addition, with Vince Cable going to the Business department rather than to the Treasury, I felt strongly that we needed a Lib Dem representative in the Treasury, which was my home turf. I had completed my degree in economics, worked in the City and then been Lib Dem economics adviser for five years. I had also held the shadow Chief Secretary post within my party for a couple of years in my first parliament, as well as being spokesman for Work and Pensions between 2005 and 2007.

So I felt that if Michael Gove was going to remain at Education, the portfolio which I wanted to 'pitch for' was that of Chief Secretary. I was also relaxed about the idea of working with George Osborne, who I like, admire and had always got on well with. It appealed to me that as number two in the Treasury I could get on with the serious public spending work, without having to be out and about giving speeches and making public appearances, which is generally the lot of those who head up departments of government.

There were broader and less personal reasons for believing that we needed a Liberal Democrat in the Treasury. I felt particularly strongly that the coalition would never work if the Treasury was wholly staffed by Conservative ministers. This was for two distinct reasons. First, it was clear that there was a good deal of unpopular work to be done in tackling the deficit, and I did not believe that we would have a stable coalition if all the tough decisions were being made by a Conservative-controlled Treasury, without any Lib Dem input.

And, second, I am very much a believer in the power of the Treasury, and its importance. The Treasury's control over public spending and taxation means that it is as much the engine room of government as is No. 10 Downing Street. Gordon Brown, when Chancellor, had shown just what a powerful position the Treasury is, at least if the Chancellor is secure in his job. It therefore seemed to me to be absolutely vital that we had a Liberal Democrat in the Treasury, to safeguard our policy interests within the coalition while working closely with George as

Chancellor. We needed to ensure that decisions on schools funding, deficit reduction, pay control, pensions reform, taxation and on other key issues, all had a Lib Dem input early on in the process. We could not possibly afford simply to be bystanders in this process, and to leave Nick Clegg or the Cabinet to address any concerns we had, once the key decisions had been taken.

Although some commentators have claimed that we were as a party mistaken to assume this responsibility, I do not believe for one moment that their analysis is right.

'Who wants to be George Osborne's axe-man?' one Lib Dem MP was quoted, anonymously, as saying to a newspaper. But who wants to be in a coalition and have no influence in the corridors of power? And who thinks for one moment that the public would exempt the Lib Dems from responsibility for cuts, simply because we did not have a minister in the Treasury?

I had, of course, no idea what Nick Clegg's view of this would be. It had been an iron law of Lib Dem coalition negotiations that positions in government were only ever discussed after talks were completed, and only by the party leaders. Anything else would risk distorting people's judgement, based on what jobs were being offered as inducements.

But it was now time to consider these issues, and I suspected – or hoped – that this was what Nick's missed call of the previous evening had been about. So after I had completed my morning media round, I decided that I should call Nick before it was too late to have any influence at all on the process of forming a government, and possibly on my own future.

When I called Nick he was still at home, and from what I could establish he was getting his children ready for school. 'I don't like to be presumptuous,' I said, 'and it may be that I am not actually going to be in the Cabinet, but if I am I really think we need someone at the Treasury.'

Nick explained that I was right in thinking that Vince Cable would be going to the Business department, and he indicated that the stories were also accurate that Chris Huhne would be going to the Climate Change department. Nick himself would be taking charge of the Constitutional Reform Agenda, he told me.

Nick said that there was an issue over whether we should be trying to secure departments which we as a party could be associated with, because of our policy priorities, and he mentioned the Transport department – without indicating that this was exactly what he and David Cameron had in mind.

I pointed out that the Treasury is the engine room of any government and that there was a real risk that if we were excluded from it, it would be more difficult to deliver on our priorities and on the coalition pledges which we had won. Nick acknowledged the point and said that he would be talking to David Cameron about the issue in a short while, but in the meantime had to sort out the top priority – which was getting his children to school. He made no mention of the Education department, which confirmed me in my view that media reports on this issue were wrong.

I returned to my office and switched on the television to see the coverage of the formation of the government. My office is in 1 Parliament Street, barely one hundred metres from Downing Street, so I could once again see the helicopters overhead and the media gathering just down the road.

I answered a few e-mails but decided to stay in my office waiting for that call which all MPs hope for when governments are being formed.

Eventually I had a pager message: 'Please call Downing Street', with a number appended to it. Without waiting for very long, I called and was put through to one of David Cameron's private secretaries, who said: 'The Prime Minister would like to see you sometime in the next half hour or so. Do you think you could be available?'

In a calm voice which sought to strike an appropriate balance between over-enthusiasm and nonchalance, I said: 'Yes, of course. I am only in 1 Parliament Street. Just let me know when.' 'How will we get hold of you?' the young lady enquired. I gave her my mobile phone number.

I waited about an hour, periodically checking my phone to ensure that Downing Street had not somehow been put through automatically to the answer phone. Eventually, just as I was wondering if there had been some hitch in the plans, the phone rang, and the same young lady said: 'If you could make your way to Downing Street now, the Prime Minister will see you in about a half an hour.'

I phoned my mother, as I knew that she would be annoyed if she learned of my journey to Downing Street via the media rather than from me. She was out, but I left a message for her. Then I walked down Whitehall, skirted round a dozen or so tourists, and presented myself to the policeman on the gates of Downing Street. My name was expected, and I was let through the security barriers into the bottom end of Downing Street.

I walked round the security hut, and strolled up Downing Street in as relaxed but businesslike way as I could manage. I have always thought that new members of the Cabinet look insufferably smug as they make their way up Downing Street and are feted by the camera crews, so I got out my pager and read through various old messages as I walked the short distance down to the door of No. 10.

The door opened and I was escorted inside. I noticed that behind the entrance the doorman had sellotaped to the side window an aide-memoire so he could recognise some of the lesser known members of the new government. Somewhat surprisingly, this appeared to have been cut out of the *Sun* newspaper, and I noticed that I was one of five or six members of my party who appeared under the uninspiring headline: 'Britain's Leading Lib Dums.'

A very well spoken and very young lady greeted me, and I assumed that she was part of the well connected Conservative advance guard who had come in with the Prime Minister. 'The Prime Minister is just speaking to the President of France,' she told me, 'and then he will speak to you.' This seemed only reasonable.

I then spotted a couple of Lib Dem officials, Jonny Oates and Lena Pietsch, wondering nonchalantly through the corridor connecting the entrance lobby of 10 Downing Street to the Cabinet Room, and said hello. It was reassuring to realise that our own staff were now being woven into the centre of government itself, that this was a real coalition, and not just a Lib Dem tail on a Conservative dog.

Inside the door of Downing Street is a modest-sized lobby, which leads straight on into a corridor of around twenty metres length. This ends in another lobby, ahead of which is the door to the Cabinet Room. Beyond the Cabinet Room are the Downing Street gardens. I was shown through to the left of the main No. 10 lobby and into a small waiting room, where I was offered a coffee. This waiting room sits on a narrow corridor which leads through from No.10 Downing Street into No. 11 – the base of the Chancellor of the Exchequer.

The walls of the waiting room were covered in drawings by the winners of a national schools Christmas card competition. I assumed that Sarah or Gordon Brown had agreed to reward the winners of this competition with this accolade.

I felt calm but excited. A coalition, and a Cabinet place, had always seemed one possible outcome of the general election, but Lib Dems are well used to great possibilities turning out to be mirages which fade away as they are approached.

However, this particular vision no longer seemed to be a mirage.

The coffee arrived. I stood up to look at the pictures. And then sat down again. And then stood up again. I was then joined by another Cabinet minister to be. I was surprised to see that it was Vince Cable, who I assumed had already seen the Prime Minister earlier in the morning. We said hello, and then the young lady returned almost immediately to escort me back down to see the Prime Minister.

I walked down the short corridor to the Cabinet Room, entered and turned left. The Prime Minister was sitting in his chair in the centre of the room, with his back to the wall – looking out over the Downing Street gardens. He welcomed me and I sat down opposite him. A photographer dashed around us to record the great event for posterity.

As I had expected, and hoped, the Prime Minister asked me to become Chief Secretary to the Treasury, working alongside George Osborne, the Chancellor. He emphasised what a huge challenge this would be, and I thanked him for the opportunity. The meeting was all over in a couple of minutes, as befits the diary of a new Prime Minister on these occasions, and then I was back out in the lobby outside the Cabinet Room. From there I was shown upstairs, where Nick Clegg and Danny Alexander were sitting talking about the other Lib Dem ministerial appointments. Nick wanted my view about who our ministers of state ought to be, and I had a quick look at the list which he had written out.

I then returned downstairs and was told that the plan was for me to head straight over to the Treasury building to meet the new Chancellor, and my new boss, George Osborne. Even though it was only a short walk round the corner, a large black ministerial Jaguar was awaiting me outside.

Once again, as the doors of Downing Street opened I did my best to look serious and unemotional, as should befit a new Chief Secretary with a tough and unpopular job to do. It was all going to plan until, as I got in the door of the waiting Jaguar, one of the press photographers who was standing opposite shouted out: 'For God's sake smile, you miserable bastard!' He then caught me in shot smiling, as I looked back over my shoulder.

The Jaguar left Downing Street, turned right, went round Parliament Square and dropped me off at the steps of HM Treasury, opposite St James's Park. George Osborne was awaiting me at the top of the steps, and a group of camera crews and assorted media were at the bottom of the steps. George and I shook hands, and we then both made brief statements saying how much we looked forward to working with each other, and how much the Treasury would reflect coalition co-operation in practice.

And thus was borne what was termed, for its all too brief existence, the Treasury team of 'Osborne and Little', a reference to our respective heights and to George's family firm.

This was, of course, a moment of huge satisfaction for me. When I was first getting involved in politics in the mid-1990s, *Tatler* magazine had – to my great pleasure – tipped me as one of the Lib Dems 'to watch for' in twenty years time. I was Lib Dem prospective parliamentary candidate in Folkestone and Hythe at the time and I went out and bought up every local copy of the magazine which I could find (two). But the magazine had then rather spoilt the effect by predicting that my hard work would lead in two decades time to the lofty position of Lib Dem Treasury spokesman – not to actually exercising any power in government. Was this all that Lib Dems could ever expect, I wondered?

I chose the Liberal Democrats to support because that is where I felt at home. I felt that the values, instincts and aspirations of the party were those that I shared. But of course I feared that by choosing a political home I felt comfortable in, I might also be removing myself from the chance of ever exercising power, of really making a difference.

When I left my job as a well paid Managing Director in the City of London to join the Liberal Democrats in 1994, we had not much more than twenty MPs, and little or no influence in Parliament. It seemed to many an odd, even eccentric, decision. Indeed, when I applied to become an economics researcher for the party on £14,000 per year, the party hierarchy found it difficult to believe my story, and assumed that I must be a Conservative spy! Lord Rennard – later our party's Chief Executive – told me that my story had to be 'checked out' before I was allowed to take up even this lowly position.

So, I believed strongly in our party, but I did not relish the idea of spending thirty years in the political wilderness. The role of opposition parties in politics is a hugely important one, but there cannot be many people who yearn to spend all their time in this position. In truth, I almost returned to the City after the general election in 1997, and got as far as signing a rather highly paid contract. But I changed my mind at the very last moment – motivated at least in part by Paddy Ashdown's dynamic leadership of the party, and his obvious determination to ensure that we were active players in the centre of British politics, and not just passive observers on the sidelines.

And now here I was, coming to the Treasury to be the first Liberal Treasury minister in almost eighty years. It was the department that I had always most wanted to be involved in – the engine room of government. 'Give me a place to stand . . . and I will move the whole world,' said Archimedes. I believe that for those who want to make a difference in British politics, there is no better place to stand than in the Treasury.

And I was coming to implement a coalition agreement which I had myself helped negotiate, and which I very much believed in. I was coming to have oversight of all public spending at a time when this would be one of the government's greatest challenges. And I was to work for, and in partnership with, a Conservative Chancellor who I liked, respected, and felt I could do business with.

Most important of all, I felt confident that I could make a difference, that I could help deliver the kind of liberalism which I believed in, dry on economic matters but also socially liberal, pushing for a fairer society through policies such as those on tax, education and welfare reform, which we had inserted into the coalition agreement.

George Osborne and I went up to our offices on the first floor of the Treasury building. At one end of the long corridor was the Chancellor's suite of offices and, turning left, the Chief Secretary's office was at the other end, thirty metres or so away.

I was met by my Private Secretary, Chris Brown, and by the seven other staff members in the Chief Secretary's office – a warm, protective, and perpetually cheerful diary secretary, Maria, the very efficient assistant Private Secretaries, Imran and Annalisa, our speechwriter, Ben, and three hard-working support staff, Alex, James and Juliet.

I was then shown through into the Chief Secretary's large office, which looks out over St James's Park. Straight ahead was a suite of armchairs and a sofa, to the right was a long conference table which could comfortably seat fifteen or sixteen people, and in the far corner was a large desk. Against the nearside wall was a management consultant's white board, apparently left over from my Labour predecessor, Liam Byrne. The walls were decorated with some suitably dull pictures of eighteenth and nineteenth century sail boats. The overall impression was one of seriousness, solidity and a degree of frugality.

I was the first Liberal minister in the Treasury since Sir John Simon in 1935, and the first ever Liberal/Liberal Democrat Chief Secretary to the Treasury. The role of Chief Secretary dates only from 1961. The post was created by the Conservative government of Harold Macmillan to help relieve the enormous workload of the Chancellor of the Exchequer. The Chief Secretary is responsible for oversight of all public spending and a number of associated issues.

Since 1961, there have been twenty-nine Chief Secretaries, and holders of the post have included many individuals who have gone on to high office – including Norman Lamont, Michael Portillo, Alistair Darling and John Major, from whom I received a very kind letter saying it was the post in government that he had most enjoyed.

After a brief chat with my Private Secretary, Chris, I was invited to join the Chancellor – who was expected to speak to Treasury officials in a large hall on the Treasury ground floor. George set out his ambitions, not least in terms of tackling the deficit, and then emphasised how proud he was to take up the post of Chancellor.

George also took the opportunity to emphasise that we were one team, even if from two different parties. I then returned to my office, and took some early decisions to cut public spending. I had already discovered that as Chief Secretary I was to have a chauffeur-driven black Jaguar permanently at my beck and call. I just could not imagine being the public spending 'axeman' while travelling around in a chauffeur-driven Jaguar. I enquired how much this had cost my predecessor's budget and was told that it was in total over £110,000 per year.

I told Chris that this luxury just had to go, and that I could easily make do without a car. He told me that the departmental administration budget was already quite tight, so that both he and the Permanent Secretary would 'welcome' this decision. Next to go was an overseas travel budget of in excess of £10,000, and half of the budget for office newspapers. In modest exchange, I asked for a screen to be placed on my desk so that I could follow developments in the financial markets.

The net effect was a saving of some £120,000 per year, and more importantly it made me confident that when people asked – as they inevitably would – what sacrifices I had personally made as part of the 'cuts agenda' I would at least have something to say.

That afternoon Chris began to induct me into the ways of the Treasury. The key seemed to be that each evening a large pile of briefing documents would arrive on my desk, which needed careful scrutiny. But many of these would not arrive until well into the evening. I was expected to read and comment on these. This evening I received the papers for the first Cabinet meeting, which was due to take place on Thursday morning at 10am.

It was clear that this would be a meeting more of introduction than of substance, though there was one paper setting out plans to cut ministerial salaries by 5%. For most of us this would seem a quite acceptable sacrifice, as going from the salary of a backbencher to that of a Cabinet minister still involved an overnight pay rise from some £65,000 to around £135,000.

But as well as these Cabinet papers, there was also a large pile of classified HM Treasury economic papers, as a briefing for the

Chancellor, Chief Secretary and the new ministerial team. Any elation that I might have felt at my new responsibilities soon fell away as I read the pile of gloomy assessments in front of me. They were the economic equivalent of a large bucket of icy water being dropped on the head from a great height.

I already knew, of course, that the old government had left us a public borrowing figure of over £150 billion per year. In other words, the government was having to borrow an extra £3bn each week just to cover the gap between its spending and what was being raised in taxes.

The reports also drew attention to the risk of economic growth forecasts for the UK having to be lowered. It had already been thought that the growth forecasts for the economy had been overestimated by the government to massage down future borrowing figures. Though civil servants clearly could not discuss what had happened under the last government, the rumours which swirled around were that Gordon Brown had put pressure on his Chancellor, Alistair Darling, to force the Treasury to use higher growth forecasts than they were comfortable with.

This is a very serious charge. However, its veracity seemed to be confirmed in Peter Mandelson's account of this period of Labour government. Writing in his memoirs Lord Mandelson reports that: 'Proper discussion of the [Budget] details was overshadowed by a tug-of-war over growth projections for the economy . . . Gordon repeatedly, and often angrily, rejected Alistair's forecasts, saying they were too conservative.' (*The Third Man*, 2010, pp. 462–3).

This is an issue which George Osborne would address early and decisively in his proposals for an Office of Budget Responsibility, to draw up independent forecasts.

Nevertheless, reading through the documents in front of me, late into the night, I could see that the Treasury's assessment of the state of the public finances was clearly bleak. The documents also outlined a range of alternative scenarios for bringing the budget deficit back down – all of these involving enormous spending cuts, with some increases in taxation.

Essentially, what was being offered to Treasury ministers was a menu of rather unpalatable options, with the clear warning that if the new government flunked these choices then there was a risk of financial crisis, and the British economy going the way of Greece and the other highly indebted European nations.

But if the Treasury were offering a menu of fiscal options, the bills which were attached to these were as formidable as those which might be attached to a range of increasingly unaffordable 'menus gastronomiques' in a very expensive French restaurant. The least expensive and painful option was clearly the one that the Treasury considered the absolute minimum necessary, and the accompanying description was clearly designed to put us off choosing it – rather like the least expensive fixed-price offering at a rather grand restaurant.

The most aggressive and expensive fiscal option seemed to me to have been inserted as an extreme outlier in order to influence our expectations, and make it easier to choose the middle option. This option detailed a degree of fiscal tightening which was greater than any other proposal I had yet seen discussed.

Even the middle option seemed to me to be a little more aggressive than I considered necessary, and required huge cuts in spending and higher taxes. I marked on my paper a fourth option, somewhere between the middle and lower options, and then put all the paperwork back on my desk to review again the next day.

Of course, what I did not yet register was that all my papers, with annotations, expletives and exclamation marks would then be taken away and fed into the Civil Service system overnight. My late-night doodlings and instant reaction would attain immediately the status of a considered ministerial response. In addition, I soon discovered that if I wanted to come back to a paper, I needed to specify this or to hide it in one of the drawers of my desk, as otherwise it would be swept up by my private office. Even my attempts to hide a few such documents away in my desk met with only limited success, as my Private Secretary clearly considered nothing to be out of bounds.

Conscious more than ever of the scale of challenge we faced on the public finances, and feeling rather less elated than I had been twelve hours before, I left the Treasury at around midnight, and walked back home, deep in thought about the huge challenges and unpleasant choices which lay ahead.

Thursday 13 May 2010

Attending the Cabinet, kissing hands with the Queen

I was in on Thursday morning at around 7.20am. I had told my private office that I would be there at 7am, and they looked rather shocked – this was clearly not the usual ministerial arrival time, but it was the start time that I was used to ever since I had begun work in the City of London in 1987.

Chris, my Private Secretary, had got in early to be there, and was waiting for me on the Treasury steps, as I had yet to be issued with my permanent pass. He had also bought an entire set of the day's newspapers, as the office papers seemed not to arrive until after 8am. I noted that this was clearly going to be a Rolls-Royce civil service operation, and I was already impressed by Chris who seemed loyal, efficient, pleasant and reassuringly human.

I ploughed through various papers at my desk, and after a while Chris came in with a sealed letter which he said I might want to see. Apparently it had been left by my predecessor as Chief Secretary, Liam Byrne MP. It was short and to the point, saying simply: 'Dear Chief Secretary, I'm afraid there is no money. Kind regards – and good luck! Liam.' My initial reaction was to laugh. But I then felt that perhaps the joke was in rather poor taste. After all, Labour had left the public finances in a complete mess, and there were signs that departments had been spending money irresponsibly before the election, in what seemed not only to be a scorched earth strategy but one focused primarily on splashing money into Labour's own parliamentary seats. I put the letter in my top draw for future reference.

At 9.50am I left for my first Cabinet meeting, accompanied by Maria, my diary secretary. Rather than take the long way round to Downing Street, via Whitehall, we turned right out of the Treasury, and strolled down the pavement, with St James's Park on our left. Under my arm I held the red bound folder embossed with the Chief Secretary's title and the Royal Crest, inside of which were all of that day's Cabinet papers.

Maria took me to the gates which give access to the back of Downing Street, and presented me to the two gun-carrying police officers, who unlocked the big gates and let me through. It was then a thirty-metre stroll past other police officers, up some steps and through the gates at the end of Downing Street.

I passed by the door of No. 11 Downing Street, home to the Chancellor of the Exchequer, and entered No. 10 along with various other new Cabinet ministers, also with their smart red folders. It felt rather like the first day at school, with a similar air of excitement and trepidation.

Outside the Cabinet Room, ministers were mingling and gossiping, and I was pleased to see that the little groups were not formed on entirely party lines – Lib Dems were engaged in relaxed discussions with their Conservative opposite numbers. We were then told firmly but politely that new mobile phones or BlackBerrys were not to be taken into the Cabinet Room. These were to be left on a rack of cubby holes which had been put up at elbow height to the left of the Cabinet Room door. Each contained a card with a number on to aid retrieval after the meeting.

We were then ushered through into the Cabinet Room, and had to find the places which had been allocated to us. As one of the more junior members of the Cabinet, I was not surprised to find myself close to the end of the great table, second from the end. There wasn't much room once we were all seated, and I squeezed in between Baroness Warsi and Eric Pickles.

However, I had the advantage of being seated on the other side of the table from the Prime Minister, so it was easy to see him, watch his reactions to the points being made, and signal a desire to contribute when necessary. Opposite me were Dominic Grieve, Jeremy Hunt and Chris Huhne.

David Cameron sat in the traditional Prime Minister's place, in the centre of the table and facing out onto the Downing Street gardens. On his left was the Cabinet Secretary, Sir Gus O'Donnell, and on his right was Foreign Secretary William Hague.

Opposite Mr Cameron was Nick Clegg, sitting in the place occupied by Gordon Brown during Tony Blair's period in office. However, it soon became clear that Nick and David Cameron got on far better together than Tony Blair and Gordon Brown, despite leading two separate and distinct parties.

The new Chancellor, George Osborne, sat to Nick Clegg's right. Again, he presented a clear contrast with his Labour predecessors, being perhaps a closer friend and ally of the Prime Minister than any other Chancellor in British history. On Nick's left sat the Cabinet's veteran warhorse, who had seen it all many times before, in the distinct shape of Ken Clarke.

The Cabinet Room has been the meeting place for governments ever since 1796, when Pitt the Younger arranged for two rooms to be knocked through into one, so that one large meeting room was available.

The present, boat-shaped, table dates only from 1959, and was commissioned by Harold Macmillan to allow people to be seen properly around the table, and to communicate more easily. On the table was some paper, a pencil for each place, some water, and a small stack of sucky sweets, presumably to ease dry throats during long meetings.

After the customary photos for the new Cabinet, we started more or less on time, and David Cameron made an eloquently impressive speech about the new government and the challenges we faced. Nick Clegg added some words of his own. Both seemed to me to have blossomed as leaders over the last few weeks. They were confident, cheerful, and looked remarkably relaxed in spite of the intense activity and strains of the last few months.

It was the first coalition Cabinet for sixty-five years, and already the mood was positive and upbeat. This was helped by the nature of the coalition negotiations over the previous week. Both sides had built up trust and respect for each other. George Osborne spoke briefly about the economic situation, and noted that the huge public sector borrowing requirement was the primary challenge for the new government. David Cameron then invited Vince Cable to speak on the economy and Vince started by prompting the Cabinet's first burst of laughter, by referring to the new coalition as an arranged marriage, and noting that his Indian relatives had once told him that arranged marriages were often more successful than the conventional kind!

The only decision-making item on the agenda was the proposal to cut 5% off ministerial pay, and to accept a pay freeze for the rest of the parliament. This axed just over £7,000 per year off a Cabinet minister's pay, taking it down to around £134,500.

The total package was set to save about £300,000 in its first year. This was a useful symbol of discipline and example, but a necessarily modest first instalment of cuts which were widely expected to require up to another £40,000,000,000 of savings by the final year of the parliament. The Prime Minister's pay also fell to £142,500, from £150,000. This was a figure for me to take note of, as my role as Chief Secretary now involved approving the employment of any public servant paid from central government funds, who was to be paid more than the Prime Minister. The requests did not take long to come in – starting with a new Chief Executive for the Royal Mail.

When the meeting ended, we were all invited out of the door at the far end of the Cabinet Room and down the steps into the Downing Street gardens.

I chatted on the way to Philip Hammond, the new Transport Secretary, who had been the Conservative shadow Chief Secretary in opposition. Philip must have had mixed feelings about moving to the Transport brief, as although it is a more senior role than that of Chief Secretary, he had clearly been preparing for the Chief Secretary post for some time. Nevertheless, he was generous in giving advice and offering to help.

Out in the Downing Street garden, we had a group photograph of the Cabinet, and then people strolled back upstairs, gossiping. I had some early approaches from Cabinet ministers who had particular spending issues which they wanted help with, and I soon realised that although I ranked near the bottom of the Cabinet pecking order, the power of the Chief Secretary is potentially huge, though this must clearly depend upon his relationship with the Chancellor of the Exchequer.

After the Cabinet meeting was over, I walked back to the Treasury. Later that day we had a meeting with George Osborne and senior Treasury officials to discuss the announcement George wanted to make on Monday 17 May. This would include plans to immediately establish an Office of Budget Responsibility, under the direction of Sir Alan Budd. The 'OBR' would ensure that in future the Budget forecasts were derived independently of ministers, and so could not be 'fixed' for political purposes. Sir Alan would also be asked to do a complete audit of the public finances, to ensure that the projections used by George in his own budgeting were credible.

We knew that there was some considerable risk that this independent audit would lead to higher borrowing figures, as the future growth forecasts used by Labour were highly optimistic. However, we also knew that in the short term tax revenues were coming in a little better than expected at the time of the Budget, and that growing confidence in the new government's determination to deal with the deficit would help keep down market interest rates. Lower interest rates would reduce projected debt interest payments, which were expected to grow rapidly as a share of total public spending, a consequence of the huge debts racked up by Labour.

We also decided to make two other announcements on Monday. One was to review all new spending decisions taken by the previous government since 1 January 2010 and the other was to promise to deliver the details of the agreed £6bn of in-year cuts by Monday 24 May. The latter would clearly require a huge amount of work by both me and the Treasury itself.

I would be leading on the work to identify the £6bn of cuts, and I had no doubt that we had a lot to do if this crucial job was to be done successfully and on time.

As soon as I got back from meeting the Chancellor, I therefore asked my office to arrange meetings for me with all of the departmental experts within the Treasury, so we could agree on the details of the savings we were seeking.

But that afternoon there was a more pressing appointment, which I could not possibly miss. The new Cabinet was due to see Her Majesty the Queen at Buckingham Palace, to receive seals of office and to be sworn into the Privy Council.

My private office suggested that I should use my chauffeur driven Jaguar to get to Buckingham Palace for the swearing in. 'Oh, I thought I had cancelled that,' I said. 'Well, sort of,' said Chris. 'But the government car service has told us that we must give something like three months notice, so we have the car for the time being anyway, whether you want it or not.' I was beginning to be wary that getting rid of my car might not be quite as easy as I had thought, but it seemed unwise to walk to Buckingham Palace and risk being late or arriving soaked in sweat. Nor did arriving in a taxi seem entirely right.

So, feeling a little guilty at the indulgence, I left the Treasury and clambered into the back of the ministerial Jaguar, and we set off down the Mall. My driver made no reference to my decision to axe the car, but soon moved on to selling me the virtues of the government car service in every way imaginable. It seemed that there was no problem in my ministerial life which was not capable of being resolved if only I had access to this service. I felt sure that the driver knew of my decision and that he knew that I knew. But I was determined to avoid having a debate over the issue, so I said little.

In a couple of minutes we arrived at Buckingham Palace and drove into the inner courtyard, which was already full of other parked black ministerial Jaguars. I climbed out of the car and up some steps, to be met by Palace officials. We were then all shown round the corner to a large room where tea and coffee were served.

After five minutes of chatter, we were called to order. The whole Cabinet was there, and for this reason we were told that the ceremony would take place in a larger room than usual, on the main floor. It was explained that the ceremony would have two parts. The first was to be sworn into the Privy Council, and the second was for Cabinet ministers to receive their seals of office from the Queen. The complex ceremony was described to us, and we all looked and listened carefully.

The ceremony involved kneeling on a stool, but with only the right knee, and in a distinctly uncomfortable 'squatting' pose that seemed designed to cause maximum awkwardness. If this were not enough, an oath had to be taken on the Bible at the same time. We then had to move forward to another kneeling position and go through something similar, with a Bible held up in our right hand. We were then told that we needed to step forward, kneel again, and kiss hands with the Queen.

We all queued outside the room in question, waiting for the Queen. Nick Clegg seemed to have most to do, given his position of Lord President of the Council, which meant that he presides on these occasions, taking precedence even over the Prime Minister.

The whole ceremony lasted about an hour. When it was over, and without any further ado, we all traipsed out to see if we could find our cars amongst the large number of black Jaguars parked outside.

Before leaving, we were each given a small Bible as a commemoration of the event.

On the way back to the Treasury, we seemed to go quite a long way round, and this gave my driver a further opportunity to sing the praises of the government car service. I said little, other than the occasional

'I see'. I suppose I should have realised that not only was taxpayer money at stake, but so were the drivers' jobs too. It was not surprising that they wanted to press their case hard. But I could not see myself, as I was told my predecessor did, heading back to my constituency each week in a chauffeur-driven black Jaguar, however convenient it was to be able to 'do my boxes' of work in the back of the car. My constituents in Somerset are a down to earth lot, and they would have thought their MP was getting well above himself if they had seen me return home in this style.

Back in the Treasury, I had my first meeting with the impressive team of civil servants who were responsible for monitoring and controlling public spending.

We all knew that we had a very big job to do if we were to meet George Osborne's target of securing £6bn of in-year savings by Monday week, though in fairness the civil servants had started work on this project during the election period, as part of their post-election planning.

I got the impression that the Treasury was relishing getting back to fulfilling its traditional role as guardian of the public finances and taxpayer interest, after a long period of public profligacy. Meetings were beginning to fill up my diary but I also realised that there was no formal steer as to how the job should be done.

It seemed to me that the choice as a minister was either to be passive and allow the system to manage you and bring papers for decision to you, or it was to take the initiative and set the agenda.

I was determined that, while working closely with the civil servants, I would set a clear pace and agenda. I knew that I had to carve out my own role as Chief Secretary, and that without my lead the 'system' would simply churn on of its own accord, with key decisions taken by the Chancellor and his advisers, rather than by me. I did not wish to act merely as a 'rubber stamp'.

I was determined that the Liberal Democrat influence in the Treasury would be real and not just a fig leaf. Indeed, without this I could not see how the coalition would survive. I saw my job as involving three key tasks: to deliver coalition economic policy, to deliver the Liberal Democrat commitments within the coalition agreement and to block measures that conflicted with Liberal Democrat policy or principles.

But I felt confident that I would have an open and productive working relationship with George Osborne. It was also soon clear that the relationship between Nick Clegg and David Cameron was a strong and open one too and that sensitive issues could be debated and resolved by the two party leaders.

Friday 14 May 2010

Celebrations in south Somerset

I hoped to get back to my Yeovil constituency on the Friday morning of 14 May, but had to delay my return for a brief morning meeting with the Chancellor, in No. 11 Downing Street, to discuss the progress on the £6 billion of cuts.

So it was late morning when I left to return to Yeovil constituency for the first time since election day, 6 May. That lunchtime we had planned a great celebration lunch at Little Barwick House, near Yeovil.

Present were Paddy and Jane Ashdown, my brilliant election agent Sam Crabb, constituency Chair Cathy Bakewell MBE and her husband, David, and my magnificent Yeovil office staff of Sue Weeks, Claire Margetts, Sarah Frapple, Sadye Mclean, and Jeremy Gale, as well as Chris Weeks, Roy Margetts and Jack Frapple.

We had a long and enjoyable lunch, and closed our Yeovil office for the afternoon.

But I collected a large amount of casework and other letters to take back home to work on. I was determined not to neglect my constituency casework and to continue to hold my regular weekly advice centres for local residents to come along and see me.

Saturday 15–Sunday 16 May 2010

A weekend in the Treasury

On Saturday morning, I held my first advice centre since the general election, and this was packed with people with the usual problems such as housing and their tax credits. After the advice centre, at lunchtime, I travelled to Norton sub Hamdon to a constituency party celebration of our general election victory.

Norton is a beautiful village which is right in the centre of the wonderful Yeovil constituency, and which has also been the home of Paddy and Jane Ashdown for around thirty-five years.

The village has a new hall, with outstanding views across the South Somerset countryside to Ham Hill. I expected a crowd of perhaps a hundred local members and councillors, but as I got closer I could see that the roads around the hall were clogged with cars which had had great difficulty in parking. There must have been around 200 members present, a much bigger turnout than expected.

I was given a fantastic welcome, and it was clear that our members and supporters were not only delighted with the scale of our election win, but were also excited and pleased with our entry into government. I was able to point out in my speech that at the last general election the Conservative candidate in my constituency had attacked me as someone who while 'nice' would have no influence in government as a consequence of being a Liberal Democrat. He had argued that the local helicopter manufacturer, Westland, would be far better off with a Conservative MP pressing their case. I could now point out that the Business Secretary was a Liberal Democrat, the Minister of State for the Armed Forces was a Liberal Democrat, and that the person who would sign off on government spending and contracts was . . . me!

This was a good response to the Conservative charge of powerlessness, though I had, however, already taken the precaution of notifying Treasury civil servants of the potential conflict of interest over Westland helicopters and I had made clear that I could take no role in approving contracts that related to their interests. This responsibility would, instead, be discharged by another Treasury minister.

After about an hour at the celebration party, I was forced to say my farewells and to travel back up to London for another meeting in the Treasury with the Chancellor and his officials. This was to discuss the announcements to be made on Monday, the work on the £6bn of early cuts and the work which needed putting in place to deliver the Chancellor's first emergency budget.

I also went into the Treasury on the Sunday to work on these issues. With the £6bn of cuts, a June Emergency Budget and an autumn Spending Review, this seemed likely to be one of many weekends spent in the Treasury over the months ahead.

Monday 17 May 2010

'There is no money left'

Today was to include the first big announcement on economic policy by George Osborne. We met early in the Treasury to run through the arrangements for the press conference, where we would be joined by Sir Alan Budd, a former Chief Economic adviser to the Treasury, who was now to be the first head of the independent Office of Budget Responsibility (OBR).

George's early announcement was designed as a development of Gordon Brown's most successful policy initiative – his decision to transfer control of interest rates to the Bank of England at the beginning of the 1997 parliament.

Of course, the introduction of the OBR was not entirely comparable, as the OBR would advise on budget forecasts rather than taking fiscal policy decisions itself.

But the change was in any case a most welcome one. It will, quite rightly, remove from politicians the power to fix the economic growth forecasts in the budget, hugely reducing the risk that future Chancellors and Prime Ministers will decide to fiddle the budget figures for their own political purposes.

The Budget growth forecasts are not merely important as an indicator of future economic growth, but they have a massive impact on the Treasury forecasts of tax revenues and spending figures. Higher growth estimates mean that the Treasury forecasts more tax revenue, lower spending on areas such as unemployment, and therefore lower borrowing or higher projected surpluses. This means that if the growth forecasts are 'fiddled' they can be used to make the case for lower taxes or greater spending – perhaps timed to occur just before a general election.

Taking away this extraordinary power to meddle can only, therefore, increase the credibility of fiscal policy. And by shining a brighter light on the credibility of government borrowing forecasts, this policy change should help to reduce, but not of course eliminate, the risks of major forecasting and policy errors in the future.

It is, of course, extraordinary that politicians ever had the power to interfere in the process of forecasting future growth rates. So, in spite of inevitable media cynicism over whether the OBR was just part of the usual incoming government way of blaming its predecessor, I doubt that a future government will want to reverse the fundamental reforms which George Osborne announced.

We also wanted Sir Alan Budd to complete a thorough spring clean of the government accounts, so that we had an entirely credible estimate of future borrowing requirements before George's first, crucial emergency Budget in June. If there were to be any surprises – good or bad – we wanted to know about them before the big fiscal policy decisions of the parliament had to be taken.

The OBR announcement was made in the conference room downstairs on the first floor of the Treasury, with a good turnout of broadcast and written media. George made his announcements first, and he also revealed for the first time that the £6bn of in-year cuts in spending in 2010/11 would be unveiled in just one week's time.

I spoke next, also confirming that we were freezing government spending announcements made since 1 January 2010, to check that the spending reflected value for money.

Sir Alan Budd then spoke about the work of the Office of Budget Responsibility.

In the question and answer session for journalists that followed, I then inadvertently gave many in the media the rather simpler headline that they would be looking for, when I made reference to Liam Byrne's letter to me, with its 'no money left' message. I had not gone to the press conference intending to make this point, and indeed had not even yet had time to show George Osborne the letter. But I decided to make reference to it in an answer to a journalist's question. I suppose I was naïve not to realise just how much would be made of this letter, and within minutes of the press conference ending I was told by our press team that journalists were asking for copies of the letter.

George and I decided not to release a copy of the letter, but we confirmed its wording.

It was an admission which put Labour on the back foot for some time to come, and which perhaps captured better than any OBR analysis could the state of the finances that Labour had bequeathed to us. I was later to discover that poor Liam Byrne did not much appreciate this exercise in open government, but it was a rather odd note to leave to an incoming government from a Chief Secretary.

In any case, I was too busy to worry about Liam Byrne's nose being put a little out of joint. I now had £6bn of cuts to find, and less than a week to do it in.

While it was true that the Treasury had been preparing its own contingency plans for the £6bn of cuts during the election campaign, there was still a long way to go to get the agreement of colleagues, and to sort out the good ideas for cuts from the bad.

Treasury civil servants had by now explained to me how the whole process would work. First, we would send out a letter to each department, telling them how much we wanted them to cut from their budgets. Only overseas aid, the health department, and defence would be spared from the exercise.

The total asked for by the Treasury would exceed the total £6bn that we needed, but not by a huge margin. Some departments might then 'settle' with us at the suggested figure, by agreement between officials. Those that didn't would have to arrange for their Secretaries of State to meet me or talk to me to explain their concerns, and to see what could be agreed. I was then required to bargain with each department to extract as much money as I could, but Treasury civil servants gave me for each department a 'bottom line' which I was advised not to go below – if I did then I would risk the whole thing not adding up.

Any Cabinet ministers who did not agree immediately to 'pay up', and who wanted to meet me, would then have to come to my office at the Treasury to see me, no matter how senior they were. It was explained to me that the Chief Secretary was not expected to go out to visit Cabinet ministers, but could stay within the Treasury 'bunker'. I liked the sound of that. On such backbone-bolstering details is fiscal discipline based, I thought.

Whether this arrangement was actually designed to bolster my credibility, or whether it was to enable Treasury officials to keep a closer eye on me, I never found out.

There were only two exceptions made to the rule that departmental bosses had to come to see me. One was for William Hague, who had agreed to settle directly with the Chancellor, perhaps in deference to his seniority. The other was that, fortunately, I was not required to negotiate with the Chancellor of the Exchequer over his own budget – though I did have a slightly odd meeting with David Gauke, as minister responsible for Her Majesty's Revenue and Customs.

The proposed HMRC cuts had been drawn up by Treasury officials. HMRC officials had then briefed their (Treasury) minister on his lines to take, while I had received further negotiating advice from Treasury officials on how hard to push if any cuts were resisted. I am sure the whole rather odd discussion kept somebody in the building amused.

As an alternative to coming to see me, Cabinet ministers could talk to me over the phone, though for this our respective Civil Service teams would expect to listen in to the conversation. For each department, the Civil Service had already drawn up a list of the scale of proposed cuts, with an indication of where these might be made – though it was up to each department to decide on the detail of the cuts themselves.

I made only one major change to this envelope of departmental cuts. I was not prepared to see the schools budget, or that for early years investment, cut. This was a key Liberal Democrat spending priority, and indeed (through a pupil premium) we wanted more money to go into schools.

I raised my concerns early on with George Osborne, and he immediately agreed to protect schools, early years and 16–19 education. This was consistent with the commitment that these cuts should not hit 'front-line services'. Our decision required the remaining departments to make bigger savings, while delighting ministers and civil servants at the department of education, who had already been told on the Civil Service grapevine to expect big cuts of between £1bn and £2bn.

I soon realised that the key for me was to be well briefed to counter the attempts by some Cabinet ministers to defend their budgets. So I needed to know the counter-arguments to those that would be put by the respective Cabinet minister. Treasury civil servants were usually good at anticipating these. What got trickier was if the Cabinet minister was well enough briefed to seek to 'counter' my 'countering' of his or her points. Then I needed a further set of arguments to secure my prize, though I could always fall back, I suppose, on 'well the Chancellor needs the money!'

I called together Treasury civil servants who shadowed each spending department, and went through the briefings with each in turn. I looked at the cuts which we were suggesting to departments, and made sure I understood the real impact and political and social implications of every change that we were suggesting.

I also threw in a few ideas of my own. Why should civil servants continue to take first-class travel, I asked, when MPs were now more or less banned from doing so? How much would be saved if we introduced restrictions into this area? Looking warily at me, one civil servant sought to parry the threat by saying: 'But Chief Secretary, the revenue from first-class ticket sales goes to the train operating companies, under their contracts. So if there were fewer first-class ticket sales, and the revenue fell, it might simply mean greater subsidy payments to the train operators to make up the difference. That would therefore save the Exchequer little or nothing. It could turn out not to be a real economy at all, Chief Secretary.'

I laughed. It was an ingenious defence, worthy of Sir Humphrey Appleby at his best, but it was not one I was prepared to accept. Yet every time I looked away, I found that this savings proposal somehow seemed to fall off the list of agreed cuts. I pushed it back in, but it would either disappear, or turn up in watered down form.

As Chief Secretary, I was to secure Cabinet agreement for this broad approach to delivering the £6bn of cuts at our second Cabinet meeting, on Tuesday 19 May. The Chancellor was due to be away, attending a meeting of European finance ministers.

I did not anticipate any serious problems, not least since the proposal was a Conservative manifesto commitment. But I didn't want to take any chances, so I had my private office fix a telephone call with former Chancellor, Ken Clarke, before the Cabinet meeting. I was put through to the Justice Secretary and started my pitch to him: 'Ken, I've got this paper coming up tomorrow at Cabinet, and as an ex-Chancellor I wonder if you could step in to support it if we have any problems.'

'No problem at all,' came back the reply, 'absolutely necessary. I will back you all the way. We just have to get on with it.' Somewhat cheekily I then added: 'It would also be helpful to say that one Cabinet minister, i.e. you, has already signed up to his cut in full. Would that be possible?' There was a brief pause on the other end of the line, and then, 'What are you asking for again? "Three something" isn't it?' 'Yes,' I said, '£325 million.' Another short pause, and then, 'Yes. Absolutely. I'll look at it but I'm sure it won't be a problem.'

The call ended and I was delighted. We had secured the support of one of the Cabinet's heavy-hitters and now already had, pretty much in the bag, our first contribution of £325 million to the £6bn of cuts which were needed.

In my outer office the Civil Service team put up a huge flip chart with the name of each department. Next to it was their target contribution asked for, along with the 'bottom line', and the amount agreed. This would allow us, in very simple terms, to follow the ongoing negotiations, and see whether we were on track for meeting the target or not.

With George away there was another meeting which I had to attend before tomorrow's Cabinet Meeting. This was a meeting of the new National Security Council. This was chaired by the Prime Minister and included, as well as senior Cabinet ministers, the heads of the security services and the top brass from our armed forces.

A large pile of briefing papers awaited me in a sealed box, which had to be opened with a special key. The papers were then to be returned to the box by me, which was to be sealed. Even my Private Secretary did not have clearance to read the material, which was 'Top Secret Classified'.

I started reading the papers on the Monday evening and some of them made even more frightening reading than the papers on the proposed cuts and budget options for incoming Treasury ministers.

On each paper was an indication of whether I was expected to speak, what I should say if I was asked to speak and the Treasury 'lines to take'. I noted down the Treasury lines to take on each of the papers, until I realised that they basically all came to the same thing. Whatever country we were looking at, whatever issue, whether it was the Middle East or the handling of the fallout from the volcanic ash cloud disrupting air travel across Europe, the Treasury line to take was always: 'We don't believe that any extra money can or should be spent on this.' This commendably consistent approach meant that it was not difficult to master the Treasury brief either for the National Security Council or for most other issues on the weekly Cabinet agenda. You just had to remember that we were not in favour of spending any more on whatever was being discussed.

Tuesday 18 May 2010

In search of £6 billion

Tuesday started with a meeting of the National Security Council at 9am. This was followed by the full Cabinet at 10am.

I again walked round by St James's Park, went through the first large security gates and was then shown in through the side entrance of No. 12 Downing Street, and up various corridors and steps until I was once more outside the entrance to the Cabinet Room in 10 Downing Street.

The National Security Council meeting was first, and there were a range of heavyweight items on the agenda. Most of these did not require a major Treasury input, but I listened carefully and reread my brief in case I was put on the spot by the Prime Minister or one of his colleagues.

The Prime Minister chaired the meeting, and present were senior Cabinet ministers, the heads of the security services, and senior members of the armed forces. I watched David Cameron chair the meeting crisply, concisely, and with a clear command of all of the topics being discussed. I concluded that he was not only rather enjoying being Prime Minister, but appeared to be rather good at it. Nick Clegg also made some important contributions, and there was a distinct sense of his special role within the government and the respect for the coalition partnership. He spoke as a real partner in government, and not just as a senior Cabinet minister.

At the end of this meeting, after a short break, the full Cabinet met. I spoke briefly on the £6bn cuts programme and to my satisfaction there were no complaints or concerns. Cabinet ministers clearly recognised that given the scale of the fiscal challenge facing us, there would not be much support for anyone who wanted to plead a special case on spending – beyond those we had already agreed.

I pointed out that all departments should now have their savings targets from the Treasury and requested agreement of the numbers by Thursday night. This would then give us Friday to sort out any problems, and the weekend to prepare for the announcement.

Outside the Cabinet, I bumped into Ken Clarke, who had not needed to throw his support behind the proposal due to its universal acceptance. 'Oh, and I agree your figure of £320 million cuts to my budget,' he said. 'Yes, I think it was £325 million,' I pointed out without wishing to seem too pushy. 'Was it 325?' he replied, 'Well, OK, that's fine by me.' If all negotiations were going to be this easy, I concluded, the whole thing could be wrapped up rather quickly.

By the afternoon, progress on the £6bn cuts was going well. I had a brief telephone call with Philip Hammond, the Secretary of State for Transport, to agree various details of his settlement, but I knew that Philip would deliver his required savings come hell or high water, given that he was the previous holder of my post in the Conservative shadow Cabinet.

The news was also good from Chris Huhne's Climate Change department, and it was clear that he felt that he could settle without a meeting and at around the required level. Wales, Northern Ireland and Scotland did not require negotiation, as they were to take the

'Barnett consequentials' of all the other agreed cuts – using a formula to calculate their share of the cuts implemented in England.

Work and Pensions were constructive and settled without a meeting with Iain Duncan Smith being required. Education was agreed quickly in a friendly meeting with Michael Gove, who was clearly relieved by the details of his settlement, and so accepted his proposed cut in full.

Delivering the cuts

The next three days were spent trying to secure the agreement of the tougher departments. Business, Local Government, the Home Office, as well as Culture, Media and Sport, all had concerns of some sort over their settlements. Indeed, Jeremy Hunt, the Culture Secretary had been lobbying me about his budget from the very first Cabinet meeting.

As a consequence, I met the Business Secretary, my own colleague Vince Cable, once and had two more telephone calls with him before we were able to settle. Vince had understandable concerns given the need to support education, retraining and business innovation during tough economic times.

Vince also went on to secure for his department a large slice of the £500 million savings which we had agreed to reinvest. These were earmarked in his department to fund extra investment in the colleges' estate, and a large number of apprenticeships.

The Home Secretary, Theresa May, also came over to the Treasury to meet me. I had been told that the Justice department and the Home Office are rather competitive, and each looks to the other for comparative treatment. I was asking for larger cash savings from the Home Office than from Justice, and ultimately the Home Office figures were not finalised until around 11pm on Friday evening.

Eric Pickles and I settled the Local Government budget after a relatively brief meeting in my office, both of us glancing occasionally at our respective briefing notes in order to grapple with the fiendish complexities of the systems of local government finance.

Treasury officials told me that 'late settlers' play a dangerous game. If the Treasury is getting all the savings it requires from other departments, then the late settlers may find that the pressure on them is rather less. However, if there is still money to be found, then the last to settle can find that they end up with a particularly tough deal.

In the meantime, all departments were embarking on a review of the spending which they had signed off on since 1 January 2010. All sixty schemes signed off since 1 January needed reapproval from the Treasury. Smaller schemes needed reapproval by the relevant department. It seemed extraordinary that with the budget in such a mess the last Labour government had signed off on so much discretionary spending in its last months in power – but it looked like both a 'scorched earth' strategy and an attempt to direct large amounts of money at Labour-held parliamentary constituencies.

For the time being, however, it was the £6bn of in-year cuts that absorbed all of my time.

I was briefed in detail before each meeting with the respective Secretary of State, and looked carefully at the savings we were proposing. We needed to make sure not only that they were deliverable but that they were socially and politically acceptable.

As the hours and days went past, the white chart on the wall in my private office was filling up with numbers. Many people were accepting their full cuts. A few others managed to settle with me at just under the requested figure.

As the cuts came in and were agreed, the Chancellor was notified, and he in turn ensured that the Prime Minister and Deputy Prime Minister were content. I was impressed to see that the Prime Minister went through the savings in great detail, asking questions in some areas, and insisting on more detail before signing off on one or two items. In spite of his close relationship with the Chancellor, David Cameron clearly took his role as First Lord of the Treasury very seriously.

One issue which I did have to discuss with the Chancellor and his advisers was the future of the Child Trust Fund. Liberal Democrat policy was to axe the Child Trust Fund in its entirety and Conservative policy was to scale back payments for those on higher incomes. Given the extent of the fiscal crisis, it was not difficult to persuade George Osborne that the more frugal of our two policies needed to be chosen, and this secured large savings over the parliament as a whole.

By 11pm on Friday we had finally agreed all the figures. The flip-chart in my office showed that we had secured £6.25 billion of cuts – just the right side of our target.

We had also agreed to allocate £500 million of these cuts for other spending to boost the economy – on social housing, business rates relief, apprenticeships and new investment in the colleges' estate.

That gave us the weekend to get the details and the presentation right. On Saturday, I came into the Treasury briefly to check everything was on track, and our hard working civil servants were in the office putting the final touches to all of the paperwork. On Sunday, I was back to personally check through the draft press releases and make sure there were no errors, and on Sunday evening I drafted my own speech for Monday's press conference.

Monday 24 May 2010

Wielding the axe

I was up early again and I went into my office in 1 Parliament Street to make final adjustments to the statement which I had to make that morning on the £6.25 billion of spending cuts.

The announcement was due to be a joint one by both George Osborne and me, and it was scheduled to take place in the huge courtyard in the middle of the Treasury building. Fortunately, the day was sunny and warm. George and I had a brief meeting in his office, and then we walked downstairs and out into the Treasury courtyard.

Two rostrums had been erected against one wall of the courtyard, and in front of us were the massed ranks of the British media, seated. It all seemed rather presidential.

Treasury officials seemed to be hanging out of every window around the courtyard to watch our performance.

George Osborne made an opening statement setting out the big picture of the cuts.

I then had the job of filling in the detail, of persuading the sceptical journalists that it all added up. It seemed to me that I needed to dare to be dull. And I was. I read out a long list of each department and the cuts that each would receive. As I did so, the sun gradually moved across the courtyard and eventually began to fall on the watching journalists.

As I looked out across the assembled media faces I could see the studied interest of the economic commentators, and then my eye caught the presence of some of the sketch writers, such as the *Mail*'s amusing and deadly Quentin Letts. A breeze blew fairly strongly across the rostrum in front of me, and I was suddenly aware of the real risk that my speech, or at least a part of it, would blow away in front of me.

This was the only copy we had available, and even the disappearance of a page would have a somewhat unfortunate affect on the impression of solidity and assurance that George and I wanted to convey. So I grasped the pages more firmly, and began to concentrate on filing away the old pages at the back of my pile of paperwork as I read on.

I spelt out that we could not afford to continue to increase public borrowing at the rate of £3 billion each week. And, in a phrase designed to please both the City and to reassure the markets, I pointed out that 'public borrowing is only taxation deferred, and it would be deeply irresponsible to continue to accumulate vast debts which would have to be paid off by our children and our grandchildren for decades to come.'

I acknowledged that this announcement was only the first step in a long road to restoring good management of our public finances, and that 'even tougher decisions await us in the Budget and the autumn spending review if we are to restore responsibility after the years of Labour extravagance and mismanagement'.

I then announced that we had exceeded the £6bn target that we had set ourselves, and that we were cutting a total of £6.260bn – £260m more than originally targeted.

And then there was the long list of spending cuts: 'Department for Transport: £683m. Communities and Local Government: £780m. Local Government DEL: £405m. Business: £836m. Home Office:

£367m. Department for Education: £670m. Ministry of Justice: £325m. Law Officers' Departments: £18m. Foreign Office: £55m. Department for Energy and Climate Change: £85m. Environment, Food and Rural Affairs: £162m. Culture, Media and Sport: £88m. Work and Pensions: £535m. Chancellor's Departments: £451m. Cabinet Office: £79m. Devolved Administrations: £704m.'

Michael White of the *Guardian* wrote that I delivered the list of figures with the 'enthusiasm of a trainee bingo caller'.

I glanced down into the media seats and noted that half seemed fascinated with the sheer detail of it all, while the others appeared to be glazing over. The element of glaze increased as I expanded first on the impact on the Devolved Administrations, and the additional flexibilities that they would be given, and then on the reduction of local government ring-fencing. There can be few people who are not bored rigid by the details of local government finance.

Some of the journalists, not least the sketch writers, then bucked up a little as I came to some of the more media-friendly parts of the announcement – including cuts in ministerial pay, ministerial cars and first-class travel. I announced that we would seek to make savings of at least a third in the cost of the government car service. 'Most ministers', I said, 'can no longer expect to have a dedicated car or driver. Ministers will be expected to walk or take public transport where possible, or use a pooled car. The pooling of cars will allow big savings to be made.' Reflecting on my own experience, I hoped that it would be somewhat easier to implement these cuts than I had actually found.

I then announced the details of our plan to axe the entire Child Trust Fund – which would save around £2.5 billion over the parliament. No longer would we be conning children that they were richer, by going out and borrowing money to give to them at age eighteen, after which they would have to pay higher taxes to pay off the public borrowing incurred to fund the scheme.

I finished by promising to 'cut with care', and made a number of 'good news' announcements. The first was to confirm our decision to protect the budgets for schools, Sure Start and 16–19 year-old education. The second was to announce that those on incomes of less than £21,000 per annum would be exempt from the Civil Service pay freeze.

Then I announced that in withdrawing the Child Trust Fund, we would do more to help disabled children, with extra money each year to be spent providing respite breaks for severely disabled children. This was a particular wish of the Prime Minister himself.

Finally, I announced that we had decided to allocate £500m of the £6.25bn in 2010/11 to measures investing in the continuing economic recovery. The largest portion of this spending was being secured by the Business department – £200m in 2010/11. This meant that their net spending reduction was to be scaled back from £836m to £636m. To help deliver up to 40,000 adult apprenticeship starts, £150m was to be used, and an extra £50m was set aside to help fund capital investment in those FE colleges most in need. An additional £170m was earmarked to fund investment in social rented housing in 2010/11, to help deliver 4,500 social housing starts.

I finally finished my speech, and George Osborne and the gathered media relaxed and looked relieved. We then took a few questions, turned and marched off, checking that our microphones were no longer switched on as we took the lift back up to the Chancellor's office.

I then did a round of media interviews, taking a little longer than planned as a consequence of not using the ministerial car to get to the Millbank media centre.

Meanwhile, the markets seemed reassured by the announcement. The economic credibility which we thought it vital for the new coalition to secure had clearly been delivered.

Tuesday 25 May 2010

Preparing for the Budget

The reaction to our announcement of cuts seemed to be generally favourable, though many commentators concentrated on the tougher decisions to come. They were right to do so. Our thinking was also moving swiftly on to the Emergency Budget, now set to take place in under a month on 22 June.

Arguably this would be the most important day of the parliament, as George Osborne would have to set out his fiscal targets, borrowing forecasts and the overall public spending envelope for the whole parliament. We would also need to take some tough decisions on taxation. Our thoughts now turned to these challenges.

I was particularly determined to carry out my own shadow spending review within the Treasury in the next ten days, so I could make an assessment of what scale of spending cuts would be consistent with delivering the kind of service levels we wanted to see.

I was determined not to set the overall public spending levels without cross-checking what the implications would be for each major part of government, to make sure that what we were doing was deliverable.

I did not, therefore, see my role merely as that of an 'axeman' – anyone can just slash planned spending levels. I wanted lower public spending totals but so we could still deliver on our key commitments on education, the NHS, pensions and other priority services.

The Cabinet met again this morning, and George and I thanked ministers for their co-operation, while warning that the toughest decisions were yet to come. Nick Clegg made a particular point of flagging up his concern that we should be sensitive to those parts of the UK with particular dependence on public sector employment. The Prime Minister and George Osborne agreed that this was important and that we would commission work to see what could be done to help.

In the morning we had the State Opening of Parliament, which I went over for. I was going to watch the Queen's Speech debate in the afternoon, but the House was so full that I took the excuse to go back to the Treasury to get on with some work.

I also spoke at a meeting of Treasury officials from the spending directorate, joking that my eyes were set on a date in July when I would no longer be the shortest serving Chief Secretary. I noted that Thomas Boardman, Chief Secretary in 1974, had served for barely two months. It was a joke I would soon come to regret.

Wednesday 26 May 2010

A Commons debut

This morning I was in meetings with Treasury officials to look forward to the next spending review and to see what cuts might be deliverable.

I was then told that Alistair Darling, now Labour's shadow Chancellor, had put down an urgent question on our cuts announcement from Monday. I had a strong suspicion that the urgent question would be granted by the Speaker, given the importance of the announcement and the fact that it could not be debated in the House on Monday. But we did not receive confirmation of the urgent statement until around 11.30am, and it was due for a response at 12.30pm.

I felt a little nervous, as the Chancellor was tied up in other meetings, and this would be my first ever appearance at the despatch box. On the other hand, not having much notice at least meant that there wasn't a lot of time to worry. Ben, my speechwriter, did a quick adaptation of my Monday statement, although unfortunately the printer then proceeded to jam, and I eventually had to rush over to the House with little time to spare, and with a heavily annotated earlier version of the statement to read from.

The House was surprisingly full, both on the government and Labour side. I was particularly reassured that so many Conservative MPs seemed to be present to offer their support, as well as a good swathe of Lib Dems.

I took an hour of questions and rather enjoyed it all. When governments have just moved to the opposition benches their hearts really aren't in it, and it is all too easy to blame them for every existing deficiency that can be identified.

Dennis Skinner, the veteran Labour MP, ranted at me towards the end. But he was not effective and apparently did not like my reply. Ann Treneman of *The Times* claimed that he mouthed 'P*** off!' to my considered response to his question, though it is recorded by Hansard as 'Get Out!', so doubtless that is what was said.

After this baptism of fire, I received generous messages of support from Lib Dem and Conservative MPs, and I then made my way back to the Treasury. I returned to my office in the Treasury feeling satisfied with my first performance as a Treasury minister. I would have been rather less elated if I had known that it was also to be my last.

Thursday 27 May 2010

The Spending Review begins

I was in early again Thursday morning, at around 7am, and was pleasantly surprised by the favourable coverage of my first despatch box performance, with articles in many of the newspapers.

Not all of it would necessarily be welcomed amongst my Lib Dem colleagues. Simon Hoggart of the *Guardian* claimed that: 'The Tories were beside themselves with pink pleasure. They had perhaps expected any Lib Dem to be a feeble milquetoast who could no more crush a spending programme than drown a little girl's kitten. Instead they had someone who made Lizzie Borden look like Pollyanna.'

The *Financial Times* was more measured, but still reported that: 'Defence of cuts wins Tory plaudits for Laws'. *The Times* reported one Conservative MP as saying: 'He's the biggest Tory in the Cabinet', which is perhaps not what my colleagues were wanting to hear, but had in many cases always feared.

It was to be another day of meeting with Treasury officials to discuss the cuts that were deliverable in each departmental area. I had started with the department of Work and Pensions, and was surprised to discover that this was one area where the previous Labour government seemed to have made no efforts at all to find savings, whereas their plans for other departments were already quite tough.

I met with defence experts within the Treasury and we went through each area in turn to consider possible savings. We still had a huge programme of work to do if I was to get through every area by Thursday week, as I had promised to write a detailed paper on the scope for spending cuts for the Chancellor to take with him to read on a trip to the Far East.

I considered asking teams to come in to see me on the Sunday and on the Bank Holiday Monday. But this would have badly disrupted the plans of many civil servants for the long weekend, and I felt that this was neither fair nor necessary. In any case, I made plans myself to work on the Sunday and Monday on the first draft of my paper.

On Thursday afternoon, I had a meeting with the Chancellor in Downing Street to talk about the Budget, and we came to some detailed interim agreements on the scale of spending cuts needed, on a possible increase in VAT and plans for pay control along with a commission to look into public sector pensions. I left my office in the Treasury late on Thursday evening. I was not to know it, but I had worked my last day as a Treasury minister.

That evening I had agreed to appear on BBC's *Question Time*, but the Downing Street press office objected to the BBC line-up of Alastair Campbell, Piers Morgan, and Sir Max Hastings. They considered that there should be a Labour MP, and not simply two Labour supporting journalists.

But *Question Time* refused to budge, so I was given the evening off. There was a minor row about the whole matter that night, when Alastair Campbell chose to reveal that I was the minister who was due to attend, but I declined to comment. On the whole, *Question Time* tends to get the better of these clashes with the government, and simply puts on another panellist who it thinks the government would least like to see represent them. When Labour was in power it was often Tony Benn. On this occasion John Redwood was invited on.

A resignation

On Friday morning, 28 May, I returned to my Yeovil constituency office. I was contacted at around 11am by the *Daily Telegraph* about my private life, my sexuality and my parliamentary expenses. It was undoubtedly the toughest time of my life, made all the more testing by having to discuss in a few short hours and over a telephone line an issue which I had always kept private from my family and closest friends.

I was given strong support by my party colleagues and by senior members of the coalition government, but I felt that I could not remain Chief Secretary while dealing both with such sensitive personal issues and with the connected issue of my expense arrangements. After a stressful and emotional thirty-six hours, I resigned from the Cabinet on Saturday evening, after driving up from Somerset to the Treasury to make the announcement. This was my decision alone, and one I would have taken more swiftly without the support and representations of senior political friends and colleagues.

At the Treasury I made a brief statement, looking exactly as I felt: shattered. I then published the following letter of resignation:

Dear Prime Minister,

The last 24 hours have been very difficult and distressing for me, and I have been thinking carefully about what action I should take in the interests of the Government, my constituents and – most important of all – those whom I love. I am grateful for the strong support which I have received from my friends, family, and from you, the Deputy Prime Minister and the Chancellor. This support has been incredibly important, but nonetheless, I have decided that it is right to tender my resignation as Chief Secretary to the Treasury. I have done so for three reasons.

Firstly, I do not see how I can carry on my crucial work on the Budget and Spending Review while I have to deal with the private and public implications of recent revelations.

At this important time the Chancellor needs, in my own view, a Chief Secretary who is not distracted by personal troubles. I hardly need say how much I regret having to leave such vital work, which I feel all my life has prepared me for.

Secondly, while my recent problems were caused by my desire to keep my sexuality secret, the public is entitled to expect politicians to act with a sense of responsibility. I cannot now escape the conclusion that what I have done was in some way wrong, even though I did not gain any financial benefit from keeping my relationship secret in this way.

Finally, and most importantly, I have an overriding responsibility to those I love most, and who I feel I have exposed to scrutiny in this way. I have pursued a political career because of my sense of public duty, but I have too often put this before the interests of those I love most. It is time to redress the balance. I want to apologise to my constituents for falling below the standards that they are entitled to expect from me. The job of being a constituency MP is no less important to me than my Cabinet responsibilities. I shall ensure that I co-operate fully with the Parliamentary Standards Commissioner in the review that I have requested. I intend to consider carefully over the period ahead how I can best serve the interests of my Yeovil constituency, which I care so passionately about.

It has been a great honour to serve however briefly in your Government and I will remain its strong supporter.

Yours sincerely,

David Laws

The Prime Minister responded:

Dear David,

Thank you for your letter tendering your resignation from the Government, which I accept with sadness.

The last 24 hours must have been extraordinarily difficult and painful for you.

You are a good and honourable man. I am sure that, throughout, you have been motivated by wanting to protect your privacy rather than anything else. Your decision to resign from the Government demonstrates the importance you attach to your integrity.

In your short time at the Treasury, you have made a real difference, setting the Government on the right path to tackle the deficit which poses such a risk to our economy.

I hope that, in time, you will be able to serve again as I think it is absolutely clear that you have a huge amount to offer our country.

Yours,

David

Danny Alexander MP was immediately appointed as my successor as Chief Secretary, and Michael Moore MP took over from Danny as Secretary of State for Scotland. Danny made a magnificent start as Chief Secretary, and quickly swept aside any doubts over his economic experience. So the work of the Treasury has gone on very smoothly without me. We all discover some time in life that none of us is indispensable.

Postscript

The coalition: its origins and prospects

Origins

The events of 6–12 May 2010 changed British politics and over-turned commonly held expectations about the relationships be-tween political parties. It is, of course, much too early to assess the long-term political implications of the coalition between the Liberal Democrats and the Conservatives, but it is difficult to believe that the dynamics that the coalition creates will not be of significance beyond the current parliament. The choices made on those few days in early May 2010 mean that the organism which is British politics will now grow and develop in ways which could not previously have been anticipated.

On 7 May, in his telephone call with Nick Clegg, Gordon Brown said that 'this is a moment of opportunity which will not return'. We were certainly conscious that the decisions we were taking in those pressured hours would shape not just the present parliament, but the future of British politics over the next couple of decades.

Few politicians and commentators had thought that a coalition between the Lib Dems and Conservatives was likely or even possible, and for three decades the expectation had been that if there was to be a coalition at Westminster it would be a 'progressive' coalition of the 'centre-left' between the Labour Party and the Lib Dems.

Such a coalition could have been established at any time between 1997 and 2010. It would certainly have changed the face of British politics. But the prospect was killed off by three factors: the scale of Tony Blair's victory in 1997, which made Liberal Democrat support unnecessary; the tribalism and lack of vision of leading figures in the Labour Party, including Gordon Brown, John Prescott and Jack Straw; and Labour's failure to replace Gordon Brown as leader from 2008–10, when it had become obvious that he would lead his party to election defeat, which helped ensure that Labour had too few seats to establish a viable coalition in 2010.

Of course, the fading prospects of a Lib Dem–Labour coalition did not mean that there was any inevitability at all about the formation of a Lib Dem–Conservative coalition. Indeed, for years, the two parties had been the bitterest of enemies at Westminster, and regarded each other with mutual suspicion and hostility.

In spite of the claims by some in the Labour Party, there was no Lib Dem leadership 'plot' to deliver the party into coalition with the Conservatives, either before the general election or during the negotiations. Instead, the decisions that we made were based on judgements about how best to deliver on our key policy priorities, how to deliver a government which could act strongly in the national interest and on hard-headed, rational judgements about promoting the party's long-term influence and effectiveness.

Indeed, as I have explained in this account, our pre-election planning for the 2010 general election was based on a central expectation that while a coalition was likely to be the best outcome for the country and the party, this was likely to prove impossible to deliver. We expected the Conservatives to emerge from the election as the largest party, but we did not expect them to compromise enough on key policy issues – including creating the opportunity for progress on electoral reform – to make a coalition possible.

Our working assumption was that the most likely outcome in the event of a hung parliament was a confidence and supply agreement with the Conservative Party, with the only question being how long such an arrangement might last. The clear risk was that it might not last long and that the Conservatives would seek a full mandate in an autumn 2010 election.

So how was it that the coalition formed took the political and media class so much by surprise? How did we find ourselves in a position on that evening of 11 May when the Parliamentary Party voted, without one voice of active dissent, for a full-scale coalition with the Conservative Party?

This political earthquake was so great that its cause cannot be attributed to one factor alone. It was, instead, the simultaneous coming together of a number of influences which succeeded in moving the tectonic plates of politics.

Some of these factors were short-term in nature, relating to the arithmetic of the new parliament, and the state of the British and international economy. The other important influences were the developments within the three main parties over the previous few years.

The single most important factor was clearly the arithmetic in the House of Commons. It is obvious that without a hung parliament there would have been no coalition. But the balance of the new parliament played a particularly crucial role in delivering a Lib Dem–Conservative coalition. The Conservatives were, clearly, the largest party, and only the Conservatives therefore offered the possibility of having a government with a strong and clear majority.

However, the Conservatives had fewer seats than Labour and the Liberal Democrats combined, and this meant that although a 'traffic-light' coalition looked unlikely, it was not impossible. This was to prove a crucial factor in the negotiations. Although David Cameron had strongly hinted in his 7 May statement, and in his discussions that day with Nick Clegg, that he preferred a full coalition to a looser confidence and supply agreement, it was not clear that he was prepared to pay the price for delivering a full coalition, which would be a referendum on voting reform.

When we failed to reach agreement with the Conservatives on voting reform, we both got as far as agreeing a draft confidence and supply arrangement to take to our parliamentary parties. Although we cannot be certain, it seems likely that this would have been the best Conservative offer and the likely post-election outcome, had there not been a real alternative on offer – following the resignation of Gordon Brown and the commencement of formal Lib Dem–Labour talks.

In any case, there would have been no Lib Dem–Conservative coalition without the guarantee of a referendum on voting reform.

The traffic-light coalition was always going to be a difficult and risky option, because it would have delivered no overall majority in the House of Commons. Although a coalition of the Labour Party and Lib Dems, with some informal agreement with the DUP, Greens, SDLP and even the Welsh Nationalists was theoretically possible, no one could be confident that it would be effective in delivering good government. Instead, with the agreement of six or more parties needing to be secured for each sensitive decision, the likelihood is that the traffic light would remain permanently on red.

But the possibility of the traffic-light coalition working, or at least being tried, wasn't zero either. And there were substantial risks for the Conservatives in remaining in opposition – not least after failing to capitalise on the economic crisis and Gordon Brown's ineffective leadership of his party. The possibility of striking deals with both other parties clearly maximised the Liberal Democrat negotiating leverage. It meant that the Conservatives had to offer an AV referendum or risk staying on the opposition benches. This in turn meant that the Liberal Democrats were offered a deal which could not easily be turned down.

A small difference in the election result could have had major consequences. A Lib Dem–Labour coalition would have delivered 315 seats to the Conservatives 306 seats. But if the Conservatives had won five more seats from Labour on 6 May, a Lib–Lab option would have looked impossible. Under such circumstances our bargaining position would have been significantly reduced and David Cameron might have felt no need to offer an AV referendum. On such thin strings did the possibility of a Lib Dem–Conservative coalition dangle.

There was a second, short-term, factor which argued for coalition rather than a more informal arrangement. This was the state of the markets, the economy and the UK public finances. Bluntly, we clearly needed a government which could take the hard decisions to bring the deficit under control. Without a credible coalition government, there would have been doubts about the ability of any single party to force through the tough decisions needed, particularly on public spending.

The markets would have responded very badly to a weak government, and the crisis which had taken hold in Greece would have been in danger of spreading to other countries – not only Italy, Ireland, Portugal and Spain, but the United Kingdom too. Although we declined to see the Governor of the Bank of England, Mervyn

King, during the election talks, I am sure this message about the importance of stability and economic credibility is one he would have wished to deliver.

Without a credible government, with tough choices ducked and the markets in turmoil, a second election could not have been long delayed. A minority government could have been toppled at any time and would probably have had to seek a new mandate in the autumn. No party could be sure of being more popular in the autumn of 2010 than they were in May 2010. David Cameron surely realised this and knew that he needed a clear majority to carry through the tough spending cuts and tax increases. A coalition with the Liberal Democrats could deliver that strong majority and also would involve sharing the responsibility for the economic pain with another party.

For the Liberal Democrats, we were always clear in our own minds that failing to deliver a strong and stable government under these circumstances would have risked not just a second general election in the autumn of 2010, but big losses of Lib Dem seats if we were seen as being to blame for failing to act responsibly.

But this was not just an issue of short-term political calculation. We also knew that the international evidence was that long term coalitions, not temporary and loose arrangements, are necessary to deliver major fiscal consolidations. And we felt a sense of responsibility at such a time to deliver a strong government for the country, in the national interest.

So, the economic environment meant that both the Liberal Democrats and the Conservatives had an interest in delivering a strong and stable government. This was clearly in the national interest, but it was also almost certainly in the political interest of both parties.

The balance of the parties in parliament, and the state of the economy, were the particular factors which paved the way for the Lib Dem–Conservative coalition.

But, equally important, were the developments in the three political parties since the 2005 general election. In all three parties there had, since 2005, been changes in leadership and political orientation. It is, indeed, possible that without these changes in each and every one of these three parties, the present coalition would not have been established.

All three parties had changed leaders since 2005. Each change made a Lib Dem–Conservative coalition more likely. It is difficult to imagine a Lib Dem–Conservative coalition government being formed if the Conservative Party had been led by Michael Howard, and the Liberal Democrats by either Charles Kennedy or Menzies Campbell. The election of the deeply tribal Gordon Brown also made a Lib Dem–Labour coalition less likely than with almost any alternative Labour leader.

The election of David Cameron as leader of the Conservative Party was clearly very significant. Ever since his election as leader, David Cameron had been seeking to lead his party back onto the centre ground. And he had made a specific pitch for liberal votes by emphasising issues such as the environment and civil liberties. This 'modernisation' was far from complete by 2010, with quite traditional Conservative positions in areas such as Europe and taxation – but there was a notable change in tone and substance nonetheless.

And if the relationships between senior Conservatives and Liberal Democrats were hardly 'close', neither were they marked by the same degree of mutual antagonism as had been the case in the past. David Cameron had talked openly of 'Liberal Conservatism', and of course he had made some modest attempts to attract Liberal Democrats to his party – including the approach he made to me through George Osborne.

It was clear after the general election that he saw the failure to secure an outright Conservative majority as both a threat and an opportunity, and he seized the opportunity boldly. His public and private statements on 7 May reflected a desire for coalition with the Liberal Democrats, something difficult to imagine the former Conservative leader, Michael Howard, sharing or being capable of delivering.

The shift in the positioning and tone of the Conservative Party also made it much easier to secure a policy agreement for the coalition. We were negotiating with a moderate and reasonable group of Conservatives, who were willing to make real concessions to reach agreement, and who behaved in an honest and constructive way, rapidly building trust.

Indeed, the relationship during the talks between the senior Lib Dems and Conservatives was notably better than that between the Lib Dems and the Labour 'top brass'. This was perhaps even more the case amongst the party leaders than their negotiating teams. And in politics, as elsewhere, relationships and trust matter.

While the Conservatives had shifted towards the centre ground of British politics since 2005, the Liberal Democrats had also moved decisively from the left to the centre, under the leadership of Nick Clegg.

The earlier generation of Lib Dem leaders and senior MPs and peers were defined to a large degree by their opposition to the Conservatives. Many senior Lib Dems had come to the party from Labour and through the SDP, after Labour's 'lurch to the left' in the early 1980s. And the Conservative government of 1979–97 had given Lib Dems a lot to be angry about, not least in the growing social divisions and inequalities of both outcome and opportunity.

But after thirteen years of Labour government, many Lib Dems were now as disenchanted with Labour as they had earlier been with the Conservatives. The war in Iraq, the undermining of civil liberties, the endless centralising and micro-managing, the failure to embrace radical constitutional reform or action on the environment, and the lack of progress on social mobility and improving public services, all gave Liberal Democrats plenty to oppose and criticise.

There was also within the Liberal Democrats a growing emphasis on the party's liberal roots, not least on economic policy, and this was expressed in the influential *Orange Book*, a collection of essays I edited with Paul Marshall back in 2004. Although the *Orange Book* provoked a strong backlash from small c 'conservative' Lib Dem activists, it helped to shift the centre of gravity in the party and led to a move away from unquestioning support for the producer interest in public services, from 'big government' solutions, and from 'tax and spend' as the answer to all economic and social problems.

The election of Nick Clegg as the new Lib Dem leader in 2007 was of particular importance. Nick was the first leader for decades who felt genuinely equidistant in his attitude to the other two parties. He was as critical of Labour on civil liberties and centralisation as he was of the Conservatives on Europe and some aspects of social policy.

Under Nick's leadership, the assumption that we could only do a 'deal' with Labour was no longer valid. Any partnership with another party would now be based solely on a hard-headed assessment of our ability to promote Lib Dem policies in government, rather than a presumption in favour of Labour as the natural partner.

This change of leader and the reassertion of liberal principles, particularly on the economy and on public service delivery, combined with the experience of thirteen years of Labour, meant that the Lib Dem policy prospectus shifted significantly over the last decade.

Out went higher taxes, and in came tax cuts for those on low incomes. Out went a commitment to a higher top rate tax of 50%, and in came a closing of unfair tax reliefs. Out went 'tax and spend', and in came 'save to invest'. Out went the automatic promotion of the producer interest in public services, and in came more focus on the consumers of public services. Out went a defence of all state-run services, and in came privatisation in areas such as the Royal Mail. Out went opposition to all provider reform in the NHS and education, and in came policies such as support for sponsor-managed schools.

There were still some areas where the party was resistant to giving up on long-held policy comfort blankets – not least in its ongoing support for the abolition of university tuition fees. But at least the party's spending priority was now shifted to investment in a pupil premium to support disadvantaged young people at school, rather than focusing available cash on better-off university graduates, where it would make little impact on improving social mobility.

The key to these changes of policy was not, as some feared, that they reflected any downgrading of our commitment to a fairer Britain, indeed precisely the opposite was the case. The changes reflected instead a reassertion of liberal economics combined with a refocusing of available resources on tackling real disadvantage, rather than providing election-winning gimmicks.

This policy realignment was hugely important in making a coalition with the Conservatives viable, though it was not inspired by this aspiration.

If we had fought the 2010 general election on the 2005 manifesto, it would have been much tougher to reach policy agreements with the Conservatives, given our previous policies on free personal care for the elderly, immediate abolition of tuition fees, higher taxes and opposition to most reforms in health and education.

The final factor which led to a Lib Dem–Conservative coalition was the nature of the 2010 Labour Party itself, and, as mentioned, the changes in its leadership since 2005. For thirteen years, the Labour Party had had the opportunity to frame a centre-left governing coalition, and for most of this time they faced Lib Dem leaders who would have leapt at this opportunity. But Labour dithered and delayed over electoral reform, and failed to establish the contacts with the new generation of Lib Dems that would be necessary to build up trust and to frame a coherent strategy. By the time Gordon Brown's conversion to the merits of coalition and electoral reform came about, it was one minute past midnight, and too late to make these changes a practical possibility. It was, indeed, a deathbed political conversion.

This was surely, for Labour, an extraordinary missed opportunity. Here was a chance to marginalise the Conservatives and reunite the centre-left. Here were three Lib Dem leaders in a row – Paddy Ashdown, Charles Kennedy and Menzies Campbell – who, under the right circumstances and in exchange for electoral reform, would have enthusiastically worked to reframe politics.

And if it wasn't necessary to secure Lib Dem votes to sustain Labour in office in 1997 or 2001 after those landslide victories, it was obvious in 2005 and 2007 that eventually only a Lib–Lab agreement would keep Labour in power.

Indeed, if Gordon Brown had had more self-awareness he would surely have known that the odds were that he would not be able to hold together the broad electoral coalition that Tony Blair had forged, at least until it was shattered by the war in Iraq.

But what did Gordon Brown do when he became Prime Minister? Instead of embarking on serious talks with the Lib Dems, and leading a debate on PR, he did next to nothing. In fact, he raised Lib Dem suspicions, and hackles, by trying to 'poach' some senior Lib Dems in 2007 to adorn his government and undermine our distinctiveness – Paddy Ashdown was even offered the post of Northern Ireland Secretary.

And this attempt to bring Lib Dems into his government was done in such a ham-fisted way that it even succeeded in undermining one of the Prime Minister's best Lib Dem friends – Menzies Campbell, who was then leader of the party. There could hardly have been an approach more likely to sow suspicion and less likely to deliver results.

Gordon Brown was a tribal politician who was never going to reach out to the Liberal Democrats until it was too late, and who was perceived by his party as an election loser for the last two years of the 2005–10 parliament. Almost any alternative Labour leader would have delivered a better result in 2010 – certainly Alan Johnson or David Miliband. But Labour flunked its chance to change its leader and so lost the real chance to secure power.

But even on 10 May, there was still a slim chance of Labour clinging on. Gordon Brown's decision to resign as Labour leader cleared the way for serious talks with the Liberal Democrats to begin.

And the Liberal Democrats took these talks seriously, not only because they strengthened our bargaining position in relation to the Conservatives, but because we wanted to explore whether a coalition with Labour was really possible and desirable. However, with the notable exceptions of Andrew Adonis and Peter Mandelson (as well as Gordon Brown), there seemed to be few Labour figures willing to work to make the coalition option a reality in May 2010.

David Miliband lay low. Alistair Darling disappeared into the Treasury. And Ed Balls, Ed Miliband and Harriet Harman seemed determined to wreck or undermine the very talks which they were engaged in. Yet again it was Labour, not the Liberal Democrats, who betrayed the hopes that many people once held out a centre-left alliance.

Although Gordon Brown's resignation cleared away one huge obstruction to a coalition, it also left a leaderless Labour Party now split between a minority who wanted to do a deal with the Lib Dems, and the majority who wanted to go into opposition, and leave the Lib Dems and Conservatives to take tough decisions on the deficit.

So Gordon Brown's deathbed conversion to the benefits of a Lib–Lab partnership was too little and too late. And when he resigned, he fired the starting gun on a leadership election which rapidly brought out the most tribal of Labour instincts.

Since the coalition negotiations, some in the Labour Party have tried to claim that a small group of Liberal Democrats – perhaps Nick Clegg, Danny Alexander and me – were always determined to deliver a coalition with the Conservatives rather than with Labour. That is simply untrue, as the account in this book reveals.

What made us conclude that a Labour coalition was impossible were three factors: the failure of the Labour team to make significant concessions to us on key priority areas, including tax, schools funding and the economy; the increasing signs that their party was split both on the desirability of coalition and on the crucial issue of the Alternative Vote; and a growing conviction that a Lib–Lab coalition government would fail to command a majority to deliver economic stability, electoral reform, and a coherent programme for government.

It did not help that the relations between senior Liberal Democrat and Labour MPs were so poor – in particular, Nick Clegg and Gordon Brown were never really comfortable with each other, and the 'truculent trio' of Ed Balls, Ed Miliband and Harriet Harman did not inspire the trust or confidence of our negotiating team.

So, it was a range of ingredients that produced the coalition pudding: the balance in the House of Commons which strengthened our negotiating position; the economic crisis that meant that stability was needed; the movement in the policy positions of both the Conservative and Liberal Democrat parties to a more liberal agenda; and the failure of Labour to take seriously a centre-left realignment after 2007, combined with their failure to deal seriously with us after 6 May 2010.

Prospects

This book is being written only five months after the coalition government was established, so it would be rash to attempt a comprehensive evaluation of what has been achieved to date, and what the prospects are for the coalition in the years ahead. The government is already navigating choppy waters and dealing with difficult issues such as the deficit and university tuition fees.

But it is fair to say that so far the coalition has developed much more smoothly than almost any informed observer might have thought possible. There is clearly a strong relationship between David Cameron and Nick Clegg, and the importance of this cannot be underestimated – it sets the tone for the government at every level.

The trust and confidence which was built up between the Conservative and Liberal Democrat negotiating teams during the coalition talks has also been crucial, and has continued into government.

There are, of course, controversial issues for the coalition, but these are as likely to be within each individual party rather than between the two. Indeed, the relationship between the two parties has been astonishingly positive and constructive, and notable so far for the absence both of significant rows and of the culture of in-fighting and spinning which marked the Blair–Brown admin-istration. It helps not just that David Cameron and Nick Clegg work well together, but that we now also have a Prime Minister and Chancellor who can talk to each other, and who are such close allies. The determination to make the coalition work is shared by all of the administration's 'big guns'.

On the policy front, both parties have had to make concessions, and these have stuck. The Liberal Democrats have signed up to tough action on the economy, and the Conservatives have agreed to action to invest in key services such as schools and ensure that as much as possible is done to protect those on lower incomes.

What is striking so far is the public's enthusiasm for the idea of the coalition.

In the past the assumption has been that England, and Britain, does not love coalitions. It is not difficult to imagine why. Coalitions require compromise, and compromise can easily lead to division or muddle.

The public no doubt like to see politicians work together, and people understand that the situation the country faced earlier in 2010 could so easily have been a national economic disaster, had the parties not been willing to put aside the usual partisanship and reach out to form the coalition.

Perhaps the public also like the policy compromises that the coali-tion has had to make, which have required both parties to drop some of their less popular or more extreme policies.

Indeed, David Cameron and Nick Clegg have challenged their own parties' naturally tribal assumptions, by arguing that the coalition is actually a better option for the British people than the programme of either party taken by itself.

The foreword to the coalition's 'Programme for Government' states bluntly that: 'We have found that a combination of our parties' best ideas and attitudes has produced a programme for government that is more radical and comprehensive than our individual manifestos.' That is a striking claim for the leaders of two party 'tribes' to make.

What is almost certainly true is that the compromises on policy made by both parties have produced joint positions which are often closer to the centre of gravity of the British people. For example on taxation, the Liberal Democrat policy on raising the personal tax allowance is arguably more relevant to more citizens than the Conservative policy of raising the inheritance tax threshold on very large estates.

On Europe, the combining of the policies of both parties has led to a rejection both of further integration and of an active antagonism towards the European Union. This probably reflects rather well the independent-minded but pragmatic position of the British people.

More generally, the coalition has managed, not least on economic policy, to blend toughness with tenderness in a way which many of the public will find attractive.

The economic liberalism of the Conservative Party and the social liberalism of the Liberal Democrats have been convincingly combined. And the liberals in both parties are now firmly in charge – creating a real possibility of a government which will be liberal politically, economically, socially and in its attitudes to personal matters.

Of course, some of the greatest challenges were always going to arise beyond the first 'flush' of coalition excitement and novelty. The coalition could hardly have been born in tougher economic times, and it will have to find its feet while deep cuts are made in many areas of public spending. This is most definitely not a benign environment for such a bold British political experiment. It will in particular be challenging to maintain harmony in 2011 and 2012, as the government has to implement some very tough decisions to restore the nation's finances. And, of course, the referendum on voting reform will test the coalition's unity in a more direct way, as coalition MPs campaign on different sides.

Delivering the cuts in public spending is bound to affect the coalition's popularity with the public – notwithstanding the general acceptance of the need to get our finances back in order. But the public does understand the scale and importance of the economic challenge, and people know that there are some tough years to come. The coalition will be judged by its ability to address the public sector deficit, and restore the conditions for sound economic growth. Much of this is within our power to determine, and the good start which has been made has restored market confidence and helped to keep interest rates low. However, there is no doubt that not all of the key influences are within our control, and much will depend on the fortunes of the global economy.

It is crucial that the reduction in the deficit is carried out while protecting as far as possible those on low incomes and the key services such as health and education. The coalition needs to go on cutting with care. We will still be spending huge amounts on our public services, and significantly more in real terms than for much of the life of Tony Blair's government.

We need to ensure that even as the tough decisions are taken we continue to hold the NHS, schools and other parts of the public sector accountable for delivering high standards of service – both through increasing consumer power and through other direct forms of accountability.

In these tough times, we need to be clear about our priorities. And we should focus on long-term delivery, and not make Tony Blair's mistake of getting knocked off course by the demand for short-term policy gimmicks. The public are sensible. They are sceptical of the daily launching of new initiatives. They want the government to focus on getting the big decisions right, and that is what we need to do.

On education, health and welfare reform, the direction of travel is good, but we need to focus on getting the big decisions right, and we need to anticipate the defects and criticisms that will emerge in one, two or three years time – and address them now. That requires a degree of pragmatism and reflection, to set alongside a clear philosophical preference for devolving power and dismantling top-down government by diktat. It requires a willingness to be bold where necessary, but also to build on what has worked, rather than forcing change for change's sake.

Deficit reduction and the economy are crucial, and of course not mutually exclusive. But the government's agenda must consist of more than prudent economic management and rather gloomy warnings for people to tighten their belts.

The coalition's effectiveness in retaining public support, and in holding together through the next few difficult years, will depend on having a commonly shared, positive, long-term vision which we are working towards – and a major part of this vision must be to make Britain a fairer place and a society of real opportunity for all citizens.

Liberals in both coalition parties cannot accept a Britain in which life chances are so determined by parental income. Britain increasingly prides itself on being a meritocracy, but – as in the United States of America – we remain a meritocracy where the chances of acquiring merit are hopelessly unequal. Too much still depends on where you were born and how well off your family is. This is a challenge to those in both parties who believe in capitalism and in freedom – and who do not accept that the two need be incompatible.

Of course, the coalition needs to redefine what fairness means. Fairness cannot mean just maintaining people above an arbitrary income line, whatever their personal circumstances. Fairness means giving people the educational and employment opportunities to ensure that they are not dependent on an over-mighty state and trapped in dead-end lives.

Fairness must mean tackling poverty, which is itself a powerful force denying people real opportunities. But fairness also means accepting our responsibilities, and accepting the boundaries that there are to the infringement of each other's liberties. For Gordon Brown, fairness means simply reducing income inequality, however this is delivered. For liberals, fairness cannot be detached from freedom and responsibility.

There are four major domestic challenges for this government, where progress should not merely wait on the restoration of budget discipline.

First, we have to reform and invest in education, to address the scandalous inequalities of outcome and opportunity which scar our society today. We need not argue about whether British society is 'broken' or not. Much of it is not broken, but none of us can regard ourselves as living in an unbroken society while we can see in so many parts of the country the broken estates and stunted lives. This extent and depth of disadvantage anywhere in British society is a challenge and threat to all of society.

That is why the second priority must be to marry the agenda of educational opportunities with new policies on employment, in particular ensuring those who can work do work, and are supported to do so. We cannot address the broken society without addressing the inequalities in employment as well as in education. Ensuring that the right incentives and support are delivered through the tax, benefits, housing and training systems is crucial, and it will not be easy. This requires a coherent long-term vision alongside patient and consistent work. And it requires priority to be given in areas such as tax and housing to policies that will help those who want to stand on their own two feet to do so.

On the NHS, the third major challenge, we have to ensure that the recent improvements in some service standards are maintained and not permitted to slip. We need those NHS managers who have become used to the years of plenty to think more creatively about delivering better services without an annual tidal wave of extra money. And we need reform which empowers the public and not the professionals, and which guarantees that patients can genuinely and effectively hold their service providers to account. We are still a long way from an NHS where the customer is king.

Finally, we have got to turn warm words on the environment into real action. The deficit cannot just be an excuse for delay. On transport, energy generation and use, and on conservation, we need to make big changes that will make a real difference. Again, these things take time, which is why we cannot afford delay.

Later in the parliament, we must hope the tough actions that have been taken now will mean that our public finances are fixed, and there is some light at the end of the tunnel. By that stage, and if we have got the policies right, there will be very little waste left in any part of the public sector. It is then that we will be able to afford to invest again in the priorities – knowing the money will be used effectively because services have been reformed. And we will need to invest. A good education and health service, and first-class transport, do not come cheap. People who pay privately know that, and in a wealthier society people want to spend more on schools and healthcare, not less.

We need to cut waste and improve delivery, but we should never think that good services can be delivered on the cheap. So later in the parliament we will have to make some difficult decisions on sharing the proceeds of economic growth. Of course, if the deficit has been dealt with, we may be able to lighten the tax burden on those on low and middle incomes, who have helped to pay the price of fiscal prudence. And eventually, when we can afford it and when debt is once again falling as a share of the economy, we will want to remove the penal tax rates of up to 50% that can only be justified by the sacrifices which are necessary in these extraordinary times.

But we will also want to pay for better schools, hospitals and transport, too, and we will want to restart some of the projects to restore our public sector estate, which Labour's 50% cuts in capital budgets have put on hold.

The coalition parties will have to talk together about our priorities, and we need to set out our vision beyond these present times of austerity.

Some, of course, will say that the coalition will have ended long before 2014 or 2015, and there are of course many challenges on the way.

Those on the right of the Conservative Party may want a conservatism that is unrestrained by Liberal Democrat values and priorities. And a few in the Liberal Democrats will be inclined to view our period in government as a brief, painful and unpleasant interlude before going back as soon as decently possible to the easy joys of opposition.

But I do not think that is the vision of the coalition party leaders. And both parties have a long- and short- term interest in showing we can deliver, and that we can take the country from the tough times back to the good times. We are in this together, and there are unlikely to be any pain-free cop-outs for those whose stomachs are unsettled by the ride.

At the next general election, of course, the Conservative and Liberal Democrat parties will stand their own candidates in individual seats. The Liberal Democrats could not remain a national political force if we removed our candidates from half the seats in the United Kingdom. The challenge is to give voters more choice and control, not the party managers – the Alternative Vote would, of course, help to give the public this additional choice and influence.

But if a single coalition candidate or a formal coalition 'coupon' is highly unlikely, the electorate will doubtless make their own judgements taking into account the performance of the coalition as a whole, and this is bound to assist incumbent coalition MPs in their existing seats, if the coalition has delivered.

And then what? Back to business as usual? That will depend largely on the electorate – they are the ultimate masters. But it will take many years to deliver on the programme and aspirations which the coalition has set out so far. This is a coalition formed in the tough times of fiscal retrenchment, one which has the potential to be a partnership for the good times too and to deliver the reform and renewal that Britain needs. After the unexpected events of May 2010, however, few people would dare to forecast with confidence how future events will unfold.

Conservative proposals: Saturday 8 May

Political Reform

A. Voting System

In his statement of 7th May, David Cameron said: "I believe we will need an All-Party Committee of Inquiry on political and electoral reform."

During the course of the initial meeting, the Liberal Democrat negotiating team asked how far it would be possible for the Conservative team to "harden up" this proposition.

During the course of the meeting, it was recognised on both sides that we were unlikely to reach an agreement on the preferred electoral system, given that the Conservative Party remains persuaded of the benefits of the first past the post system (despite the effect on the number of Conservative seats at present) whereas the Liberal Democrat Party have long argued for a move to proportional representation.

Given this background, it seems likely that any agreement at this stage will need to focus on process rather than on specific outcomes.

As a result, we have considered how it might be possible for the Conservative team to respond to the request that David Cameron's proposition should be "hardened up" by defining:

a. how the all-Party Committee of Inquiry would operate; and
b. the process that would be followed once the all-Party Committee had reported.

The Operation of the All-Party Inquiry

So far as the all-Party Inquiry is concerned, we now propose that:

a. the Inquiry should be conducted by two representatives of each of the three main parties represented at Westminster, together with a single representative of the minority parties represented at Westminster;
b. the purpose of the Inquiry would not be to identify a single preferred system, but rather to present a menu of options for the voting system and for other political reforms (see Part B below). Any proposition favoured by any of the representatives constituting the Committee would be included within the report;
c. each of the identified options would be presented as a motion suitable for placing immediately on the Order Paper of the House of Commons;
d. the terms of reference of the Committee would mandate the Committee to agree on the options to be presented as motions for the Order Paper by 31st October 2010.

The Process following the report of the All-Party Inquiry

Following the report of the All-Party Inquiry on 31st October 2010, Conservatives and Liberal Democrats would ensure that all options identified by the Committee were placed on the Order Paper for debate and would provide Government time in the House of Commons, to ensure that each of the motions emerging from the Committee were debated and voted upon.

Crucially, Conservatives and Liberal Democrats would ensure – and would call upon other parties to ensure – that voting on each of the motions emerging from the Committee took place on the basis of a free vote.

Further motions would be placed on the Order Paper by the Conservatives and Liberal Democrats. These motions would provide for the House of Commons to vote on the holding of a referendum about any of the motions arising from the Inquiry. Conservative and Liberal Democrat members would again be given a free vote on these further motions, and we would again call on other parties to provide a free vote for their members.

B. Other Political Reform

Conservatives and Liberal Democrats would ensure that the report of the Committee of Inquiry included motions relating to:

a. fixed-term parliaments;

b. the ability of voters to force a by-election for any MP found to have engaged in serious wrong-doing;

c. reducing the number of Members of Parliament.

d. equalising the size of constituency electorates;

e. a largely or wholly elected House of Lords;

f. individual voter registration;

g. rules enabling propositions that obtain large degrees of public support to be debated in the House of Commons; and

h. rules ensuring that England-only (or England and Wales)

legislation has to obtain the support of a majority of Members representing English (or English and Welsh) constituencies.

In relation to each of these motions, Conservatives and Liberal Democrats would hold discussions outside the Committee of Inquiry and would agree on the precise terms of the motions that Conservative and Liberal Democrat representatives would place before the Committee for inclusion in the report of the Inquiry.

In relation to these motions, as opposed to motions on the voting system, Conservative and Liberal Democrat members could be subject to a whipped vote.

Deficit, Schools Spending and Tax Measures

A. General Approach to Deficit Reduction.

In his statement of 7th May, David Cameron said: "No Government will be in the national interest unless it deals with the biggest threat to our national interest – and that is the deficit. We remain completely convinced that starting to deal with the deficit this year is essential."

During the initial meeting, the Conservative team explained our belief that the achievement of a further spending reduction of £6 billion in 2010 would be regarded by the financial markets as a test of whether a Conservative/Liberal Democrat Government was capable of carrying through the necessary deficit reduction plan. This view is shared by the Treasury and the Bank of England.

The Conservative negotiating team also takes the view that reassurance of the financial markets (and hence maintenance of a low interest rate economy) depends on:

a. an explicit agreement between the two parties that the bulk of the structural deficit will be eliminated over the course of the next five years; and

b. a further explicit agreement between the parties that the necessary fiscal tightening will be achieved mainly through spending reduction rather than tax increase.

At present the Conservative position is that the split between spending reduction and tax increase should be 80-20, whereas the Liberal Democrat position is that the split should be closer to 70-30 (as calculated by the independent Institute for Fiscal Studies).

We are prepared to discuss figures between 70-30 and 80-20.

B. Spending Review
General Approach to the Spending Review
During the election the Conservatives promised an emergency budget within 50 days of the election, which would set out:

a. a forecast for the borrowing requirement over the forecast horizon;

b. the overall envelopes for spending and tax revenues over the same period;

c. the composition of any necessary tax measures; and

d. a statement of the Government's fiscal target.

We also said that the economic and fiscal forecasts underpinning the Budget should be independently verified by an interim Office for Budget Responsibility headed by a respected independent figure such as Sir Alan Budd. The Treasury have already made arrangements for this, and we regard this as a crucial step in establishing credibility with financial markets and restoring trust in official forecasts.

The Conservative position is that decisions over the allocation of spending should then be made in a Spending Review over the summer, reporting in the Autumn, These decisions include:

a. the division of spending between DEL and AME, to the extent that this is influenced by policy decisions;
b. the division of DEL between departments, and between current and capital spending within departments; and
c. spending priorities within departments.

We have made only two commitments about the allocation of spending between departments:

a. year on year real increases in health spending (defined as the total DEL limit for the department of health); and
b. meeting the 0.7% of GNI target for Overseas Development Assistance spending by 2013.

The second of these commitments is already agreed between the Conservatives and the Liberal Democrats. We propose that the first commitment – to real terms increases in health spending – should also be part of our agreement.

Pupil Premium and School Spending
Neither the Conservative manifesto nor the Liberal Democrat manifesto makes any commitment over the size or growth rate of the total DCSF budget. However, both manifestos are committed to:

a.   making savings from cutting wasteful spending within DCSF; and
b.   a pupil premium.

Only the Liberal Democrat manifesto puts a number on the size of the pupil premium, of £2.5 billion. The Liberal Democrat negotiating team made it clear that this was additional money, and that they regard this as a crucial aspect of any agreement.

We are prepared to discuss figures for the pupil premium of up to £2.5 billion.

We are also prepared to discuss funding this from outside the schools budget by reductions in spending elsewhere, either within or outside DCSF.

C. Tax Measures

During the initial meeting the Conservative negotiating team explained that avoiding the most damaging part of the planned increase in Employee and Employer National Insurance Contributions was a key component of our election campaign and our economic policy. We therefore wish to maintain this commitment as part of the agreement between the two parties. We note that the approach we would take to avoiding the most damaging part of the NICs increase is to raise NI thresholds, which is consistent with the approach taken to personal taxation by the Liberal Democrats.

The Conservative negotiating team also explained that we support the principle of raising the income tax threshold to £10,000. The issue for us is how this could be financed.

We are prepared to discuss tax measures that would help to finance the raising of the threshold.

We cannot accept the Liberal Democrat proposals for a mansion tax or for increased taxes on pensions saving.

However we are prepared to discuss taxing capital gains on non-business assets at closer to personal income tax rates, provided there is an explicit and generous exemption for entrepreneurial investments in businesses. We will also pursue further anti-avoidance measures.

We are prepared to discuss the relative priority accorded to other tax proposals made by the two parties.

Banking Reform

A. Bank Levy

We have already proposed a levy on banks, and we are prepared to discuss the form or forms that this should take (along the lines of the IMF proposals for a balance sheet levy and/or a Financial Activities Tax on profits and bonuses).

B. A More Competitive Banking System

We are agreed that the banking system needs to be more competitive and that the sale of taxpayer stakes in the banks should be used to achieve this aim.

We also agree on the need for more diverse sources of credit, including mutuals and credit unions, and we have made proposals for a Big Society Bank funded by unclaimed bank deposits.

C. Bank Lending

We agree that constraints on the supply of bank lending to small businesses are a considerable risk to the recovery.

We do not agree with the Liberal Democrat proposals for mandatory lending targets, but we hope to agree on a major loan guarantee scheme to facilitate increased bank lending to small businesses during the recovery.

D. Separating "Casino Banking" from Retail Banking

We already agree that the riskiest investment banking activities should be separated from retail banking. We also agree that this is a complex issue that will take time to resolve, and our preference is for any changes to be made on the basis of international agreement.

We therefore propose, as part of this agreement between our two parties, some form of independent commission into structural reforms of the banking system.

E. Reforming the Regulatory System

We are agreed on the need for regulatory reform. There is disagreement between us on how far this should go. We propose, as a method of resolving this disagreement:

a.   "twin peak" style separation within the FSA of prudential regulation and consumer protection;

b.   the immediate creation of a Financial Policy Committee within the Bank of England responsible for macro-prudential regulation and oversight of micro-prudential regulation, chaired by the Governor and including within its membership both the Chairman of the FSA and the co-chief executive responsible for prudential regulation, as well as external members; and

c.   following the completion of these changes, moving prudential regulation from the FSA to the Bank of England subject to final confirmation by our two parties.

Conservative–Lib Dem confidence and supply agreement: Monday 10 May

"An Offer to the Liberal Democrats of a Confidence and Supply Agreement for a Conservative Minority Administration." (Final Draft: 10th May 2010)

In return for the guarantee of support for a minority Conservative Administration in any confidence vote and in the votes on the supply of finance, as well as the understanding that the minority administration will put before Parliament a programme based on the bulk of the Conservative manifesto, the Conservative Party has agreed the following.

In order to provide stability and confidence in the lasting nature of this agreement, the Government will make provision for fixed Parliaments of four years.

1. Deficit Reduction

On the fundamental issue of the public finances, we commit to:

A significantly accelerated reduction in the structural deficit over the course of a Parliament, with the main burden of deficit reduction borne by reduced spending rather than increased taxes; arrangements that will protect those on low pay and those in most need from the effect of public sector pay constraint and other spending constraints; protection of jobs through the cutting of Labour's proposed jobs tax; and formal participation of Liberal Democrat representatives in a Financial Stability Council that will be consulted on budget judgements and the allocation of spending reductions between departments.

2. Liberal Democrat priorities

We agree to satisfy the four tests set by the Liberal Democrats by implementing the following measures:

› On fair taxes, the first Budget will include an increase in income tax thresholds funded by increased capital gains tax on non-business assets. We will also give clear political priority over other tax cuts to further increases in income tax thresholds over the course of a Parliament.

› On political reform, we guarantee a free vote in the House of Commons in the current year on a motion to hold a referendum on the introduction of the Alternative Vote system for the House of Commons. In addition to the political reforms set out in the section 3 below, we will also introduce provisions for an elected House of Lords, with interim provisions agreed between the two parties.

› On the pupil premium, we will fund a significant premium for disadvantaged pupils from outside the schools budget by reductions in spending elsewhere.

› On the green economy, we will implement in full a combined Liberal Democrat and Conservative policy programme contained in our two manifestos to establish a low carbon economy, as set out in section 3 below.

1. Further specific areas of agreement

In addition we agree to the following:

› On civil liberties, a comprehensive programme of measures to advance liberty and roll back state intrusion. This will include a Freedom or Great Repeal Bill with the scrapping of the ID card scheme, the National Identity Register, the Contact Point Database, and the finger-printing of children at school without parental permission; the extension of the scope of the Freedom of Information Act to provide greater transparency; adopting the protections of the Scottish model for the DNA database; the protection of historic freedoms through the defence of trial by jury, the restoration of rights to non-violent protest; the review of libel laws to protect freedom of speech; safeguards against the misuse of anti-terrorism legislation; further regulation of CCTV; and the ending of storage of internet and e-mail records without good reason; a new mechanism to prevent proliferation of unnecessary new criminal offences.

› A radical package of political reform including the recall of MPs who have engaged in serious wrong-doing; individual voter registration; debates in Parliament on propositions that obtain large degrees of public support; the implementation of the Calman reforms; the grant of a referendum to Wales on further powers to the Welsh

Assembly, if the Assembly seeks such powers; measures to curb the influence of lobbyists; a radical devolution of power and greater financial autonomy to local government and community groups.

> A series of steps to improve the banking system. The priority is to increase bank lending to small businesses to create and protect jobs and boost the recovery, with discussion between our two parties to identify the most effective way of achieving this; other measures will include a bank levy; an independent commission on structural reform of the banking system reporting within a year; and over the longer term efforts to recover the taxpayer money that has been invested in the banks.

> Specific measures to fulfil our joint ambitions for a low carbon and carbon friendly economy, including: the establishment of a smart grid and the roll-out of smart meters; the full establishment of feed-in tariff systems in electricity – as well as maintenance of banded ROCs; measures to promote a huge increase in energy from waste through anaerobic digestion; the creation of a green investment bank; the provision of home energy improvement paid for by the savings from lower energy bills; retention of energy performance certificates while scrapping HIPs; measures to encourage marine energy; the establishment of an emissions performance standard that will prevent coal-fired power stations being built unless they are equipped with sufficient CCS to meet the emissions performance standard; the establishment of a high-speed rail network; the cancellation of the third runway at Heathrow; the refusal of additional runways at Gatwick and Stansted; and the replacement of the Air Passenger Duty with a per flight duty; the provision of a floor price for carbon, as well as efforts to persuade the EU to move towards full auctioning of ETS permits;

measures to make the import or possession of illegal timber a criminal offence; measures to promote green spaces and wildlife corridors in order to halt the loss of habitats and restore biodiversity; mandating a national recharging network for electric and plug-in hybrid vehicles; continuation of the present Government's proposals for public sector investment in CCS technology for four coal-fired power stations; and a specific commitment to reduce central government carbon emissions by 10 per cent within 12 months.

Reform of the voting system – a bankable offer from the Conservatives, Monday 10 May

In his statement of 7th May, David Cameron made it clear that he would welcome the formation of a full coalition between the Conservatives and Liberal Democrats to deliver a stable and lasting Government in the national interest.

Throughout our negotiations with the Liberal Democrat negotiating team, the Conservative side has made it clear that our preference is for a full coalition in which senior Liberal Democrats participate as Cabinet Ministers and at all levels of the Government, and in which the coalition partners take joint responsibility for governing the country.

During the course of our discussions, it became clear that Liberal Democrats would not find it acceptable to enter into such a coalition without a "bankable" commitment from the Conservative Party in relation to the Alternative Vote system for elections to the House of Commons.

In response to this demand, the Conservative negotiating team offered a free vote in Parliament on a referendum on AV – with the most senior Conservatives committed to voting in favour of a referendum.

The Liberal Democrat negotiating team made clear that this was not a sufficiently bankable proposition – and this led to the construction of a "supply and confidence" agreement.

It has now become clear that Liberal Democrats do not find the prospect of a "supply and confidence agreement" attractive under current circumstances – and that an agreement between Liberal Democrats and Conservatives will therefore be possible only on the basis of a full coalition Government lasting for a full (and fixed) Parliamentary term.

Since such a coalition is also the preferred option from the Conservative point of view, we are more than willing to return to discussions on this basis.

We recognise, however, that this will necessitate agreement by the Conservative Party to a "bankable" commitment on the question of the Alternative Vote system for elections to the House of Commons.

Accordingly, over the course of the last few hours, David Cameron convened a special meeting of the Conservative Shadow Cabinet and subsequently a special meeting of the Conservative Parliamentary Party. As a result of these meetings, David Cameron obtained the permission of both the Shadow Cabinet and the Parliamentary Party to offer a "bankable" commitment in relation to AV.

If the Liberal Democrats enter into a full coalition Government alongside the Conservatives, the Conservative Party will undertake to legislate for a referendum on the introduction of the Alternative Vote for elections to the House of Commons. We will whip the Conservative Parliamentary Party to vote in favour of such legislation so that, together with the votes of the Liberal Democrats, its passage can be guaranteed. We are prepared to offer either a pre-legislative or a post-legislative referendum.

We are also prepared to discuss in detail a timetable for the introduction and passage of the relevant legislation.

Given that a coalition Government of Conservatives and Liberal Democrats will have a majority of over 70 in the House of Commons, the result of votes on such legislation is substantially more assured than the result of any legislation proposed by a Labour-Liberal Democrat coalition which would depend on a range of minority parties and which would have (even with these minority parties) only a slim overall majority.

Labour 'offer' document: Saturday 8 May

Democratic and Constitutional Reform

› An Early Referendum on Electoral Reform.
› A Second Chamber with consultation on full election by open list proportional representation.
› Fixed term Parliaments.
› Right of recall of MPs.
› A statutory register of lobbyists.
› Review of citizenship education to prefigure votes at 16.
› Agreement on a convention for moving to a written constitution.
› Implementation of the Calman proposals and a referendum for Welsh Assembly powers.

Tax and Spending

› A plan for securing the economic recovery, with measures to stimulate job creation, help the unemployed back to work and ensure investment in the transition to a low carbon economy.
› Agreement to bring forward a Budget that will meet the test

of fairness, with more help for low paid workers and pensioners, and support for families, alongside measures to tackle unfair
tax reliefs.

› Agreement not to cut public spending overall in 2010/11 but to
bring forward a spending review to set out departmental spending
allocations to 2013/14.

› Agreement to a bank levy (working alongside other governments
on "parallel tracks" to a global levy).

› Agreement to pursue a European Union Growth Strategy working
with our European Partners – and the wider G20 – to develop a
concrete plan as an essential element of our domestic economic
policy.

› Establishment of a local government finance commission to report
on moving to a fairer system of local government financing, including consideration of local wealth and income taxes.

› Royal Mail modernisation.

Public Service Reform

› Education Reform – A potential £1/£1.5bn injected into schools
for expanding 1-1 tuition for deprived pupils, with a local pupil
premium. Further measures could include an expansion of Teach
First, greater freedoms for the best schools, with more takeovers
and mergers. School Report Cards would replace League Tables as
the primary means of ensuring school accountability. A working
group on 14-19 qualifications reform to be established.

› Social Care Reform – establishment of a commission to examine
options for financing a comprehensive system of social care; ex-
amination of measures to support carers with more respite care.

› NHS – An agenda to provide more healthcare services in the home and community, enshrine citizen guarantees to key standards, and promote greater local accountability of health services.

› Welfare Reform – provide guarantees of jobs or training for out of work young people and the long term unemployed; ensure welfare to work for the inactive who can take jobs. Tougher conditionality to deliver savings.

› Family Policy – extend the right to request flexible working to all employees, expand pre-school childcare and nursery places, and re-index pensions to earnings from 2012.

Environment/Green Economy/Transport

› Take forward plans for high speed rail.

› Create a green investment bank.

› Promote port development to provide wind turbine manufacturing facilities.

› Establish pay as you save home energy loans.

› Implement a "zero waste" policy and bans on recyclable and biodegradable materials to landfill.

› Agree a White Paper on enhancement of the natural environment and biodiversity.

› Promote reform of the Common Agricultural Policy to support nature conservation.

› Create a supermarket ombudsman.

› Take forward green tax reform in the Budget.

Home Affairs/Civil Liberties

> Criminal Justice Reform: examine sentencing reform for short sentences; increasingly move offenders with custodial sentences who have mental health and drug problems into secure accommodation; and promote new forms of community justice and restorative justice.

> Discussion on establishing a Fundamental Review of legislation impacting civil liberties and security, in light of evolving terrorist threat (covering i.e. control orders, pre-charge detention and the use of intercept evidence in courts).

> Statement that ID cards – like passports – are purely voluntary and self-financing over the Parliament; review data requirements for biometric passports.

> Police Reform – examine new measures to make police authorities more accountable and to promote the takeover/merger of failing forces.

> Reform libel laws.

Housing

> Reform the Housing Revenue Account and build 10,000 council homes a year.

> Develop a comprehensive empty homes strategy.

> Scrap home information packs.

> Maintain home buy direct and develop new forms of affordable homes to rent for low income working families.

Defence

> Conduct a Strategic Defence and Security Review.

> Maintain an independent nuclear deterrent, reviewing our requirements in light of NPT negotiations.

Labour Party proposals: 'Liberal Democrat–Labour Party Discussions', Monday 10 May

The new Government will be founded on a core commitment to fairness. It will pursue the key objectives of economic growth, democratic and political reform, social justice and environmental sustainability. It will be pro-European and internationalist, offering engagement and leadership to its international partners.

1. Economy

1.1 The new government will ensure that the health of the public finances is restored as quickly as possible, while taking no action to jeopardise the recovery. In the light of market concerns, tough action will be taken to reduce the deficit.

1.2 Both parties recognise the importance of ensuring stability in the market and protecting Britain's standing. At the start of our discussions we recognise our common responsibility to do whatever is necessary to deliver a strong deficit reduction plan, through economic growth, fair taxes and cuts in lower priority public spending.

1.3   We also agree to pursue a European Union growth strategy, working with our European partners – and the wider G20 – to develop a concrete plan as an essential element of our domestic economic policy.

1.4   An economic statement will be made immediately following the Queen's Speech on the measures we propose. This statement will:

1.4.1   Set out overall fiscal projections consistent with the eradication of the structural deficit over a responsible timescale.

1.4.2   Confirm planned increases in National Insurance to enable the protection of frontline spending on childcare, schools, the NHS and policing.

1.4.3   Reallocate a proportion of any identified in year 2010-2011 savings to the promotion of growth and jobs including the implementation of low-carbon industrial support and energy-saving schemes, and protection for young jobseekers.

1.5   The new government will also:

1.5.1   Introduce a new Banking Levy [[on a basis agreed with France and Germany] [and in parallel tracks with America]].

1.5.2   Increase the personal allowance for pensioners over 65 years of age to £10,000 in 2011/12; and instigate a review of personal income tax allowances and tax credits with a view to relieving lower-paid working families from income tax and National Insurance Contributions on the first £10,000 of household income, and reducing unfairness in tax reliefs.

1.5.3   Set out our commitment to enforce lending arrangements with the semi-nationalised banks and make provision for a major loan guarantee scheme.

1.5.4   Set out our commitment urgently to investigate the separation of high risk and low risk banking with the emphasis on the requirements associated with risk.

1.5.5   Make proposals to tackle irresponsible bonuses within the banking sector [including a one year continuation of the bonus tax].

1.5.6   Include proposals to create a Green Investment Bank with a mandate to invest in low carbon infrastructure, with a view to widening its scale and remit.

1.5.7   Include proposals for the roll out of green loans to improve home energy saving.

1.5.8   Set a remit for the Low Pay Commission to ensure that the National Minimum Wage rises at least in line with average earnings over the period to 2015; and ask Whitehall Departments to pay a living wage, resourced by constraint on high pay in the public sector.

1.5.9   Create a People's Bank at the Post Office offering trusted and accessible banking services in the community.

1.5.10   Confirm plans to ensure universal access to broadband.

1.6   A Comprehensive Spending Review will be held throughout the summer reporting in autumn 2010. This CSR will consult widely throughout the public sector, the private sector and with other interested stakeholders.

1.7 The new government will remain committed to the principle of increasing conditionality and enforcement in the benefits system in order to support its goals for fairness and fiscal sustainability.

2. Political Reform

2.1 In line with the principles adopted by our two parties as the basis of the new constitutional settlement, the new government will adopt a radical, far-reaching agenda on political and constitutional renewal and reform. The programme for government will include the following elements.

    2.1.1 Immediate legislation to set the date of the next election for the first Thursday in May 2014, and establish the principle of four-year, fixed-term Parliaments in future;

    2.1.2 Immediate legislation to introduce the Alternative Vote for elections to the House of Commons. This will be confirmed in a referendum.

    2.1.3 A party funding bill to introduce caps on donations and spending limits, based on the proposals of the Hayden Phillips committee, as part of wider party funding reform.

    2.1.4 Reform to the House of Commons based on the Wright Commission proposals.

    2.1.5 Proposals for consultation on a House of Lords fully elected by open list proportional representation [to be enacted within four years].

2.1.6   The early introduction of a Power Of Recall for MPs who have committed serious wrongdoing.

2.1.7   The implementation of the proposals of the Calman Commission and a referendum on increasing the powers of the Welsh Assembly, with orders to be laid to that effect, subject to the views of the Electoral Commission, by 18th June.

2.1.8   A cut in the number of government ministers and in ministerial pay.

2.1.9   Regulation of lobbying to include a statutory register.

2.1.10   No further action to be taken in this Parliament on the ID card scheme for British nationals.

2.1.11   We will introduce a Bill to protect civil liberties and rights, including reforming the Regulation of Investigatory Powers Act; regulating the use of CCTV to maximise crime prevention while protecting privacy; restoring the right to protest in the vicinity of Parliament Square; increasing the number of people constituting a public assembly; repealing the offence of trespassing on a designated site; restoring the public interest defence for whistleblowers; restricting the offences exempt from double jeopardy; repealing changes to bailiff powers which allow the use of force in a person's home; strengthening freedom of information laws and the powers of the information commissioner, including to investigate private sector bodies; requiring parental consent for biometrics to be taken from children; and reforming the rules on retention of DNA in line with the Scottish model.

2.1.12   Enforcement of the provisions of the Equality Act 2010.

2.1.13   A review of citizenship education to prefigure reducing the voting age to 16.

2.1.14   Creation of a Convention on moving to a Written Constitution.

3.   Wider social, environmental and public service reform

3.1   The new government will adopt a decentralising, reforming agenda in relation to Britain's public services. It will put tackling climate change and protecting the environment at the heart of its programme. The government programme will include the following elements:

3.1.1   The restoration of the earnings link for the Basic State Pension, moving to a triple guarantee such that pensions are uprated in April 2011 by the higher of prices or 2.5 per cent, and in April 2012 and beyond by the higher of earnings, prices or 2.5 per cent.

3.1.2   A pupil premium to target additional funding to the million most deprived children, with a guarantee of 1-1 catch up tuition for children who need it. This will be fully funded [within three years].

3.1.3   Substantial increases in freedom for schools and hospitals, devolving accountability throughout our public services. All hospitals will become Foundation Trusts within the next four years, and up to 1,000 secondary schools will become part of the Accredited School Groups.

3.1.4   Greater provision of healthcare services in the home and the community, with guarantees of service standards for citizens, such as minimum waiting times and GP access, enshrined in the NHS Constitution.

3.1.5   A cross-party commission on finding a sustainable settlement on the funding and provision of a comprehensive social care system, delivered by a new National Care Service, which builds on the implementation in 2011 of free personal care at home for those with the greatest needs and the two-year cap on the costs of residential care from 2014.

3.1.6   Extension of childcare and nursery places and provision for shared parental leave, as well as the introduction of a new Father's Month with four weeks of flexible paid leave rather than the current two.

3.1.7   Guarantees of work for young people unemployed for six months, and adults out of work for two years, with mandatory participation or less of benefits.

3.1.8   Tuition fees for 2010/2011 are currently capped at £3,290. We will carry out a national debate on the future of higher education funding, with full consultation following the Browne review.

3.1.9   Extension of the right to request flexible working to older workers, and an end to the Default Retirement Age at 65.

3.1.10   A new target that 40 per cent of electricity will be from low-carbon sources by 2020.

3.1.11   Reviewing the support regime for low-carbon energy generation as part of the Energy Market Assessment.

3.1.12   A commitment to reduce carbon emissions from central government [the public sector] by 10 per cent within 12 months.

3.1.13   Taking forward plans for High Speed Rail with legislation to be introduced within four years. No plans will be taken forward for additional runways in the South East in this Parliament.

3.1.14 Police reform, including provisions for greater local accountability and the takeover of police forces and Borough Commands that consistently fail their communities.

3.1.15 Extensive roll-out of restorative justice and citizen engagement in justice, through Neighbourhood Justice Panels, Community Prosecutors, and supporting magistrates to consult with Neighbourhood Policing Teams – working closely with local government.

3.1.16 A review of under six-month prison sentences to see how they can be reduced in favour of tough community sentences where that is shown to reduce reoffending and protect the public, whilst maintaining action to reduce violence against women.

3.1.17 Strengthen the points based system and extend it to applications for citizenship or permanent settlement.

3.1.18 A fundamental review of local government finance reform, to include consideration of the localisation of business rates.

3.1.19 Reform of the Housing Revenue Account, to enable local authorities greater freedom to build and maintain social housing, with 10,000 new council homes a year built by the end of the Parliament.

3.1.20 A comprehensive empty homes strategy, continued support for Home Buy Direct, and the development of new forms of affordable homes to rent for low income working families.

3.1.21 Reform of libel laws.

3.1.22   An unequivocal commitment: we will not torture; we will not ask others to torture on our behalf; any allegation or evidence of torture will be subject to full, independent investigation; and any official involved in torture, in the past or in the future, will have broken the law and be liable for prosecution.

4.   Britain in the World

4.1   The new government will place a high premium on Britain's reputation around the world, including constructive leadership in the European Union.

4.2   A Strategic Defence Review will be held alongside the CSR. Both parties are committed to the UK maintaining a credible [and continuous] independent nuclear deterrent. The SDR will review how best to achieve this and how the UK can make the most effective contribution to nuclear non-proliferation and multi-lateral nuclear disarmament.

4.3   Legislation for an Armed Forces Charter – the British version of the GI Bill – entrenching the entitlements of the Armed Forces, their families, and Veterans including accommodation, health and mental health, education, and wider welfare.

4.4   Both parties remain committed to the UK's role in the international effort in Afghanistan, based on a combined military and political strategy, with an increasing focus on training the Afghan Army and Police and strengthening national and local governance, and committed to a process of transitioning provinces and districts to Afghan control starting in the next year.

4.5   Both parties remain committed to a comprehensive approach to protecting the UK from the threat of international terrorism, which includes a strong emphasis on tackling the long term causes and drivers of terrorism. The National Security Committee and Secretariat will be developed into a National Security Council [with a single National Security Adviser].

Liberal Democrat draft confidence and supply agreement: April–May 2010

"Stability and Reform: An Agreement for Stability, Confidence and Supply and for the Government of the United Kingdom, May 2010."
Joint Statement by Party Leaders

In the General Election of 6th May 2010, the people of the United Kingdom did not give a mandate for Government to any one political party.

We believe that there is now a responsibility placed upon all political parties to accept the result of this election, and to work together sensibly to deliver economic stability and political and social reform.

We must act to ensure that the modest economic recovery now underway is sustained, and that there is a credible and decisive plan to reduce Britain's unacceptably large budget deficit. We have also agreed a series of political, economic and social reforms to clean up our politics and to make Britain a fairer place in which to live.

To help deliver the stable government needed to restore this same stability to our economy, we have agreed to legislate for four year, fixed term, parliaments. This Stability and Reform Agreement is signed for a period of 4 years, with Annual Renewal so that there is a mechanism for consulting on and agreeing the broad programme for Government.

We enter this agreement with a determination to consult on key government plans and to deliver good government for the people of the United Kingdom.

Economic Recovery, Debt Reduction, and Public Spending Priorities

Policy Principles

The first priority is to ensure that economic recovery continues. Economic recovery is crucial for protecting jobs, reducing unemployment, bringing down the deficit, and for providing the revenues to invest in our front-line public services.

The Government will take no action which would tip the economy back into recession.

The Government will take early action to set out clear, credible and decisive plans to tackle the UK's budget deficit, and by doing this we will restore confidence in the financial markets and help keep interest rates low.

The Government will take action to ensure that the banks lend again to businesses.

The Government will promote fairness in our tax system, and environmental sustainability in our economy.

The Government will invest in education, and deliver a fairer deal for pensioners.

Policy Initiatives

We agree the following actions by the new Government:

›   Within 40 days of the signing of this Agreement the Government will present to Parliament a clear, credible and decisive plan to reduce the Budget Deficit. This plan will at least halve the structural deficit over 4 years, and will eradicate the structural deficit within 8 years. The Liberal Democrats commit to allow the passage of this Budget on condition that its major proposals have been first consulted on and agreed between the Chancellor of the Exchequer and the Liberal Democrat Shadow Chancellor of the Exchequer prior to the Budget Statement itself, and on Privy Council terms.

›   This Budget Statement will include plans for a Levy on UK Bank profits.

›   This Budget Statement will include plans for a Fundamental Review of Public Spending, which will be concluded by December 2010. The Chancellor of the Exchequer shall consult with the Liberal Democrat Shadow Chancellor before publishing the conclusions of this Review.

›   The Budget Statement will include plans for a Green Strategy for the UK, which will be published by October 2010, and which will set out plans to make Britain carbon neutral by 2050, along with decisive early action to meet interim carbon reduction targets.

›   The Budget Statement will include plans to lift the tax free personal allowance to £10,000 per annum.

›   The Budget Statement will include plans for restoring the link between annual increases in the basic state pension and average earnings increases. From April 2011, the basic state pension will rise each year by the greater of average earnings, RPI inflation or 2.5%.

> The Budget Statement will include plans to introduce a Pupil Premium from September 2011 onwards. This Premium will deliver an extra £2.5bn per year to the frontline budget for schools and colleges, and it will be targeted at disadvantaged young people and designed to close the gap between the performance of young people from advantaged and disadvantaged backgrounds.

Political Reform

Policy Principles

Our political system is broken and discredited. We need to clean up politics, make Parliament more effective, and give power back to the people. We must tackle the unfairness of our voting system for the House of Commons.

Policy Initiatives

To deliver this reformed political system we will:

> Immediately legislate for 4 year, fixed term, Parliaments. The next General Election will be fixed for the first Thursday in May 2014.

> Ensure that the MPs expenses system is cleaned up, and that all MPs and Members of the House of Lords pay full British taxes.

> Cut the cost of British politics, and immediately cut the pay of all Ministers.

> Immediately legislate for a "recall" system so that MPs who are suspended from the House of Commons for serious wrongdoing have to face a by-election in their constituencies.

> Immediately establish a review of the electoral system for the

House of Commons, and hold a referendum by no later than June 2011 to give the British people a choice of whether to move to a fairer voting system.

> Cap political donations at £10,000 per year, and limit spending throughout the political cycle.

> Replace the House of Lords with a fully elected Senate, with a dramatic reduction in the number of members.

> Devolve more powers to the Scottish Parliament and Welsh Assemblies.

> Commission a Review of Local Government Finance, to replace the unfair council tax and to give local authorities greater financial freedom and accountability.

Operational Annex

The Leaders of the "X" and Liberal Democrat parties will make suitable arrangements for ongoing consultation on the Government's developing programme. The Liberal Democrats will not be under any obligation to support measures in Parliament which are not included in this agreement or which have not been consulted on and agreed between the Parties.

The Liberal Democrats will not oppose the Government on issues of confidence and supply, provided that the measures set out in this Agreement are honoured.

This Agreement is for a period of four years, with annual review and renewal.

Final coalition agreement, Tuesday 11 May

"Conservative-Liberal Democrat coalition negotiations; Agreements reached; 11th May 2010."

This document sets out agreements reached between the Conservatives and Liberal Democrats on a range of issues. These are the issues that need to be resolved between us in order for us to work together as a strong and stable government. It will be followed in due course by a final Coalition Agreement, covering the full range of policy and including foreign, defence and domestic policy issues not covered in this document.

1. Deficit Reduction

The parties agree that deficit reduction and continuing to ensure economic recovery is the most urgent issue facing Britain. We have therefore agreed that there will need to be:

› a significantly accelerated reduction in the structural deficit over the course of a Parliament, with the main burden of deficit reduction

borne by reduced spending rather than increased taxes;
> arrangements that will protect those on low incomes from the effect of public sector pay constraint and other spending constraints; and
> protection of jobs by stopping Labour's proposed jobs tax.

The parties agree that a plan for deficit reduction should be set out in an emergency budget within 50 days of the signing of any agreement; the parties note that the credibility of a plan on deficit reduction depends on its long-term deliverability, not just the depth of immediate cuts. New forecasts of growth and borrowing should be made by an independent Office for Budget Responsibility for this emergency budget.

The parties agree that modest cuts of £6 billion to non-front line services can be made within the financial year 2010-11, subject to advice from the Treasury and Bank of England on their feasibility and advisability. Some proportion of these savings can be used to support jobs, for example through the cancelling of some backdated demands for business rates. Other policies upon which we are agreed will further support job creation and green investment, such as work programmes for the unemployed and a green deal for energy efficiency investment.

The parties agree that reductions can be made to the Child Trust Fund and tax credits for higher earners.

2. Spending Review – NHS, Schools and a Fairer Society
The parties agree that a full Spending Review should be held, reporting this Autumn, following a fully consultative process involving all tiers of government and the private sector.

The parties agree that funding for the NHS should increase in real terms in each year of the Parliament, while recognising the impact this decision would have on other departments. The target of spending 0.7% of GNI on overseas aid will also remain in place.

We will fund a significant premium for disadvantaged pupils from outside the schools budget by reductions in spending elsewhere.

The parties commit to holding a full Strategic Security and Defence Review alongside the Spending Review with strong involvement of the Treasury.

The Government will be committed to the maintenance of Britain's nuclear deterrent, and have agreed that the renewal of Trident should be scrutinised to ensure value for money. Liberal Democrats will continue to make the case for alternatives. We will immediately play a strong role in the Nuclear Non-Proliferation Treaty Review Conference, and press for continued progress on multilateral disarmament.

The parties commit to establishing an independent commission to review the long term affordability of public sector pensions, while protecting accrued rights.

We will restore the earnings link for the basic state pension from April 2011 with a "triple guarantee" that pensions are raised by the higher of earnings, prices or 2.5%, as proposed by the Liberal Democrats.

3. Tax Measures

The parties agree that the personal allowance for income tax should be increased in order to help lower and middle income earners. We agree to announce in the first Budget a substantial increase in the personal allowance from April 2011, with the benefits focused on those with lower and middle incomes. This will be funded with money that would have been used to pay for the increase in Employee National Insurance threshold proposed by the Conservatives, as well as revenues from increases in Capital Gains Tax rates for non-business assets as described below. The increase in Employer National Insurance threshold proposed by the Conservatives will go ahead in order to stop Labour's jobs tax. We also agree to a longer term policy objective of further increasing the personal allowance to £10,000, making further real steps each year towards this objective.

We agree that this should take priority over other tax cuts, including cuts to Inheritance Tax. We also agree that provision will be made for Liberal Democrat MPs to abstain on budget resolutions to introduce transferable tax allowances for married couples without prejudice to this coalition agreement.

The parties agree that a switch should be made to a per-plane, rather than per-passenger duty; a proportion of any increased revenues over time will be used to help fund increases in the personal allowance.

We further agree to seek a detailed agreement on taxing non-business capital gains at rates similar or close to those applied to income, with generous exemptions for entrepreneurial business activities.

The parties agree that tackling tax avoidance is essential for the new government, and that all efforts will be made to do so, including detailed development of Liberal Democrat proposals.

4. Banking Reform

The parties agree that reform to the banking system is essential to avoid a repeat of Labour's financial crisis, to promote a competitive economy, to sustain the recovery and to protect and sustain jobs.

We agree that a banking levy will be introduced. We will seek a detailed agreement on implementation.

We agree to bring forward detailed proposals for robust action to tackle unacceptable bonuses in the financial services sector; in developing these proposals, we will ensure they are effective in reducing risk.

We agree to bring forward detailed proposals to foster diversity, promote mutuals and create a more competitive banking system.

We agree that ensuring the flow of credit to viable SMEs is essential for supporting growth and should be a core priority for a new government, and we will work together to develop effective proposals to do so. This will include consideration of both a major loan guarantee scheme and the use of net lending targets for the nationalised banks.

The parties wish to reduce systemic risk in the banking system and will establish an independent commission to investigate the complex issue of separating retail and investment banking in a sustainable way; while recognising that this would take time to get right, the commission will be given an initial time frame of one year to report.

The parties agree that the regulatory system needs reform to avoid a repeat of Labour's financial crisis. We agree to bring forward proposals to give the Bank of England control of macro-prudential regulation and oversight of micro-prudential regulation.

The parties also agree to rule out joining the European Single Currency during the duration of this agreement.

5. Immigration

We have agreed that there should be an annual limit on the number of non-EU economic migrants admitted into the UK to live and work. We will consider jointly the mechanism for implementing the limit. We will end the detention of children for immigration purposes.

6. Political Reform

The parties agree to the establishment of five year fixed-term parliaments. A Conservative-Liberal Democrat coalition government will put a binding motion before the House of Commons in the first days following this agreement stating that the next general election will be held on the first Thursday of May 2015. Following this motion, legislation will be brought forward to make provision for fixed term parliaments of five years. This legislation will also provide for dissolution if 55% or more of the House votes in favour.

The parties will bring forward a Referendum Bill on electoral reform, which includes provision for the introduction of the Alternative Vote in the event of a positive result in the referendum, as well as the creation of fewer and more equal sized constituencies. Both parties will whip their Parliamentary Parties in both Houses to support a simple majority referendum on the Alternative Vote, without prejudice to the positions parties will take during such a referendum.

The parties will bring forward early legislation to introduce a power of recall, allowing voters to force a by-election where an MP was found to have engaged in serious wrongdoing and having had a petition calling for a by-election signed by 10% of his or her constituents.

We agree to establish a committee to bring forward proposals for a wholly or mainly elected upper chamber on the basis of proportional representation. The committee will come forward with a draft motion by December 2010. It is likely that this bill will advocate single long terms of office. It is also likely there will be a grandfathering system for the current Lords. In the interim, Lords appointments will be made with the objective of creating a second chamber reflective of the share of the vote secured by the political parties in the last general election.

The parties will bring forward the proposals of the Wright Committee for reform to the House of Commons in full, starting with the proposed committee for management of programmed business and including government business within its scope by the third year of the Parliament.

The parties agree to reduce electoral fraud by speeding up the implementation of individual voter registration.

We have agreed to establish a commission to consider the "West Lothian question."

The parties agree to the implementation of the Calman Commission proposals and the offer of a referendum on further Welsh devolution.

The parties will tackle lobbying through introducing a statutory register of lobbyists. We also agree to pursue a detailed agreement on limiting donations and reforming party funding in order to remove big money from politics.

The parties will promote the radical devolution of power and greater financial autonomy to local government and community groups. This will include a full review of local government finance.

7. Pensions and Welfare

The parties agree to phase out the default retirement age and hold a review to set the date at which the state pension age starts to rise to 66, although it will not be sooner than 2016 for men and 2020 for women. We agree to end the rules requiring compulsory annuitisation at 75.

We agree to implement the Parliamentary and Health Ombudsman's recommendation to make fair and transparent payments to Equitable Life policy holders, through an independent payment scheme, for their relative loss as a consequence of regulatory failure.

The parties agree to end all existing welfare to work programmes and to create a single welfare to work programme to help all unemployed people get back to work.

We agree that Jobseeker's Allowance claimants facing the most significant barriers to work should be referred to the aforementioned newly created welfare to work programme immediately, not after 12 months as is currently the case. We agree that Jobseeker's Allowance claimants aged under 25 should be referred to the programme after a maximum of six months.

The parties agree to realign contracts with welfare to work service providers to reflect more closely the results they achieve in getting people back into work.

We agree that the funding mechanism used by government to finance welfare to work programmes should be reformed to reflect the fact that initial investment delivers later savings in lower benefit expenditure.

We agree that receipt of benefits for those able to work should be conditional on the willingness to work.

8. Education

Schools

We agree to promote the reform of schools in order to ensure:

› that new providers can enter the state school system in response to parental demand.
› that all schools have greater freedom over the curriculum; and,
› that all schools are held properly accountable.

Higher Education

We await Lord Browne's final report into higher education funding, and will judge its proposals against the need to:

› increase social mobility;
› take into account the impact on student debt;

> ensure a properly funded university sector;
> improve the quality of teaching;
> advance scholarship; and,
> attract a higher proportion of students from disadvantaged backgrounds.

If the response of the Government to Lord Browne's report is one that Liberal Democrats cannot accept, then arrangements will be made to enable Liberal Democrat MPs to abstain in any vote.

9. Relations with the EU

We agree that the British Government will be a positive participant in the European Union, playing a strong and positive role with our partners, with the goal of ensuring that all the nations of Europe are equipped to face the challenges of the 21st century: global competitiveness, global warming and global poverty.

We agree that there should be no further transfer of sovereignty or powers over the course of the next Parliament. We will examine the balance of the EU's existing competencies and will, in particular, work to limit the application of the Working Time Directive in the United Kingdom.

We agree that we will amend the 1972 European Communities Act so that any proposed future Treaty that transferred areas of power, or competences, would be subject to a referendum on that Treaty – a "referendum lock". We will amend the 1972 European Communities Act so that the use of any passerelle would require primary legislation.

We will examine the case for a United Kingdom Sovereignty Bill to make it clear that ultimate authority remains with Parliament.

We agree that Britain will not join or prepare to join the Euro in this Parliament.

We agree that we will strongly defend the UK's national interests in the forthcoming EU budget negotiations and that the EU budget should only focus on those areas where the EU can add value.

We agree that we will press for the European Parliament only to have one seat, in Brussels.

We agree that we will approach forthcoming legislation in the area of criminal justice on a case by case basis, with a view to maximising our country's security, protecting Britain's civil liberties and preserving the integrity of our criminal justice system. Britain will not participate in the establishment of any European Public Prosecutor.

10. Civil Liberties

The parties agree to implement a full programme of measures to reverse the substantial erosion of civil liberties under the Labour Government and roll back state intrusion.

This will include:

›   A Freedom or Great Repeal Bill.
›   The scrapping of the ID card scheme, the National Identity Register, the next generation of biometric passports and the Contact Point Database.
›   Outlawing the finger-printing of children at school without parental permission.
›   The extension of the scope of the Freedom of Information Act to provide greater transparency.
›   Adopting the protections of the Scottish model for the DNA database.

- › The protection of historic freedoms through the defence of trial by jury.
- › The restoration of rights to non-violent protest.
- › The review of libel laws to protect freedom of speech.
- › Safeguards against the misuse of anti-terrorism legislation.
- › Further regulation of CCTV.
- › Ending of storage of internet and email records without good reason.
- › A new mechanism to prevent the proliferation of unnecessary new criminal offences.

11. Environment

The parties agree to implement a full programme of measures to fulfil our joint ambitions for a low carbon and eco-friendly economy, including:

- › The establishment of a smart grid and the roll-out of smart meters.
- › The full establishment of feed-in tariff systems in electricity – as well as the maintenance of banded ROCs.
- › Measures to promote a huge increase in energy from waste through anaerobic digestion.
- › The creation of a green investment bank.
- › The provision of home energy improvement paid for by the savings from lower energy bills.
- › Retention of energy performance certificates while scrapping HIPs.
- › Measures to encourage marine energy.
- › The establishment of an emissions performance standard that will prevent coal-fired power stations being built unless they are equipped with sufficient CCS to meet the emissions performance standard.

> The establishment of a high-speed rail network.
> The cancellation of the third runway at Heathrow.
> The refusal of additional runways at Gatwick and Stansted.
> The replacement of Air Passenger Duty with a per flight duty.
> The provision of a floor price for carbon, as well as efforts to persuade the EU to move towards full auctioning of ETS permits.
> Measures to make the import or possession of illegal timber a criminal offence.
> Measures to promote green spaces and wildlife corridors in order to halt the loss of habitats and restore biodiversity.
> Mandating a national recharging network for electric and plug-in hybrid vehicles.
> Continuation of the present Government's proposals for public sector investment in CCS technology for four coal-fired power stations; and a specific commitment to reduce central government carbon emissions by 10 per cent within 12 months.
> We are agreed that we would seek to increase the target for energy from renewable sources, subject to the advice of the Climate Change Committee.

Liberal Democrats have long opposed any new nuclear construction. Conservatives, by contrast, are committed to allowing the replacement of existing nuclear power stations provided they are subject to the normal planning process for major projects (under a new national planning statement) and provided also that they receive no public subsidy.

We have agreed a process that will allow Liberal Democrats to maintain their opposition to nuclear power while permitting the government to bring forward the national planning statement for ratification by Parliament so that new nuclear construction becomes possible.

The process will involve:

> the government completing the drafting of a national planning statement and putting it before Parliament.
> specific agreement that a Liberal Democrat spokesman will speak against the planning statement, but that Liberal Democrat MPs will abstain; and
> clarity that this will not be regarded as an issue of confidence.

Liberal Democrat ministers in the coalition government: May 2010

Deputy Prime Minister and Lord President of the Council: Nick Clegg MP

Secretary of State for Business, Innovation and Skills: Vince Cable MP

Secretary of State for Energy and Climate Change: Chris Huhne MP

Secretary of State for Scotland: Danny Alexander MP (to 29th May); Michael Moore MP

Chief Secretary to the Treasury: David Laws MP (to 29th May); Danny Alexander MP

Minister of State, Foreign Office: Jeremy Browne MP

Minister of State, Ministry of Defence: Nick Harvey MP

Minister of State, Department of Work and Pensions: Steve Webb MP

Minister of State, Department of Health: Paul Burstow MP

Minister of State, Department for Education: Sarah Teather MP

Minister of State, Ministry of Justice: Lord McNally

Parliamentary Under Secretary, Home Office: Lynne Featherstone MP

Parliamentary Under Secretary, Department of Business, Innovation and Skills: Ed Davey MP

Parliamentary Under Secretary, Department for Communities and Local Government: Andrew Stunell MP

Parliamentary Under Secretary, Department for Transport: Norman Baker MP

Deputy Leader of the House of Commons: David Heath MP

Deputy Chief Whip: Alistair
Carmichael MP

Assistant Government Whip and
Chief Adviser to the Deputy
Prime Minister: Norman
Lamb MP

Assistant Government Whip: Mark
Hunter MP

Advocate General for Scotland: Lord
Wallace

Deputy Chief Whip (Lords): Lord
Shutt